Social Welfare Policy, Programs, and Practice

Social Welfare Policy, Programs, and Practice

Elizabeth A. Segal
Arizona State University

Stephanie Brzuzy
Arizona State University

F. E. Peacock Publishers, Inc.
Itasca, Illinois

To my parents—thank you for a lifetime of support.
EAS

To my grandfather, who shared with me the joy of learning, and to my parents, who nurtured that joy. Thanks.
SB

Advisory Editor in Social Work
Donald Brieland

Cover image:
Copyright © Michael Lenn/SIS

Copyright © 1998
F.E. Peacock Publishers, Inc.
All rights reserved
Library of Congress Catalog Card No. 97-67452
ISBN 0-87581-411-5
Printed in the U.S.A.
Printing   10   9   8   7   6   5   4   3   2
Year   03   02   01   00   99   98

Contents

Chapter 4
Social Welfare Policy Analysis   59

Part Two   Key Content Areas of Social Welfare Policy   75

Chapter 7

Social Welfare Policies Affecting Children and Families   127

Chapter 12

Sources of Information for Social Welfare Policy Analysis and Practice   229

Chapter 13

Policy Practice: Influencing the Course of Social Welfare Policy   245

Chapter 14

The Role of Social Work   263

Preface

Social welfare issues affect every member of our society. During a typical day in the United States, we might learn that the president and Congress cannot agree on how to balance the federal budget, growing numbers of people are affected by AIDS, states are voting to decide whether immigrants should receive health coverage, and jobs have been lost because another factory has closed. These events are all social welfare concerns. Anyone who receives a paycheck from which taxes have been withheld is an active participant in our social welfare system, and anyone who drives a car on public roads or visits a public library is a beneficiary of government services. Social welfare policy touches every facet of our professional and personal lives.

This book is designed to help students understand what drives social welfare policy, how it affects people's lives, and ways to influence it. Three general areas are covered. In part one we introduce the fundamental concepts, theories, and history of social welfare policy. In part two we describe the social welfare policies and programs relevant to key areas of interest. In the final section, part three, we present social welfare policy practice techniques.

By emphasizing both theory and practice, this book also makes a unique contribution to the study of social welfare policy. Most social welfare policy books present theoretical material, and a few books help the student to act as a policy practitioner. This book does both. We describe the resources necessary for policy research and outline techniques for taking policy action. Our hands-on approach to social welfare policy analysis and practice reflects our experience as classroom instructors, policy researchers, and employees in state and federal government.

In chapter 1 we introduce students to the general study of social welfare policy. In chapter 2 we trace the history of social welfare policy in the United States. The theories, values, and beliefs that have influenced social welfare policy development are covered in chapter 3. Guidelines for analyzing policy follow in chapter 4.

Chapters 5 through 10 are organized by social condition and populations. Social welfare policy evolves in response to social problems or needs, and these tend to be concerns related to a population group, such as children or seniors, or to a social condition, such as poverty or lack of civil rights.

Chapters 11 through 14 are designed to guide the student in policy practice: the process of influencing and changing social welfare policies. Resources are included that are readily accessible to students exploring social welfare policy. Key concepts and exercises are provided at the end of each chapter.

Newcomers to the study of social welfare policy will find this book helpful. The American system of social welfare is so broad and complex that it would be impossible to include in-depth coverage of every policy issue. Instead, we provide a comprehensive overview of the social welfare policy arena. This text is designed to introduce students to social welfare policy concepts and to serve as a guide for conducting social welfare policy analyses. We examine the major social welfare policies and programs in the United States from colonial times through the 1996 legislative year, which saw the most significant changes to social welfare policy since the 1960s. Reading through the entire book will help students to become "policy literate"—able to understand, analyze, and influence public policies.

Policy practice can be as simple as casting a vote or as involved as lobbying or even running for public office. We hope this book will encourage social workers to be policy practitioners, committed to promoting social justice and influencing social change.

Part One

Foundations of Social Welfare Policy

Our focus in this section is on the foundation and structure of the social welfare system in America and how social welfare policy develops. In the first chapter, we address the need to understand the social welfare system and how it affects the practice of social work. We also define key terms that are often misunderstood by students and the general public. In chapter 2, we look at the history of social welfare policy in America exploring how today's policies are based on beliefs and values that date back to the beginnings of this nation. A thorough understanding of the current social welfare system requires a solid grasp of the history of social welfare policies and programs. Chapter 3 begins our discussion of how social welfare policy is actually created. We provide the definitions and concepts needed to analyze current policies and assess their impact on our nation. In chapter 4, we continue this discussion and outline techniques for conducting policy analysis. A model for social welfare policy analysis will be presented and examples of the model will be demonstrated throughout part two. Social workers who are able to analyze the impact of social welfare policies can advocate more effectively for the needs of their clients.

Chapter 1

What Is Social Welfare, and Why Is It Important?

Have you ever held a job and received a paycheck with part of your earnings deducted under a heading called FICA? If so, you are part of the largest social welfare program in America, commonly known as "Social Security." Almost every job in this country is part of the Social Security system, and the Federal Insurance Contribution Act (FICA) is the law requiring your employer to withhold a percentage of your salary and send it to the Social Security Trust Fund. Whether or not you choose to do so, you are an active participant in our network of social welfare policies and programs. However, how much do you know about the programs? Do you know the exact percent withheld from your paycheck? Do you know what you will receive in return for this contribution? Should you know, and if so, why?

Why Study the Social Welfare System?

To understand our social welfare system is to gain power—the power to question, to advocate for change, and to make good decisions about our lives. If you know the strengths and weaknesses of social programs, you can better plan for your future. As a professional in the field of human services, you can be a better leader and a better source of information for your clients.

Social work, by its nature and professional ethics, is concerned with the well-being of all members of society. According to Section 6 of the National Association of Social Workers' Code of Ethics, "Social workers should promote the general welfare of society." The code states in Section 6.04(a) that "Social workers should be aware of the impact of the political arena on practice and should advocate for changes in policy and legislation to improve social conditions in order to meet basic human needs and promote social justice" (National Association of Social Workers, 1997). The study of social welfare policy, programs, and practice is thus an imperative part of your preparation as a social worker.

There are several general ideas upon which this book is based. First, each of us is part of the social welfare system. At different times in our lives our roles will vary, but simply by being members of society we are automatically part of the system.

Second, this book is posited on the idea that all of us are both providers and recipients of social welfare. Every time you earn a paycheck, taxes are withheld so that the government can pay to provide services. Each year we are required by law to file our income tax returns and to report and pay federal and state taxes. Sales tax on certain purchases helps to pay for public services. Many of those services, such as interstate highways and public parks, are used by everyone. Some services, such as literacy training or home-delivered meals, are used only by those who need them.

The government's use of tax dollars to provide social welfare services is considered a provider role. Every time you drive on a public road, take a book out of the public library, rely on fire or police protection, or go to school, you are receiving public social welfare services. These are considered recipient roles. For example, most universities and colleges, public or private, receive some government assistance. Whether it is in the form of state tax dollars, federal money for financial aid, or tax-exempt status for being a non-profit institution, all schools are recipients of social welfare.

Third, citizens are also involved in making social welfare policy. Participating in an election contributes to the making of social welfare policy by electing officials who develop and enact public laws. Not voting is also participating in policy-making by letting those who *do* vote make the choice. Other ways of participating in policy-making are outlined in chapter 13.

Fourth, private efforts are also part of our overall social welfare system. The United Way or a shelter for physically abused women are examples of private services that promote societal well-being. Private efforts usually are intertwined with public services, adding to the breadth of our social welfare system.

The roles of provider and recipient change from situation to situation. The foundation of a social welfare system is that people contribute to care for others and for themselves. The system exists for two primary reasons: (1) to create a "safety net" on which we can all rely if needed, such as emergency services; and (2) to provide services that cannot be effectively or efficiently provided on an individual basis, such as fire protection and interstate highways. It is unrealistic to rely on individuals to pave their own roads or protect themselves from emergencies such as fires. The larger society needs a social welfare system to economically and efficiently provide for social needs. The analysis of social welfare policy allows us to assess whether the system achieves the goal of providing for our social needs. At times, social problems arise and demonstrate that the social welfare system is not effective. Through social welfare policy analysis we can determine what works, what does not, why it is not working, and how we might change the system. This ability to analyze social welfare policy is an integral part of the social work profession.

Finally, another premise of this book concerns the overall foundation of our social welfare system. The system is based on social values and beliefs that shift over time. In chapter 3, we will discuss in detail the different theories, perspectives, values, and beliefs on social welfare policy. As you will find, no one theory completely describes our system. Nevertheless, there are several significant concepts that provide a foundation for further analysis. These principles provide a point of reference and a context from which to discuss and analyze social welfare policy.

The newcomer to social work and social services will find this book of great assistance in understanding our social welfare system. We begin by outlining the history of social welfare policies in America and providing the theoretical foundation for our social welfare system. The tools needed to analyze policy are covered, followed by key areas of social concern. We conclude the book with a discussion of the policy-making process and the role of social work. This book will serve as a guide to understanding the overall structure of our social welfare system and as a resource to help social workers effect change in our social welfare system.

Why This Social Welfare Policy Book?

Courses and books about the social welfare system often seem very dry and unimportant to the person interested in helping individuals by being a social worker. However, understanding our social welfare system is essential for any member of our society, particularly for those who are actors within the system. The best of intentions and clinical training cannot help create new jobs in a community where a local factory has closed. A person with physical disabilities requires emotional and psychological support, as well as an accessible home and transportation. The social welfare system covers all these aspects of our social well-being. To best serve people, today's social worker must possess a working understanding of that system.

This book is designed to educate and provide the necessary background for the reader to become "policy literate." A policy-literate individual understands the general structure of our social welfare system and knows how to communicate with social policy makers and administrators. Policy literacy helps us make sense of the political responses by those in power to people's needs.

Are you policy literate? How good is your knowledge of our social welfare system? To find out, answer the general questions listed in the Policy Questionnaire on the next page. Were you able to correctly answer all of the questions, some, few, or none? Most students (and people in general) do not know the answers to these questions, yet these questions represent basic information that is fundamental to understanding our social welfare system. This lack of knowledge and understanding limits our ability to assess the social well-being of people and to make constructive changes in the social welfare system.

Therefore, every student of social work should study the social welfare system. We need to understand the social forces that affect our clients. As a result of this understanding, we gain valuable insight into the social environment and the interaction between it and the individual. With this understanding, we can become knowledgeable advocates to serve as resources and call for change when the system is not responsive to people's needs. Moreover, for our own professional and personal lives, it is necessary to understand and navigate the system that affects our social well-being.

No matter what aspects of social work you choose to pursue, social welfare policy plays a significant role. This book presents the skills and tools you will need to gain social welfare policy knowledge. With the knowledge and skills gained from studying this book, you can achieve social welfare policy literacy.

An Ecological Systems Perspective

The concern to promote the general welfare of society often focuses on the individual's relationship with his or her social environment. Concern with our surroundings and their impact on the individual's well-being set social work apart from other professions.

A social system is composed of several interrelated parts. The components of a system interact, react, and depend upon each other for survival, resulting in a reciprocal quality to our relationships. For example, siblings who are part of a family system may interact with each other by playing together, and the family system may interact with a social service agency from which it receives child care or health services, and the agency is part of a community that may regulate the provisions of the agency according to guidelines established by the state and federal government. We interact with many different systems on many different levels, including personal, environmental, cultural, social, national, and international systems (Chetkow-Yanoov, 1992).

Policy Questionnaire

1. What percent of your paycheck is taken out to pay for "Social Security"?
2. What percent of children younger than 18 years of age are living in poverty?
3. How many members of Congress are there?
    (a) How many are in the House of Representatives?
    (b) How many are in the Senate?
4. What is the name of the federal medical assistance program for the poor?
5. What is the name of the federal medical insurance program for the elderly?
6. What is the federal/state cash assistance program designed to aid poor children?
7. What major social welfare act was passed by Congress in 1935?
8. Which social welfare program is the most costly for the federal government?
9. What is the current hourly minimum wage?
10. How many judges sit on the Supreme Court?
11. What percent of eligible voters actually voted in the 1996 presidential election?
12. How many Cabinet positions are there?

Answers
1. 7.65% (as of 1997)
2. 20.8% (as of 1995)
3. 535
    (a) 435
    (b) 100
4. Medicaid
5. Medicare
6. Aid to Families with Dependent Children (AFDC)/Temporary Assistance for Needy Families (TANF)
7. The Social Security Act
8. Social insurance or Social Security
9. As of September 1, 1997: $5.15
10. 9
11. 50%
12. 14 (as of 1997)

The emphasis of social work on the person in his or her social environment demands that we look at each person as a part of a larger system. The ecological systems perspective means that the social worker is concerned with a person's individual, family, and community circumstances. This perspective requires us to take a large-scale, or "macro," view of people's lives.

In this book, we focus on the larger domain of social well-being that gets translated into social welfare policy and programs. The ideological components, as well as the concrete programmatic aspects of our social welfare system, are presented and analyzed from a social work perspective. The social welfare system is both very broad and very detailed. Rather than try to cover both aspects, this book covers the broad scope of our social welfare system.

What Is Social Welfare?

The terms *social welfare*, *social welfare system*, *social welfare policy*, and *social welfare program* are sometimes used interchangeably, but they have distinctly different meanings. **Social welfare** is the condition or well-being of a society. Social welfare encompasses people's health, economic condition, happiness, and quality of life. As citizens and human service professionals, every aspect of our social well-being affects our daily lives. For example, segments of our population do not receive any type of health care coverage either through private insurance or public care. Eventually, these individuals will need some kind of medical attention. As a result of not having private or public coverage, that medical attention may come long after the need first arises. The consequence is a more severe (and costly) medical problem.

Consider the child with an earache who is not covered by health insurance and does not receive medical care. In time, the earache could get worse and the child could suffer acute infection and other medical complications as a result of delayed care. The likely point of service delivery will be emergency care. The cost of the emergency medical care will need to be covered, at a greater expense to the family and society than would have been needed initially. Who pays for this care? Ultimately, the hospital which provides the emergency care must cover the cost. To do so, the hospital charges more to others who can pay. These charges are passed on through higher costs to insurance providers, the government, and individuals who directly pay for their own care. While the physical costs of waiting to receive care are borne by the child and the family, the financial costs are eventually covered by all of us. This example highlights the social connectedness of each person's health and well-being.

Our **social welfare system** consists of the organized efforts and structures used to provide for our societal well-being. In its simplest form, the social welfare system can be conceptualized as four interrelated parts: (1) social issues; (2) policy goals; (3) legislation/regulation; and (4) social welfare programs. The social welfare system starts with an identified social issue. Once the issue is recognized to be a social concern, the next step is to articulate policy goals. These goals can result in a public position created through legislation or regulation. Finally, the legislation is translated into action through the implementation of a social welfare program (see Figure 1.1).

For example, there has been a great deal of public concern over the increase in the severity of family problems that result in the need for foster care of children. This social issue has been identified as a problem in need

Figure 1.1

Social Welfare System

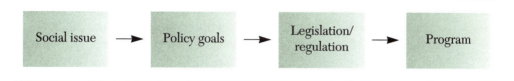

Social issue → Policy goals → Legislation/regulation → Program

of social intervention. Politicians and concerned social service professionals articulated the goal of supporting families and keeping them together. In response to this public goal, federal legislation was passed in 1993 to fund family preservation services (P.L. 103–66). The result of this legislation has been the development and implementation of state and local programs that offer intensive intervention with families in order to improve parenting skills and prevent the need for foster care placements (U.S. General Accounting Office, 1995). This example highlights how federal action directly influences the services offered in communities. The implementation of these programs is possible through the federal government's enactment of legislation that authorizes the provision of money to state and local governments for the development of direct services to families.

One should ask the following basic questions when studying the social welfare system. Following each question is the term that is often used to discuss these social welfare system questions:

Who gets services?	Eligibility
Why do they get services?	Program goals
What do they receive?	Benefits
How do they receive services?	Service delivery system
What does it cost?	Cost analysis
Who pays for it?	Financing

In order to understand the American social welfare system, these questions must be asked, and the answers must be analyzed. In chapter 4, we present an in-depth way to analyze the social welfare system, and in chapter 12, we offer resources to aid in this process.

Social welfare policy is the organized response or lack of a response to a social issue or problem. Policy implies assuming a position, but that position does not necessarily require action. It can be an all-out effort to eradicate a social problem or a choice to ignore a social problem. For example, from 1983 to 1990 the federal government did not intervene with any public policy related to AIDS. Although the illness was documented as a growing national concern since 1983, there was no federal legislation until 1990. In part, this represented a federal decision to let local communities and social service agencies deal with AIDS. It also reflected a decision not to treat

AIDS as a national, macro concern. The choice *not* to intervene represented a policy. Thus, social welfare policy is a position to act, or not to act, on a social issue or problem on behalf of society.

Social welfare programs are the products of social welfare policies. An example of a social welfare program that touches all of us is public education. Historically, numerous social conditions gave rise to the publicly acknowledged awareness that children lacked sufficient education. Promoters of compulsory education during the mid-1800s claimed school attendance would reduce crime and poverty, thereby improving social conditions (Katz, 1986). A general consensus led to agreement on the policy goal to improve social conditions through publicly mandated education. The result was the development of compulsory education as a social program. Over time, the public and policy-makers became convinced of the value of public education to reduce juvenile crime and idleness.

As is true of so many social welfare policies, the public realization of a social problem long precedes the actual policy and programs designed to address the issue. Public education for children took more than fifty years to establish. Finally, by the 1920s, the force of government legislation in all states supported compulsory education. The result of this social welfare effort is today's public education system, in which public schools are financed in large part by communities and regulated by local, state, and national government bodies. While this example of public education is simplified, it demonstrates the process under which social concerns lead to social welfare programs.

Why Do We Have a Social Welfare System?

The United States is considered the primary working example of capitalism and a marketplace economy. This means that we operate through an exchange of goods and services: for our work we receive a salary, which in turn allows us to purchase what we need or want. This system does not cover all members of our society, however. For those who cannot work because of health or physical limitations, for those who cannot find work, or for those who are excluded because of their race, sex, age, physical ability, or sexual orientation, there is no market exchange of salary. As a result, the market system does not provide sufficient resources for some people.

To provide for those outside the market system and to keep the system in check, the government plays a crucial role in maintaining the social well-being of the country. For example, the federal government provides services to help people find work through programs such as Job Corps and the Job Training Partnership Act. The government also provides for those who cannot work because of physical disabilities through programs legislated under the Social Security Act. These are examples of federal government intervention in the marketplace economy. State and local governments operate in much the same way. For example, schools are run by local people elected to serve on school boards. Their decisions direct and control the public education each child receives.

Although the underlying principle of the social welfare system is government involvement, not all people agree with this position. Since the earliest history of this nation, people have argued for and against government involvement in the social arena. Those arguments and the types of government roles and systems developed over the history of this nation are also the domain of this book.

Difficulties of Identifying Social Problems and Solutions

The definitions of the social welfare system, social welfare policy, and social welfare programs appear rather clear. In reality, however, our social welfare system is often confusing, convoluted, and both overlapping and lacking. The system has been patched together throughout the history of this nation. The piecemeal nature of our responses to social issues created a system that is not always logical nor coherent. While this book attempts to organize and explain the social welfare system in clear ways, it is not a simple system. To become an expert in our complex and ever-changing social welfare system takes considerable study. To illustrate this complexity, consider the following exercise.

In a small group, discuss and come to a consensus about what the top five social problems are that face the United States today.

Can you come to agreement?

Are there too many to list just five?

Are they distinguishable from each other, or is there tremendous overlap?

Did your group mention poverty, inadequate education, lack of health care, substandard housing, crime, or others?

How can poverty be separated from lack of health care or inadequate education?

Haven't some researchers linked crime to poverty?

Which social problem needs the greatest attention?

Can such an identification be made?

This group activity is not meant to frustrate you, but simply to begin to illustrate the complexity of social problem identification and solutions. Two people may agree that drug abuse is a serious social problem. One may call for a strong police force to arrest those who use illegal drugs, while the other may advocate for rehabilitation programs to help people stop using drugs. These choices represent different values and ideologies that influence social welfare policy decision-making. The first approach punishes people for illegal behaviors, and the second approach teaches people different behaviors.

Given the difficulties you had in agreeing on what constitutes a major social problem, now imagine hundreds of elected officials representing thousands of constituents trying to come to the same consensus you faced in your small group. While the task can seem overwhelming and impossible, social welfare policies and programs are regularly instituted. Our study of the social welfare system attempts to analyze the outcomes of those public policy choices.

Approaches to the Development of Social Welfare Policy

Several key concepts constitute the foundation for our discussion of the social welfare system. These concepts include residual, institutional, universal, and selective approaches to the development of policy. Understanding these concepts is important to our ability to analyze social welfare policies and programs.

Residual Versus Institutional Approaches to Policy-Making

Historically, both changing economic and social conditions moved the country from reliance on private social welfare programs to acceptance of public social welfare programs. This shift is characterized by two competing conceptions of social welfare policy: *residual* and *institutional* approaches (Wilensky & Lebeaux, 1965).

The first concept, **residual social welfare policy**, calls for organized public intervention only when the normal resources of family and marketplace break down. Social welfare services are called into play *after* a problem is identified that cannot be addressed through a person's own means. Social services become available in an emergency. The focus is on individual behaviors and responsibility.

The second concept, **institutional social welfare policy**, calls for the existence of social welfare programs as part of the social structure and as part of the normal functioning of society. Social welfare programs are seen as a preventive effort built into the social system. Institutional social welfare policy regards providing services as a legitimate function of society. The complexities and difficulties of modern life are ever-present. Therefore, it is normal for individuals at times to require the assistance of social institutions. Institutional social welfare policy focuses on prevention and collective responsibility.

Examination of a social concern helps to illuminate the differences between residual and institutional approaches to social welfare policy and programs. Teenage pregnancy is commonly viewed as a social problem by politicians, the public, and social service providers. When young women become mothers at an early age, often their opportunities for education and employment are limited. For the children born to young mothers, opportunities can also be limited due to emotional, economic, and social stress. A residual approach to the social issue of teenage pregnancy would focus on providing services *after* the teenager becomes pregnant. Residual programs might include specialized prenatal care for teenage mothers, school programs for teenage mothers held on weekends and nights, and parenting skills classes. An institutional approach would be to target all teenagers *before* pregnancy occurred. Institutional programs might include establishing in all schools family planning education courses which stress delaying parenthood and access to birth control clinics for all youths.

The difference between the residual and institutional approaches embodies the struggle in developing social welfare policy and programs. To what extent should individuals be responsible, and to what extent should society be responsible? For the most part, social welfare policy in this country has followed the residual approach. Most social programs were created to respond to an identified need after it has occurred. The result of this approach is a categorization system used to identify who should receive services and who should not.

Universal Versus Selective Provision of Services

The principle of **universality** calls for social services that provide benefits to all members of society, regardless of their income or means. **Selectivity** means that services are restricted to those who can demonstrate need through established eligibility criteria. A major difference between universal and selective programs is the extent of stigma attached to receiving services. Universal services are available to all, while the recipients of selective services are identified as incapable of providing for themselves.

The advantage of universal coverage is that everyone is covered and therefore many social problems can be prevented. A major disadvantage of such an approach is its cost. Selective coverage ensures that only those most in need will be covered. Such targeted coverage is less expensive, but it stigmatizes the recipient and can be too narrow. Those who do not meet the prescribed criteria will not receive anything.

Blending Social Welfare Policy Approaches

How do the concepts of residual and institutional approaches fit with universal and selective approaches? Table 1.1 demonstrates how some common programs fit these conceptions of social welfare policy. Most social services are residual and selective: they are developed in response to breakdown and are available only to those who demonstrate a need.

Table 1.1
Social Welfare Policy Blend

	Residual	**Institutional**
Universal	• Federal Emergency Management Agency services	• Public education • Fire and police protection
Selective	• Aid to Families with Dependent Children/ Temporary Assistance to Needy Families • Food stamps • Medicaid	• Social Security • Medicare

Examples of selective residual services include public cash assistance and most other aid given to those who are poor. Very few residual services are universal. However, Federal Emergency Management Agency services are available in a crisis such as an earthquake, regardless of whether or not a person has financial means. This is an example of a universal residual program.

The clearest examples of universal institutional services are public education and fire and police protection, which are available to all regardless of income. Some institutional services are selective. Many may argue that the program commonly referred to as "Social Security" is a universal institutional program. The program is actually a selective institutional program: only those who have worked in covered employment are eligible to receive benefits, and benefits are determined according to the person's history of contributions. The structure of the Social Security program is discussed in greater detail in chapter 9.

There are some social welfare programs that can be defined as institutional and universal, yet the actual implementation of many of these programs suggests otherwise. For example, public education is available to all, yet the resources and quality of education vary by region and community. Author Jonathan Kozol, in *Savage Inequalities: Children in America's Schools* (1991), argues that there are great inequalities in our educational system. School spending on children in the suburban communities outside of New York City, for example, is more than twice as high as spending for children in city schools. Such disparity in resources for public education demonstrates that although all children in this country are entitled to public education, they do not all receive the same benefits.

Finally, there is a flow between residual and institutional approaches to the development of social welfare policies. Let us return to the example of public education. We have been discussing it as a universal institutional social welfare program, but it has not always fit into this category. As previously described, public education began as a residual response to the problem of juvenile crime and idleness. Public education was not originally conceived of nor developed as an institutional program, but rather evolved into one. Many of our institutional social welfare policies and programs originated as residual policy responses.

The American Social Welfare Policy Response

In conclusion, there are different ways to respond to social need. The most prevalent response of our social welfare system has been to take a residual approach to social problems. Such an approach rests on a "wait and see" attitude. Our social welfare policy is usually made in response to social breakdown, creating a policy or program *after* a problem is identified. Prevention is seldom practiced in our social welfare system. There are advantages and disadvantages to the residual approach. Throughout this book, we will demonstrate that while the residual approach is the most prevalent policy response, often it is not the best. Preventing a problem from occurring, rather than waiting until a social problem exists, is a much better choice.

While prevention sounds simple and logical, we will see how difficult it has become to implement such an approach in our social welfare policy arena. The ideological, political, and social implications of institutional over residual responses will be stressed throughout the book.

Key Concepts

social welfare	institutional social welfare policy
social welfare system	residual social welfare policy
social welfare policy	selectivity
social welfare program	universality

Exercises

1. Develop a list of all the social welfare programs in which you are a participant. How important are these services in your everyday life? Can you identify whether each program is residual or institutional? Can you determine whether it is universal or selective?

2. Read through a newspaper or a news magazine such as *Time* or *Newsweek*. How many articles are related to social welfare issues? How are the issues presented? Does the discussion seem relevant to social work practice? How do these issues affect you, your family, and your friends?

References

Chetkow-Yanoov, B. (1992). *Social work practice: A systems approach*. New York: The Haworth Press.

Katz, M.B. (1986). *In the shadow of the poorhouse*. New York: Basic Books.

Kozol, J. (1991). *Savage inequalities: Children in America's schools*. New York: Crown Publishers.

National Association of Social Workers. (1997). *NASW Code of Ethics*. Washington, DC: Author.

U.S. General Accounting Office. (1995). *Child welfare: Opportunities to further enhance family preservation and support activities*. Washington, DC: Author.

Wilensky, H.I., & Lebeaux, C.N. (1965). *Industrial society and social welfare*. New York: The Free Press.

University of Illinois at Chicago, The University Library, Jane Addams Memorial Collection

Chapter 2

History of Social Welfare in America

Today's social welfare policies have been shaped by historical events and molded by changing social values. Therefore, exploring the history of social welfare policy in the United States can help us better understand today's social welfare system.

The political system of a democratic government rests on the principle that people or their elected representatives make policy decisions. Elections and decisions are usually decided by the majority. In our country, that majority mirrors those who control the most resources, typically white Euro-American men. Thus, American social welfare policy has evolved in ways that reflect the majority culture. Typically, that majority has been concerned with maintaining the status quo, rather than risking social upheaval. Examples of efforts to maintain the status quo can be seen in the treatment of women and minorities. Social welfare policy in this country has tended to reinforce traditional family ethics that kept women at home (Abramovitz, 1996) and restricted minorities and immigrants from full economic participation (Katz, 1989).

In spite of the overriding goal of protecting the status quo and maintaining majority control, change has occurred from colonial times to the present. Some social welfare policy changes were dramatic and far-reaching. Others were slow and gradual. Because our social welfare system reflects economic fluctuations, political changes, and shifting American social values, it is important to examine the system within the context of history.

Colonial Period (1690–1800)

Social welfare, the concern with societal well-being, dates back to the time of the earliest European settlers. The colonial period in this country was a time of great uncertainty. To the Europeans who first landed on this continent, North America seemed to possess no established social, political, or economic system. The settlers lacked awareness of native cultures that had inhabited the land for centuries before. Those who came here during the late 1600s and early 1700s tended to ignore cultures and mores that were not their own. Consequently, the earliest settlers chose for their first social welfare system one with which they were most comfortable, based on laws they brought with them from their countries of origin.

The earliest form of legislated social welfare policy in the colonies came with the importation of the **Elizabethan Poor Laws** (Trattner, 1994). Passed in 1601 in England, the Elizabethan Poor Laws embodied the first public legislation outlining a public response to social welfare needs. As the feudal system was changing in England, the obligation to assist people in dire need surfaced as a public concern. The Laws were passed primarily out of necessity, not because of a commitment to social well-being. Landowners and church leaders were not able to care for everyone in economic need. Therefore, the Elizabethan Poor Laws were passed to designate a system of care for the poor and indigent.

A number of key components characterized the Poor Laws (Axinn & Levin, 1992). Categorization of need was developed by distinguishing between those deserving of aid, the "worthy poor," and the undeserving, or "unworthy poor." The **worthy poor** included widows, orphans, the elderly, and people with disabilities. These groups were viewed as worthy because their circumstances of need were perceived to be beyond their control. The **unworthy poor** were able-bodied single adults and unmarried women with out-of-wedlock children. These groups were considered unworthy because they either could work and were not doing so, or they did not follow the expected social norms. These distinctions are important to understand, because they permeate our social welfare system to this day.

In addition to the categorization of people in need, the Elizabethan Poor Laws institutionalized other structures that remain a part of our social welfare system. The Poor Laws outlined, first and foremost, that the economic support of those in need must first come from within the family. Only when the family could not afford to care for a person did the local authorities take public responsibility for his or her care. Another stipulation was that the person in need had to be a legal resident of the community. In this way, the generosity of the local government would be provided to community residents rather than to outsiders. Funding for this public assistance came through money collected from local residents who could afford to pay. The tendency to support those known to us over strangers continues to be a very strong sentiment today.

The Elizabethan Poor Laws also established a single relief system coordinated by civil authorities. It was intended to provide support for those who deserved assistance, not as a way to eradicate poverty. The colonists believed strongly in the work ethic: those who could work should do so. They also believed strongly that there were sufficient jobs available for anyone willing to work. Hard work was believed to lead to moral uprightness and individual well-being.

These earliest social welfare laws set the stage for all social welfare policy to come. In summary, the major principles of the Elizabethan Poor Laws included (1) a distinction between worthy and unworthy poor; (2) the idea that the family is responsible first and foremost for the care of its members and that only after family failure should local authorities intervene; (3) the stipulation that only those who are residents are eligible to receive assistance; and (4) provision of assistance only when dire necessity requires it, ending when the recipient achieves the ultimate goal of employment or marriage to someone who is employed. Recognition of poverty was seen as an individual shortcoming, not as a structural or societal failure. However, one key outcome of the colonial period was the belief that social welfare was a partnership between private care and public aid.

The South, while similar to the North in adherence to the Elizabethan Poor Laws, differed in regard to its economic structure. The agricultural economy of the South relied on large numbers of laborers. African slaves provided an inexpensive source for that labor. From the 1600s through the late 1700s, almost 600,000 Europeans came to America and 300,000 Africans were brought here as slaves (Daniels, 1990). Almost all the Africans were located in Southern states where they worked as slaves. The Europeans, the majority of whom were British, controlled the economic and social order of Colonial America. Thus, by 1661, the South had institutionalized slavery, and care of slaves rested with their owners. The Elizabethan Poor Laws were not applicable to slaves, who had no legal claim to social welfare support from local governments. As in the North, these policies set the foundation for the public response to social welfare needs for centuries.

During the colonial period, America was perceived as a land of abundant resources with plenty of room for growth. The native people, like African slaves, were regarded by the colonists as non-persons with no rights to the land or resources (Day, 1997). The American Indians were considered a nuisance blocking the growth of the colonial empire (Nabokov, 1991). The differences in culture between the colonists and those who were native were significant and bred misunderstanding and mistrust for centuries. For the American Indian tribes, the white colonists, in the words of a member of the Santee, were

> a heartless nation. They made some of their people servants.... We have never believed in keeping slaves, but it seems that these Washichu [white people] do.... The greatest object of their lives seems to be to acquire possessions—to be rich. They desire to possess the whole world. For thirty years they were trying to entice us to sell them our land. Finally the outbreak [of illness] gave them all, and we have been driven away from our beautiful country (Nabokov, 1991, p. 22).

With such differences in beliefs and plenty of land to push the American Indian people back, the colonies grew and prospered. Because of economic growth and a rich base of natural resources, the belief that poverty was inevitable or structural never became part of the national consciousness. In fact, because of America's abundant resources and expansion, poverty was viewed as a personal misfortune, not a public responsibility.

Pre–Civil War Period (1800–1860)

After the American Revolution in 1776 and the formation of the United States, economic, political, and social forces changed the face of the nation. The economic structure of the country shifted from primarily agrarian to primarily industrial. More and more immigrants from European countries were settling in America. With growing immigration and industrialization, workers in search of employment gravitated towards cities, and the America of the 1800s became more urbanized.

The social welfare system in the United States changed with the increase in industrialization, immigration, and urbanization. Although the fundamental precepts of the Poor Laws were still accepted, local authorities were facing greater social problems and need. Certain conditions such as mental illness, disabilities, and orphaned children seemed impossible to solve through distribution of aid to individuals. One solution was the creation of residential institutions designed to care for such people (Leiby, 1978). Institutions were believed to be the way to eliminate social problems through rehabilitation and setting examples of proper ways to live (Rothman, 1971). The focus on institutions, also known as "indoor relief," included the establishment of hospitals, almshouses for the poor, and orphanages for children (Axinn & Levin, 1992).

Colonial and pre–Civil War America reflected a strong religious background which greatly influenced how social problems were viewed (Jansson, 1997). The dominant ideology centered around a religious, moralistic perspective that regarded individual behavior as the root of most problems. This perspective reinforced the emphasis on correcting people's behavior through rehabilitation and life in institutions. Although the intent of institutional living was to rehabilitate people, the reality was very different.

Institutions often became places where people who were destitute and people who were suffering from mental illness were warehoused and left without any efforts at rehabilitation. The conditions were often substandard, and inmates were treated very poorly.

The concept of rugged individualism permeated the society of the 1800s. America was still seen as a nation rich in resources, and opportunities for hard work were perceived to be plentiful. Therefore, anyone unemployed or poor was regarded with suspicion. Poverty was viewed as an individual condition and responsibility.

In reality, however, the concept of available work for every person who wanted it was (and continues to be) a distortion of historical reality (Katz, 1986). As has been true during many periods of history, viable employment for unskilled or semi-skilled workers was not universally available. While there have always been rich and poor in American society, the industrialization of the 1800s began to create broader differences and a greater disparity in resources between those at the top and those at the bottom.

Civil War and Post-War Period (1861–1874)

The Civil War awakened the new nation to social unrest, regional nationalism, and economic disparity. The difference between the North and South was not simply a matter of abolition versus institutionalization of slavery. The industrialized North had an economic base that differed from the more agrarian economy of the South. The Civil War and its aftermath created tremendous need for relief efforts. As a result of poor sanitary conditions, public health emerged as a social welfare concern, as did the need for government intervention.

For the first time in the nation's history, the federal government made a brief foray into providing social welfare benefits. Before the Civil War, all social welfare programs fell under the control of private charity groups and local governments. With the magnitude of the Civil War and the North's successful efforts to abolish slavery came the post-war need to provide for those displaced by the war. In 1865, the new federal government established the Freedman's Bureau, which provided temporary relief to newly freed slaves, managed abandoned and confiscated property, helped to reunite families, provided medical supplies and food rations, and established institutions such as hospitals, schools, and orphanages (Trattner, 1994).

The Freedman's Bureau was placed in the War Department, which ensured that it remained temporary; indeed, it was disbanded in 1872 (Jansson, 1997). The development of the Bureau raised the question of what should be the role of the federal government in the creation of social welfare policy and the provision of services. Seen only as a wartime effort, the Bureau was not designed to alter the social or economic structure that had given rise to the Civil War. It provided the minimum services needed immediately after the war.

Although slavery officially ended with the Civil War, the impact of racial differences remained deeply imbedded in American society. African-Americans, while technically freed, were still subject to the will of the majority. Even Northern abolitionists who had fought for the end of slavery perceived African-Americans as morally inferior (Jansson, 1997). Forcing people to leave their native land and culture and then depriving them of any chance to develop their own resources and culture set the stage for long-standing racial imbalances. How could African-American freed slaves begin to achieve the social, political, and economic success that the founders of this country had secured for themselves almost 200 years before? Early settlers had access to land and resources, and by the 1800s controlled the political and social economy. Even with the end of the Civil War, African-Americans were not included in those systems. Freed slaves had no belongings, no land, had been kept from education, and therefore had no chance to integrate into the mainstream society. What institutional slavery accomplished before the Civil War, social values and structural systems maintained after the war.

Women fared a bit better after the Civil War. The war had drawn women out of their homes and into the social structure to a greater degree. Women found a place for themselves in social welfare services and public health careers. Following the war, the country experienced enhanced economic wealth and an improved standard of living. Women from families who were economically well off found opportunities to do social welfare service work outside the home.

During the years following the Civil War, white Americans decimated the resources and culture of American Indians. Thousands of miles of railways opened the way for westward expansion. In 1887, the Dawes Act destroyed American Indian culture by dividing the land among individuals. Needing resources, many sold their land for little money or were cheated out of it, and 90 million acres were transferred to whites while 90,000 American Indians were left homeless. Also in 1887, the government provided funds to missionary groups to create boarding schools. American Indian children were forced to attend these schools and consequently lost contact with their families, communities, and culture (Day, 1997).

The period from the 1870s through the turn of the century was characterized by rapid economic growth, renewal of immigration, increased industrialization, and urbanization. The industrial development fostered by the war laid the foundation for post-war expansion and the growth in individual wealth (Axinn & Levin, 1992). It also set the foundation for intensified economic disparity, poverty, regional differences, and racial strife. The high level of unemployment during the latter 1800s challenged the American belief in the idea that anyone looking for work could find it (Bremner, 1956). People began to accept the possibility that there might be structural reasons beyond the control of the individual that contributed to poverty. Severe bouts of economic depression, particularly during the late 1800s, gave rise to a tremendous need for social welfare intervention and recognition of the large-scale needs of many population groups. Out of this period came the birth of professional social services and the beginnings of social work as we know it today.

Progressive Era (1875–1925)

The late 1800s and early 1900s witnessed two opposite but related trends: economic growth and increased poverty. Urban areas grew tremendously, and industry expanded. Immigrants were hired to perform dangerous and low-paid jobs, with the concentration of wealth in the hands of the few who were at the top. Poverty was prevalent among industrial workers, immigrants, and rural Southern African-Americans (Wenocur & Reisch, 1989). The wide schism between the "haves" and "have-nots" produced great social need. Change was rapid, and the social problems that surfaced were far beyond the capabilities of the existing private charities.

The growing disparity between rich and poor fueled political and social dissatisfaction that in turn gave rise to a new political movement. This period, the Progressive Era, witnessed a shift in social welfare policy and programs from family and private responsibility to community and government responsibility. Unlike the expansionary years after the Civil War, economic conditions at the turn of the century worsened, and the nation began to regard social problems such as poverty as social concerns rather than individual problems (Trattner, 1994). This new concern with social problems included closer examination of the structural forces that led to personal misfortune.

Among the numerous social problems during this period were terrible labor conditions, particularly for women and children; poor health, especially among those living in crowded urban tenement areas; lack of understanding of mental health needs, which led to mistreatment of those deemed to be "insane"; poor treatment of children and lack of educational opportunities; and overall poverty among a significant portion of the population.

Social welfare programs and the provision of services during the Progressive Era were embodied in two distinct movements, the Charity Organization Societies and the Settlement Movement. Together, they serve as the foundation for the profession of social work today. They also represent two different perspectives and traditions for serving those in need.

Charity Organization Societies

Modeled after groups in London, the first Charity Organization Society was established in 1877 in Buffalo, New York. Charity Organization Societies (COS) were developed to eliminate poverty through discovering its causes among individuals and then removing those causes from society (Erickson, 1987). Objective techniques stressing scientific methods were considered the best way to solve the problem of poverty. Through coordination of relief giving and modeling of appropriate behavior by "friendly visitors," families would receive relief without duplication of services and would be shown how to live a respectable life. Those most involved in the COS believed that poverty was rooted in the personal character of the poor person (Germain & Hartman, 1980).

Three main principles guided the COS: (1) urban poverty was rooted in moral and character deficiencies of the individual; (2) by helping poor people recognize and correct their flawed character, poverty could be abolished; and (3) to accomplish the goal of ending poverty through character rehabilitation, charitable societies needed to cooperate and organize so as to stop providing overlapping resources (Boyer, 1989).

Perhaps the most famous COS worker was Mary Richmond. She began work in Baltimore in 1891 as an administrator and as a friendly visitor. Over the years, she advocated for the training of social work professionals. She wrote *Social Diagnosis*, which presented theory and practice in how to identify clients' problems. Her work served as the foundation for establishing professional social work (Erickson, 1987).

Although the COS were widespread, their focus on individual change in spite of terrible economic and social conditions was not sufficient to eradicate the poverty of the early 1900s. Recurring economic depressions and mass destitution were beyond the reach of the COS movement (Katz, 1986). Moreover, efforts to reform individuals through assistance administered on the basis of scientific assessment of needs tended to be paternalistic, and blaming the individual for his or her condition (Ehrenreich, 1985). Charity Organization Societies did nothing to change the environmental conditions that contributed to impoverishment, such as unequal opportunities, illness, and lack of social support.

Although the COS movement failed to eradicate poverty or to significantly improve the lives of those in need, it made lasting contributions to our social welfare system and the development of the social work profession (see Table 2.1). It introduced the concept that provision of social services should be handled by formal organizations with training in providing support and relief funds. These organizations should focus on the unique concerns of individuals and not assume all situations are alike. In addition, the COS movement introduced the concept of scientific methods, paving the way for research and investigation of individual and family needs. The COS were the forerunners of today's family service agencies (Erickson, 1987).

Settlement Movement

The Settlement Movement also arose at the turn of the century. The work of the Settlements was based on a completely different perspective from the COS regarding the causes of poverty and social need. The Settlement Movement began in this country in 1887 with the establishment of the Neighborhood Guild in New York City. It was based on a similar model in England, the famous Toynbee Hall (Reid, 1981). The philosophy behind

Table 2.1

Contributions of Early Approaches to Social Work

Charity Organization Societies	Settlement Movement
• Specialized focus on individuals and families	• Focus on individuals as part of their communities
• Casework	• Group work
• Coordination and organization of formal social services	• Community organizing
• Scientific methods used to determine need	• Emphasis on social reform and political action
• Training of professional social service providers	• Research on the community
• Research on the individual	• Social needs assessment
	• Understanding strengths of cultural diversity

the Settlement Movement was that social workers should live among the people in order to best serve communities. Established as neighborhood centers where all were welcome, settlement houses served both as housing for settlement workers and meeting places for local people. The Settlement Movement philosophy combined the achievement of individual growth with satisfying social relations and social responsibility. Unlike the narrow individual focus of the COS, the Settlements emphasized community and society. The Settlements held a holistic perspective of the person in society and regarded a person's inner well-being as inseparable from external forces. The Settlement philosophy held that people could become full citizens through participation in social systems including the family, neighborhood, ethnic groups, and place of employment.

Discussion of the Settlement Movement would not be complete without mention of Jane Addams. For more than thirty years, Jane Addams was a powerful force behind the Settlement Movement (Germain & Hartman, 1980). In 1889, she and Ellen Gates Starr founded Hull House in Chicago, the most famous of the Settlements. Hull House was located on the west side of Chicago where poor immigrant groups lived in crowded, unhealthy, and unsafe conditions. The goals and activities of Hull House set the tone for Settlements across the nation.

Most Settlement houses were founded in poor neighborhoods occupied mostly by recent immigrants. Their early goals were to help socialize people to their new homeland and alleviate the tremendous economic and social disparity between the newcomers and the established, wealthier classes. The Settlement leaders emphasized the need to direct reform efforts toward the environment. Activities within the Settlement Movement included social clubs which provided vocational training and educational opportunities, recreational programs, playgrounds and gymnasiums, and classes in drama, music, and the arts. Although socialization was a key element, the goals of helping immigrants adapt to their new home and shrinking the gap between the wealthy and the poor were always significant parts of Settlement work. The Settlements, more than any other institutions in America, emphasized work with immigrants through intelligent and sympathetic approaches (Kogut, 1972).

After establishment of Hull House, the Settlement Movement grew rapidly. In 1891 there were 6 Settlements; by 1897 there were 74; and by 1900, more than 100. The Movement peaked in 1910 with 400 Settlements (Davis, 1984). The Settlements provided places for local people to meet and discuss the politics of the day. The Settlement houses became clearinghouses for urban reform and played a vital role in the Progressive or "social justice" political movement of the 1900s (Trattner, 1994).

The Settlement Movement is credited with contributing to the establishment of a number of social reforms. These include regulation of child labor, compulsory school attendance laws, maximum hours and minimum wages for female workers, workers' compensation, mothers' pensions, new standards for public sanitation and health, special courts for juvenile offenders, visiting nurses, and visiting teachers (Chambers, 1974).

Jane Addams herself was very involved in efforts toward environmental reform and political reform. She was a powerful public speaker and prolific writer who used both avenues to reach the American people. After twenty years of public admiration, she fell out of favor with the public because of her opposition to World War I. She was an outspoken leader of the peace movement and one of the founders of the Women's International League for Peace and Freedom (Addams, 1922, 1937). Years after the war, her efforts on behalf of world peace were recognized. She received the Nobel Peace Prize in 1931. Although she was at odds with those social workers who focused on individual change rather than social reform, she was universally admired.

Settlement workers believed they could solve social problems by living in poor neighborhoods. They were reformers who helped people who lacked power to organize locally and nationally. Settlements were a strong force during the Progressive Era and contributed to the development of social welfare policies and organizations including the National Child Labor Committee, the National Women's Trade Union League, the National Association for the Advancement of Colored People, and the American Civil Liberties Union (Davis, 1984). When the American public shifted its focus during World War I, however, the Settlements declined in importance. The prosperity of the post-war period masked the concerns of the poor, and the pressing social needs that had given rise to the Settlement Movement seemed to dissipate. Nevertheless, the contributions of the Settlement Movement to our approach to providing social welfare services were significant.

The Settlement Movement provides a model for social workers' involvement in social welfare policy and political action (see Table 2.1). Group work, community organization, and social action emerged from the Settlements. Settlements such as Hull House were very involved in gathering data on their surrounding communities and in turn used their findings to document the need for social change. The Settlement Movement embodied the values of the Progressive Era: to help economically and socially disadvantaged people integrate into society, while simultaneously working for structural changes designed to improve labor conditions and alleviate poverty.

Consequences of the Progressive Era

The Progressive Era witnessed tremendous political change. For the first time in America, industrial workers began to organize and demand better working conditions and wages. Although management was still in control of production, unions organized among numerous trades and provided new-found strength for workers. Women found a place in the changing economic and political environment, becoming employed in social welfare services and seeking increased political involvement. The Suffrage Movement gained public attention and culminated in 1920 with passage of the constitutional amendment awarding women the right to vote. Women fought for and achieved access to higher education and professions (Boulding, 1992).

African-Americans did not fare as well as other groups did during the Progressive years. While white workers, women, and children gained rights, most of the freed slaves of the South remained in poverty. Many became tenant farmers, economically enslaved to their former owners. Some moved North to find jobs in urban centers. While their lives were better than those who lived in the South, Northern African-Americans were barred from union membership and did not benefit from the progress made for white workers (Jansson, 1997). Although the African-American community organized from within and established the National Urban League in 1910 and the National Association for the Advancement of Colored People (NAACP) in 1912 (Axinn & Levin, 1992), the racial division and hierarchy between whites and African-Americans in America was firmly rooted.

In spite of political change and progress, the underlying economic and social structure of the United States remained intact. The severe economic depressions of the turn of the century gave way to a resurgence of social stability. World War I brought a sense of common purpose to the nation, put people to work, and halted immigration, giving the country time to absorb the diverse cultures that had flocked to America in the late 1800s and early 1900s. By the 1920s the nation was relatively prosperous and the social changes of the Progressive Era had slowed. "Old American values" resurfaced, and a return to majority conservatism dominated (Daniels, 1990, p. 281).

Social welfare policy still remained in the hands of private charities, states, and localities. The role of the federal government was yet to come, although the seeds of federal involvement in social welfare had been sown during the Progressive Era. The federal government had passed legislation regulating work, protecting women and children, placing restrictions on factory owners, and protecting American workers.

The Great Depression and the New Deal (1925–1940)

Economic instability and depression were remote concerns during the 1920s. The "Roaring Twenties" were years of economic prosperity and extravagant living. Certainly there were poor people, but their problems were geographically and socially confined. Those in political power and those who controlled industry remained oblivious to the needs of the poor. Much of the population was living beyond their means, buying on credit and saving little or nothing. Market speculation and fraudulent stock deals were common. Shrewd business dealings that resulted in profit were viewed as acceptable. There was a general belief that anyone who worked hard and had some business savvy could "make it" economically.

The stock market crash of October 1929 brought an abrupt end to the strong faith in the market system and the prosperity of the 1920s. The warning signs of extended credit, little savings, and market speculation had gone unheeded. The nation's social structure and charitable organizations were totally unprepared to meet the incredible social needs and demands of Americans during the Great Depression of the 1930s. The economic changes were staggering: in 1929 almost 1.6 million people were unemployed, in 1931 8 million were unemployed, and by 1933 almost 13 million were out of work—more than 25% of the civilian labor force (U.S. Bureau of the Census, 1975). In addition, the Gross National Product fell from $103 billion in 1929 to $56 billion in 1933 (U.S. Bureau of the Census, 1975). Millions of families were impoverished by unemployment of the main breadwinner.

Existing social services and relief organizations could not deal with the millions in need. The private charitable groups of the 1920s had been concerned with individuals and small-scale need, and they lacked the skills and resources to deal with the tremendous social and economic upheaval of the Great Depression. Public opinion changed with the magnitude of the Depression. People who were hard-working and trusted the market system suddenly found themselves without work. They lost savings and had no prospects for self-support. These occurrences were contrary to the American belief in individualism and reward for hard work and honesty. The market system had failed, and poverty had become a societal concern. The combined failures of the economic system, private charitable agencies, and state and local governments to address economic need placed social welfare on the agenda of the federal government:

As a result of the Depression, many people came to realize that the fortunes of individual Americans were interdependent, and many adopted the belief that it was the duty of the federal government to prevent new depressions (Grönbjerg, Street, & Suttles, 1978, p. 46).

Prior to the 1930s, the federal government played a secondary role to states and localities in social welfare policy. The federal government had begun to intercede through regulation, but for the most part it had left the market system alone. Thus, those who were outside of the benefits of the market—poor workers, women and children, racial minorities, and immigrants—had received no federal government support. The economic upheaval of the Great Depression changed that.

The shock of the Great Depression paved the way for the election of Franklin Delano Roosevelt to the presidency. The nation was in the depths of severe economic destitution and ready for a new leader with new ideas.

> One of the factors that made Roosevelt a great leader was that his beliefs so neatly coincided with popular values in the thirties.... What was good, decent, fair, and just—what was "right"—was also what a majority of people wanted and, hence, what was expedient (McElvaine, 1993, p. 325).

Roosevelt had a genuine concern for others, a noblesse oblige combined with his understanding of struggle based on his own experience with polio. He believed that the Depression was the result of factors that could be changed through federal action. His policies, referred to as the **New Deal**, were designed to reverse the economic misfortunes of the nation.

The Social Security Act of 1935 was the single most significant federal legislation to develop out of the Great Depression and Roosevelt's New Deal efforts. It represented a major change in the country's approach to social welfare policies and programs. Although a number of smaller federal efforts were undertaken during the early 1930s, the groundwork for passage of the Social Security Act was set from three efforts: the Federal Emergency Relief Act (FERA), the Civilian Conservation Corps (CCC), and the Works Progress Administration (WPA) (Axinn & Levin, 1992; Trattner, 1994).

The FERA established the first federal economic relief agency since the brief years of the Freedman's Bureau after the Civil War. The magnitude of poverty led to a consensus that the federal government needed to be the direct provider of relief to local public agencies through which individuals would receive aid. The intent was that the relief was to be temporary, just until people had become employed.

Thus, by 1933, the creation and provision of jobs was the dominant goal of the social welfare policies under the New Deal. The CCC and the WPA were created to develop employment for those on relief. The WPA provided 8 million government jobs ranging from heavy construction to orchestral performances (Axinn & Levin, 1992). Examples of WPA projects included the building of post offices, schools, and government buildings. The CCC provided employment for thousands of young men by putting them to work on conservation projects, including reforestation and flood control (Trattner, 1994).

The Roosevelt administration planned to use the FERA to provide direct relief and the WPA and CCC to provide temporary employment through the worst of the Depression. Once basic relief had been achieved, permanent solutions were needed. Two key advisors to the president at this time were both social workers: Harry Hopkins and Frances Perkins. Harry Hopkins, born in Iowa, started his social work career as a Settlement house worker in New York City. He went on to work as an advocate for the poor and served in the New York State Bureau of Family Rehabilitation and Relief. Hopkins served as the director of the Federal Emergency Relief Agency and acted as a personal advisor to Roosevelt. Frances Perkins, the first woman appointed to a Cabinet position, served as secretary of labor throughout the Roosevelt administration. Frances Perkins had begun her career as a public investigator of labor conditions and was deeply committed to improving the lives of workers. Her work as a member of FDR's Cabinet demonstrated her commitment to enhancing labor conditions and promoting federal social welfare services. Perkins chaired the Committee on Economic Security, which developed the Social Security program we have today (McSteen, 1985; Severn, 1976).

The Great Depression disproved the concept that poverty was always the result of personal laziness and unworthiness. During the Depression millions of hard-working, responsible, and previously economically stable workers found themselves without work. The circumstances of their poverty were beyond their control. The economic upheaval of the Depression altered public opinion toward social welfare policy and programs. The overall failure of economic institutions lessened the resistance of the voting public toward adopting a national social welfare policy (Dobelstein, 1980).

The failure of the economic system brought the federal government into the direct provision of social welfare services. The enactment of the Social Security Act established the two main social welfare programs of today: social insurance and public assistance (Berkowitz & McQuaid, 1988). The Social Security programs reflected Roosevelt's New Deal efforts of providing relief in times of economic downturn while stressing employment as the key to economic well-being.

The Social Security Act, which went into effect in August 1935, represented a compromise between radical and conservative ideologies. Conservative interests were concerned that federal social welfare policy would destroy individual responsibility and self-determination. Radical proposals called for large payments and federal responsibility for the economic well-being of all Americans. In response to these competing political pressures, the Act included provisions for economic security for the aged, unemployment insurance, assistance for dependent children, as well as funds for states to provide services to promote vocational rehabilitation, infant and maternal health, public health, and aid to children and people with disabilities. The overall aim was to reinforce the work ethic by rewarding employment while at the same time providing a federal safety net of economic relief for those most in need.

The Social Security Act created two main social welfare programs: (1) social insurance, including Old-Age Insurance and Unemployment Insurance, and (2) public assistance, including Old-Age Assistance, Aid to Dependent Children and Aid to the Blind. Over the years the Act has been amended numerous times to include other provisions. The details of economic assistance and the Social Security Act are explained more fully in chapters 5 and 8 as part of the discussions on assistance to the poor and elderly.

The Social Security Act legislated two very different approaches to providing people with economic assistance. **Social insurance** is a collectively funded program for workers and their dependents to provide economic resources at the conclusion of employment due to retirement, disability, or death. It is *social* because anyone who works is covered as are his or her survivors and dependents, provided he or she has paid in while working, and it is *insurance* because the payments guarantee coverage for the rest of the recipient's life. **Public assistance**, on the other hand, does not require any involvement prior to economic need. It is a government-funded effort to provide economic assistance to people who fall below a certain income level and are considered to be in poverty. It is *public* because it is funded through general revenue collected by the government, and it is *assistance* because it is meant to be temporary and aid people in distress, not to provide lifetime support.

The social insurance provisions of the Social Security Act were appealing for a number of reasons. Initial acceptance was aided by the bias in the system: early entrants, were favored with a high benefit-to-cost ratio. That means that in the early years of the program, people would receive benefits after paying into the program for a short time. The program was incremental: the costs started low and increased gradually, making it more acceptable to the tax-paying public. Also, the design of the program promised benefits without any stigma in return for one's payroll taxes. A person earned credits through working and never had to prove financial need.

The public assistance provisions did not receive as much popular support. Because of the tremendous poverty of the Great Depression, people needed immediate economic aid. The overall plan was that public assistance was to be temporary. Once the immediate economic crisis had passed and all were employed (or related to someone who was employed) there would no longer be a need for public assistance. Public opposition and reluctance to accept both social insurance and public assistance were diminished by the severity of the Great Depression and the political savvy of Roosevelt and his supporters. In the end, the Social Security Act reflected many compromises and contained many ambiguities so that different interest groups could support it (Derthick, 1979).

The establishment of the Social Security Act in 1935 marked the beginning of a new era in social welfare policy. The Act ushered in a significant change in the ideological stance of the federal government. It marked the beginning of the modern welfare state. Since 1935, almost all significant social welfare policy has been enacted as part of the Social Security Act or as an outgrowth of it. Its programs account for the majority of coverage, recipients, benefits, and expenses for social welfare from 1935 to the present. In addition, the creation of social insurance and public assistance through the Social Security Act gave rise to several major shifts: there has been tremendous growth in the federal bureaucracy and in the number of personnel working on social welfare issues, and it established the federal government as the institution to take on projects disowned or ignored by the private sector (Berkowitz & McQuaid, 1988).

The decade of the 1930s, then, brought about significant social welfare policy shifts. Human rights came before property rights, movement toward equality in access to employment and education was initiated, legislation to promote better health and economic security was passed, and federal intervention into the economy was instituted, all of which helped to push forward the development of professional social work (Fisher, 1980). Although in the years to come there would be many challenges by those opposed to government involvement in personal life, the federal government was firmly entrenched in the provision of social welfare services by the end of the 1930s.

World War II and the Development of the Post-War Economy (1940–1960)

Challenged by international events, President Roosevelt was forced to focus on World War II and abandon his primary concern with the social reforms of the New Deal. World War II did what all the employment programs of the New Deal could not: it put most Americans back to work. The war effort employed millions through enlistment in the armed services and employment in war-related industries and technologies. Socially, it simultaneously closed the country to immigration and exposed military personnel to international ways and experiences. It brought full employment and finally ended the economic downturn of the Great Depression.

In addition to bringing the economy out of the Depression, World War II permanently expanded the social role of the federal government.

> New Deal spending in the years 1937 through 1941 averaged $9.2 billion a year. By the years 1947 to 1950, however, federal expenditures averaged $37.8 billion. A four-fold increase in government spending had occurred almost unnoticed (Berkowitz & McQuaid, 1988, p. 147).

The military also changed the social environment. With so many men in the military, women were brought into the work force and introduced to non-traditional jobs. The famous image of "Rosie the Riveter" exalted the work efforts of women in jobs formerly held by men. As the war drew on, social mores gave way to military necessity. African-Americans were brought into the military and slowly began to be integrated into the larger military system. In spite of these gains, however, the liberation of women and the integration of African-Americans were short-lived. After the war, the nation shifted into a period of private interest, focus on the family, and a conservatism not witnessed since the 1920s.

Immediately following the war, the federal government passed the Servicemen's Readjustment Act of 1944, commonly known as the GI Bill. It reflected the national sentiment that the nation owed its veterans and therefore funded provisions for education and training, home and business loans, and employment services designed to help the returning soldiers adapt to civilian life (Axinn & Levin, 1992). While today the GI Bill is viewed as a major piece of legislation, its original sponsors never planned it to be more than a modest support for readjustment (Lemann, 1993). However, millions of people took full advantage of the educational provisions, leaving a lasting positive view of the federal response to returning veterans.

The 1950s witnessed a postwar prosperity that emphasized a focus on private well-being. Although the federal government was permanently drawn into the provision of social welfare services during the 1930s and 1940s, the efforts of the 1950s centered around incremental change and services that reinforced the private domain. Federal subsidies for housing, mortgages, and transportation made it possible for post-war families to leave cities and live in newly developed suburban areas (Ehrenreich, 1985).

The one major social welfare policy development of the 1950s was the addition of disability insurance to the Social Security Act. This addition exemplifies the development of social welfare policy during the 1950s. It took years to convince policy-makers to extend social insurance to cover workers and their families in the event these workers became disabled. This social welfare policy shift reflected the mood of the times: it demonstrated how difficult it was to expand the coverage of the existing Social Security Act. Under this conservative mood, developing any new social welfare policies was extremely difficult. Thus, major social welfare policy changes would not come about for another decade.

Social Reform (1960–1970)

The private focus and relative economic stability of the 1950s was broken by the revelations of the 1960s. While generally the economy had prospered, research uncovered tremendous segments of the American population who did not benefit from the post–World War II prosperity and were living in poverty. Michael Harrington's book *The Other America: Poverty in the United States* (1962), which described the economic misfortunes of many Americans, is credited with initiating the **War on Poverty**. Massive migration of African-Americans from the South to the North had created densely populated urban areas untouched by the economic prosperity of the 1950s (Jansson, 1997).

The 1960s, like the 1930s and the early 1900s, was a period of social welfare policy development. In response to the "rediscovery" of poverty and the demographic shifts, two major social welfare policy initiatives were achieved by 1964: the Civil Rights Act and the War on Poverty. The Civil Rights Act codified protection of minorities by requiring desegregation of public facilities and prohibiting discriminatory hiring practices (Jansson, 1997). President Johnson launched the War on Poverty as an effort to start his own New Deal (Trattner, 1994). Included among those efforts was the Economic Opportunity Act, which outlined the administration's anti-poverty attempts. Among the provisions were the Job Corps program to aid youths in preparing for employment; VISTA (Volunteers in Service to America), which stressed community service in impoverished neighborhoods; and Community Action Programs, which provided federal funds for community programs working toward the elimination of poverty (Axinn & Levin, 1992). Also in 1964, the Food Stamp Program was enacted to address the growing need to alleviate hunger in America.

Additional legislation was enacted in 1965. The Older Americans Act developed a nationwide network to coordinate services for the elderly. The coverage of the Social Security Act was expanded by the addition of two major social welfare programs, Medicare and Medicaid, to address health care for the elderly, poor, and people with disabilities. Early efforts during the 1920s and 1930s to include health coverage in the Social Security Act had failed. Supporters of health care insurance and assistance had spent thirty years lobbying for health coverage. As part of the War on Poverty, they were successful in gaining passage of Medicare, which is part of the social insurance program of the Social Security Act, and Medicaid, which provides health coverage as part of public assistance. The addition of Medicare broadened the safety net of Social Security for the elderly and workers who became disabled, and the constellation of health services for the poor was expanded through Medicaid.

In addition, the War on Poverty extended to cover other areas of social welfare. As a result of the Economic Opportunity Act, Head Start was established in 1965. The goal of Head Start was to prevent poverty through services to aid poor preschool children and their families. The services included medical care, nutrition, school preparation, and parental education (Gustavsson & Segal, 1994).

The Shifting Focus of the 1970s and 1980s

For social welfare activists, the 1960s must have seemed like a time of optimism, when it seemed that all social problems could and would be addressed. Policies and programs were created and supported by government and voters alike. No matter how liberal and reformist the new legislative efforts might have been, however, conservative ideologies were still evident. By the later 1960s, efforts were begun to curtail the social largess of the decade. Public assistance, developed as part of the New Deal, had shifted from aid to the elderly, those with disabilities, and widows and their children to a new population: dependent children of unmarried, abandoned, or divorced women (Berkowitz & McQuaid, 1988).

By the late 1960s, the growth in the caseloads of single mothers and families of color in the Aid to Families with Dependent Children (AFDC) program (expanded in 1962 from the original Aid to Dependent Children program of the Social Security Act) prompted more punitive measures. The program was perceived as having changed from one of income support to the worthy poor—widows and orphans—to one of subsidizing women whose lifestyles differed from the norm and did not comply with the nation's family ethic (Abramovitz, 1996). The economy began to stagnate, and inflation from government expenses for the Vietnam War effort started to catch up with the nation. People began to view government skeptically, "as an enemy" (Jimenez, 1990, p. 8). Thus, during the 1970s, there was a reversal of the efforts of the previous decade.

Despite the shifting ideology of the 1970s and President Richard Nixon's conservative policies, however, incremental change gave rise to a number of policy initiatives. In 1973, the federal government passed the Comprehensive Employment and Training Act (CETA), designed to help the unemployed, and a year later Title XX was added to the Social Security Act to provide funds directly to the states for social welfare services for the poor. Both initiatives reflected the more conservative elements of the times, with reliance on local authority and the private market for implementation rather than the federal government (Trattner, 1994).

The activism of the 1960s did not disappear during the 1970s. The women's movement gained momentum in the struggle for equal rights and protection from discrimination. The National Organization for Women (NOW), organized in 1966, established itself as a national representative of women's issues. In 1973, the landmark legal case of *Roe v. Wade* legalized abortions and in the process gave women of all economic and social backgrounds access to the medical procedure. Gay rights advocates mark the 1969 Stonewall riot as the beginning of the gay rights movement. The riot was a violent confrontation between police and gay patrons of the Stonewall Bar in New York City that lasted for five days. The confrontation politicized many gays and resulted in intensified organizing for equal rights and protection from discrimination (Marcus, 1992).

Nevertheless, the renewed conservatism of the 1970s became more entrenched during the 1980s. Represented by the presidency of Ronald Reagan, the 1980s were a full decade of preoccupation with private interests. The Reagan administration focused on three fundamental goals: shifting responsibility and power from the federal government to states and localities; relying on the private sector to provide for social welfare needs; and reducing federal programs and spending for social welfare initiatives (Rochefort, 1986).

Social welfare policy legislation enacted during the 1980s was meager and often punitive, taking resources away from social welfare services under the guise of less government. This punitive response was particularly felt by poor women who relied on government cash benefits to support their families. After cuts in AFDC were regulated into law in 1983 under President Reagan, the Family Support Act of 1988 was passed to amend the AFDC program. Described as "welfare reform," the Act was punitive and restrictive, giving poor women less support and protection from economic hardship (Segal, 1989).

When social welfare policy was enacted during the 1980s, it often came long after a social problem had gained national attention. For example, in 1987, years after researchers and mayors of urban cities recognized the problem, the federal government finally passed legislation to provide support for people who were homeless. The Stewart B. McKinney Homeless Assistance Act was passed in July 1987 but was never fully funded. From 1987 to 1991, Congress authorized $3.3 billion, yet only $2.4 billion was actually appropriated to be spent on services for people who are homeless (U.S. General Accounting Office, 1992).

Just as slow in coming was the federal response to AIDS, a disease which had gained public attention as early as 1983 (Shilts, 1987). In spite of this knowledge, the federal government did not respond with AIDS-related legislation until 1990 with the Ryan White Comprehensive AIDS Resources Emergency (CARE) Act, designed to provide services to people with AIDS. As with other legislation of the time, full funding was not forthcoming. In 1991 and 1992, the Act received less than one-fourth the authorization of almost $900 million (Select Committee on Children, Youth, and Families, 1992).

At the same time that social welfare services were being rescinded and underlying social problems were being ignored, the federal government invested untold billions in supporting corporate America. The $7.5 billion bailout of Continental Bank in 1984 (Congressional Quarterly, 1985) and the more than $100 billion spent between 1989 and 1993 for covering the savings and loan scandal (Congressional Quarterly, 1993) are the most publicized instances. Other subsidies of agriculture, energy, and technology groups occurred to significant degrees. In summary, the decade of the 1980s was characterized by decreased government support for poor and disenfranchised people and increased government support for corporate America. This shifting emphasis reflected the priority of support for private interest rather than for social welfare programs.

Turning Tide of the 1990s?

The early years of the 1990s seemed to represent the start of a shift away from private interest and disregard for those who were disadvantaged and disenfranchised. In 1990, the Americans with Disabilities Act was passed, mandating protection from discrimination for people with disabilities. In 1991, after years of chipping away at the efforts of the 1960s, the Civil Rights

Restoration Act expanded many of the protections of the earlier legislation. In the spring of 1993, gay advocates organized the largest civil rights demonstration in American history with the March on Washington. Nearly a million people demonstrated for equal rights and an end to discrimination based on a person's sexual orientation.

The election of Democrat Bill Clinton to the White House in 1992 ended twelve years of Republican control. Under President Clinton, several major pieces of legislation were passed, after having languished for years during Republican administrations. After suffering two presidential vetoes by George Bush in 1988 and 1990, the Family and Medical Leave Act (FMLA) was passed and signed into law in January of 1993. While minimal in its coverage and far short of what activists had hoped to achieve, the FMLA marked the first time in history that the federal government mandated employers to guarantee unpaid leave for workers after the birth or adoption of a child, or during the illness of a dependent or family member. Other social welfare legislation passed under President Clinton includes the Brady Bill, which enacted controls on the purchase and ownership of handguns, and the Anti-Crime Bill, which outlawed automatic assault weapons. These two bills had been introduced in Congress during the Reagan and Bush administrations and had met with defeat each time.

Democratic control of Congress was short-lived. After the 1994 election, Republicans took control of both the House and the Senate for the first time in more than forty years. The Republican platform called for retraction of social welfare services and a shift away from federal support. The Republican "Contract with America" pledged to decrease federal control of social welfare services with a move to turn over the responsibility to state and local governments. These positions built on those espoused during the 1980s under the Reagan presidency. The Republican agenda of limiting social welfare programs and removing the federal government from the social welfare system was reflected in the Personal Responsibility and Work Opportunity Reconciliation Act, signed into law by President Clinton in August 1996. This piece of social welfare policy represents a radical shift in public assistance. Since 1935, the AFDC program guaranteed cash assistance to any family with very low income. The new legislation cancelled a guarantee that had been in place for more than sixty years. The AFDC program will be phased out and replaced by the Temporary Assistance for Needy Families (TANF) program.

Analysis of the new legislation reveals there will no longer be unified federal guidelines for the program (Center on Budget and Policy Priorities, 1996). Now public assistance programs vary from state to state. If a state runs out of money in a given year, it can stop providing economic aid. Poor families will have to wait until the following year for assistance. In addition, there is a time limit on cash assistance. No family can receive more than five years of assistance over its lifetime. The Children's Defense Fund (1996) estimates that as a result of this bill, child poverty will increase by 12%, poor families will lose an average of $1,300 a year in income, more than 300,000 children with disabilities will lose assistance, and the food stamp program will be cut $28 billion over the next six years. The new law is very complicated and contains numerous sections. It remains to be seen what the full impact of this policy change will be in the years to come.

Final Thoughts on the History of Social Welfare

The impact of recent legislation will unfold as the United States enters the new millennium. What remains clear is that there is a strong move toward shifting the social welfare system away from the federal government and back to states and communities. The impact of this shift will be strongly felt by social work practitioners, who provide much of the personnel for our social welfare programs.

Whatever social welfare policy decisions are made in the future, it is certain that changes will be built upon the achievements and failures of the past. In order to be prepared to participate in the dialogue for social welfare policy change, it is imperative to understand its history. In this chapter, we have provided an overview of the history of social welfare policy in America that should serve as the foundation for understanding our social welfare system.

Key Concepts

Elizabethan Poor Laws	New Deal
"worthy" versus "unworthy" poor	Social Security Act of 1935
Progressive Era	social insurance
Charity Organization Societies	public assistance
Settlement Movement	War on Poverty

Exercises

1. Ask someone significantly older than you to reminisce about social conditions throughout his or her life. Was this person alive during the Great Depression? Does he or she remember World War II? Was this individual involved in social movements of the 1960s? Does she or he remember the struggle over civil rights? Try to link these personal experiences with the historical events outlined in this chapter.

2. Read a historical novel to help bring to life some of the periods highlighted in this chapter. As a class project, groups of students can be assigned to research different time periods. The task of each group is to find a novel written about that time period and analyze the experiences

of the characters in relation to the historical events of the era. For example, you might read *The Grapes of Wrath* for the Great Depression or *Forrest Gump* for the 1960s. Are the books realistic portrayals? Why or why not?

References

Abramovitz, M. (1996). *Regulating the lives of women: Social welfare policy from Colonial times to the present.* Revised edition. Boston, MA: South End Press.

Addams, J. (1922). *Peace and bread in time of war.* New York: Macmillan.

Addams, J. (1937). *Twenty years at Hull House.* New York: Macmillan.

Axinn, J., & Levin, H. (1992). *Social Welfare: A history of the American response to need* (3rd ed.). New York: Longman.

Berkowitz, E., & McQuaid, K. (1988). *Creating the welfare state* (2nd ed.). New York: Praeger.

Boulding, E. (1992). *The underside of history.* Volume 2. Newbury Park, CA: Sage.

Boyer, P. (1989). Building character among the urban poor: The Charity Organization Movement. In Colby, I.C. (ed.), *Social welfare policy: Perspectives, patterns, insights*, pp. 113–134. Chicago: Dorsey.

Bremner, R.H. (1956). *The discovery of poverty in the United States.* New York: New York University Press.

Center on Budget and Policy Priorities. (1996). *The new welfare law.* Washington, DC: Author.

Chambers, C.A. (1974). An historical perspective on political action vs. individualized treatment. In P. Weinberger (ed.), *Perspectives on social welfare.* New York: Macmillan.

Children's Defense Fund. (1996). *Legislative Update (8-2-96).* Washington, DC: Author.

Congressional Quarterly. (1985). *Congress and the nation, 1981–1984.* Volume VI. Washington, DC: Author.

Congressional Quarterly. (1993). Hill votes more funds for thrift bailout. *1993 CQ Almanac*, 150. Washington, DC: Author.

Daniels, R. (1990). *Coming to America: A history of immigration and ethnicity in American life.* Princeton, NJ: Harper Perennial.

Davis, A.F. (1984). *Spearheads for reform.* New Brunswick, NJ: Rutgers University Press.

Day, P.J. (1997). *A new history of social welfare* (2nd ed.). Boston: Allyn and Bacon.

Derthick, M. 1979. *Policymaking for Social Security.* Washington, DC: Brookings Institution.

Dobelstein, A.W. (1980). *Politics, economics, and public welfare.* Englewood Cliffs, NJ: Prentice Hall.

Ehrenreich, J.H. (1985). *The altruistic imagination: A history of social work and social policy in the United States.* Ithaca, NY: Cornell University Press.

Erickson, A.G. (1987). Family services. *Encyclopedia of social work, Volume 1*, pp. 589–593. Silver Spring, MD: National Association of Social Workers, Inc.

Fisher, J. (1980). *The response of social work to the Depression.* Boston: G.K. Hall & Co.

Germain, C.B., & Hartman, A. (1980). People and ideas in the history of social work practice. *Social Casework, 61* (6), 323–331.

Grönbjerg, K., Street, D., & Suttles, G.D. (1978). *Poverty and social change.* Chicago: University of Chicago Press.

Gustavsson, N.S., & Segal, E.A. (1994). *Critical issues in child welfare*. Thousand Oaks, CA: Sage.

Harrington, M. (1962). *The other America: Poverty in the United States*. Baltimore: Penguin.

Jansson, B.S. (1997). *The reluctant welfare state* (3rd ed.). Pacific Grove, CA: Brooks/Cole.

Jimenez, M.A. (1990). Historical evolution and future challenges of the human services professions. *Families in Society: The Journal of Contemporary Human Services*, 71, (1), 3–12.

Katz, M.B. (1986). *In the shadow of the poorhouse*. New York: Basic Books.

Katz, M.B. (1989). *The undeserving poor: From the war on poverty to the war on welfare*. New York: Pantheon Books.

Kogut, A. (1972). The settlements and ethnicity: 1890–1914. *Social Work, 17* (3), 22–31.

Leiby, J. (1978). *A history of social welfare and social work in the United States*. New York: Columbia University Press.

Lemann, N. (1993). GI Bill nostalgia. *Washington Post National Weekly Edition* (September 6–12).

Marcus, E. (1992). *Making history: The struggle for gay and lesbian equal rights*. New York: HarperCollins.

McElvaine, R.S. (1993). *The Great Depression: America, 1929–1941*. New York: Times Books.

McSteen, M.A. (1985). Fifty years of social security. *Social Security Bulletin, 48* (8), 37–44.

Nabokov, P. (ed.). (1991). *Native American testimony*. New York: Penguin.

Reid, K.E. (1981). *From character building to social treatment*. Westport, CT: Greenwood Press.

Rochefort, D.A. (1986). *American social welfare policy: Dynamics of formulation and change*. Boulder, CO: Westview Press.

Rothman, D.J. (1971). *The discovery of the asylum: Social order and disorder in the new republic*. Boston: Little, Brown.

Segal, E.A. (1989). Welfare reform: Help for poor women & children? *Affilia, 4* (3), 42–50.

Select Committee on Children, Youth, and Families. (1992). *A decade of denial: Teens and AIDS in America*. House of Representatives Report 102–1074. Washington, DC: U.S. Government Printing Office.

Severn, B. (1976). *Frances Perkins: A member of the cabinet*. New York: Hawthorn Books.

Shilts, R. (1987). *And the band played on*. New York: St. Martin's Press.

Trattner, W.I. (1994). *From poor law to welfare state* (5th ed.). New York: The Free Press.

United States Bureau of the Census. (1975). *Historical statistics of the United States*. Washington, DC: U.S. Government Printing Office.

United States General Accounting Office. (1992). *Homelessness: McKinney Act programs and funding through fiscal year 1991. GAO/RCED*–93–39. Washington, DC: U.S. Government Printing Office.

Wenocour, S., & Reisch, M. (1989). *From charity to enterprise: The development of American social work in a market economy*. Urbana, IL: University of Illinois Press.

Chapter 3

Theories and Concepts in Social Welfare Policy

Changes in social welfare policy usually represent the culmination of a large number of social, political, and economic events. A particular policy can be shaped by the concerns of its supporters, social conditions, economics, timing, or any combination of these and other factors. Many different theories have been devised to explain why policy evolves the way it does. To understand social welfare policy, students should become familiar with some of the leading theories of policy evolution.

In this chapter, we present several theories that attempt to explain why and how social welfare policy develops. Underlying influences, such as social conditions and values that shape social welfare policy, are discussed. The synthesis of these ideas serves as the foundation for our analysis of social welfare policy and programs throughout the remaining chapters of this book.

Theories of the Evolution of the Social Welfare System

As outlined in chapter 2, social welfare policies and programs evolve over time. How did the current social welfare system come to be? What factors precipitated the development of today's social welfare policies? Several theories have been developed to explain why the social welfare system evolved as it did. Five of these theories are discussed here.

Industrialization and the Social Welfare System

The structure of the modern social welfare system traces its beginnings to the passage of the Social Security Act in 1935. As discussed in chapter 2, this legislation placed the federal government in the permanent role of guardian of social well-being for the entire nation. The passage of the Act marked the culmination of earlier events and social conditions that contributed to its development.

According to the industrialization theory outlined by Wilensky and Lebeaux (1965), today's social welfare state traces its beginnings to the advent of the industrial era. From the 1850s to the 1920s, the United States was characterized by tremendous industrial expansion and urbanization. The result of these trends was both a greater need for social welfare services and the means to cover that need: industry and urban crowding gave rise to social conditions that demanded attention, and greater productivity gave rise to greater economic resources to address human needs.

Industrialization led to new methods for manufacturing and new types of jobs. It also led to modernization and attempts to produce more goods at less cost. Workers' standard of living improved with increased production and incomes, but the desire to maximize profits also caused poor working conditions to proliferate. The changes in the workplace led to worker dependence on the owners of business. This dependence gave rise to concerns about unemployment, job-related disability, health care for workers, and the care of dependent children and widows when a worker was disabled or died.

Social conditions were also changing during the industrial era. With improvement in health care and modernization of living conditions, life expectancy increased and retirement became a real possibility. Family incomes rose, and people became more mobile. Consequently, the extended family of previous generations disappeared, and with it the safety net it had provided.

The above-mentioned changes in economics, communities, and family relations forever altered the provision of social welfare services in this country. Although the individual was still primarily responsible for his or her well-being, workers also expected industry and government to ensure that certain basic needs were met. Those needs included safety at the workplace, a guarantee of a minimum wage, regulated work hours and conditions, social insurance for retirement, and disability and survivors' benefits in the event of death. Industrialization had led to a common acceptance that the federal, state, and local governments had key roles in maintaining the social well-being of all citizens. While there were times throughout early American history that the government had provided social welfare services, by the 1950s there was general acceptance of the government as a permanent part of the social welfare system.

Social Values and Cycles of History

As discussed in chapter 1, the majority of social welfare programs and services in this country are residual in response and selective in coverage. The residual and selective design of social welfare policy largely reflects the ideologies and values of our society. This country was founded on the values of individualism and self-care. Government intervention is contrary to this philosophy, yet Americans also believe in helping those in need. The interplay between these two **social values**, individualism and social responsibility, has played a key role in the development of social welfare policy.

Schlesinger (1986) views American history as a cycle between individualism and social responsibility. He describes a "continuing shift in national involvement between public purpose and private interest" (p. 27). The shift between cycles represents each period running its course and bringing about change. The periods of public purpose see sweeping changes in a short period of time, but sustained public action requires energy and a high capacity for political commitment. People tire of this level of activity and need to regroup. Thus, periods of public purpose are followed by times of private interest when people become immersed in their personal lives. During periods of private interest, the changes brought about from public action are absorbed and people focus on privatization and personal acquisition. Eventually, however, private interest leads to dissatisfaction because acquisition is not equal for everyone and segments of society fall behind. People begin to feel that the system is not fair and they press for public change and responsibility. Thus, history shifts from private interest to public purpose.

The cycles shift with generations. Schlesinger posits thirty-year cycles moving between public purpose and private interest. During the twentieth century, the nation moved several times from a focus on private interest and acquisition to public concern back to private interest. For example, at the turn of the century the Progressive Movement called for public action. This period was followed by the materialism and acquisition of the 1920s, only to be followed by the Great Depression and an outcry for public action. The public action of the 1930s was represented by the New Deal era and government provision of social welfare services to individuals. This period was followed by a return to private interest characterized by the conservatism and material growth of the 1950s. Again, a shift occurred, and the 1960s became a period of public action. Interest and energy ebbed, and by the 1980s the nation had once again settled into a period of private interest. According to the historical cycles theory of social welfare policy development, the 1990s began a new period of public action and social change.

Social Control

Some theorists view social welfare policy as a tool of **social control**. Those in positions of power use the institutions of the social welfare system to control and direct the behavior of the needy. Piven and Cloward (1971) in *Regulating the Poor* cited public assistance as a tool used by those in political power to quell social unrest and reinforce the employment system. By creating a residual social welfare program and keeping benefits low, the powers-that-be ensure that most people will not be inclined to rely on public assistance and will instead be willing to work, even at low-paying jobs. In time, when benefits remain too low to meet people's basic needs, social unrest develops. In response to the social unrest, programs expand. Thus, shifts are made in benefit amounts and eligibility, but the system remains intact.

Like the historical cycles theory, the social unrest theory views social welfare policy as alternating between periods of narrow benefits and periods of broader social welfare services. The movement on this continuum reflects ongoing efforts by those in political power to keep social unrest at a minimum by providing more generous benefits, then encouraging people to work by cutting back on benefits and tightening eligibility requirements. This fluctuation is reflected through history. Piven and Cloward point to the 1930s and the 1960s as times when coverage and benefits for public assistance expanded. These periods are viewed as evidence of attempts to regulate the poor through social control. Both the 1930s and 1960s began with social movements and closed with expansions in the social welfare system. After the expansions, social unrest dissipated. The poor were successfully regulated through changes in social welfare benefits.

Elite Power

The elite power theory, built on the idea that a handful of people control the policies that govern all of society, is related to social control theory. Domhoff (1990) describes the elite control of public policy as the domination of the nation by a small capitalist class. This dominant and elite class is well connected to those who make public policy.

> There usually are very narrow limits to what can be accomplished by poor people, minorities, trade unionists, and liberals through elections and the legislative process. The costs of running for office are enormous for average people in terms of time and money, and the impediments to change built into the legislative process make it very hard to sustain a pressure-group coalition or legislative social movement that does not have a great amount of money and patience (Domhoff, 1990, p. 260).

Domhoff agrees with social control theory that power gets redistributed when average people organize to disrupt the system. Although the conditions and reasons that motivate people to disrupt the system vary and cannot be predicted, history demonstrates that the process can occur and social change can be supported by those in power. That support is, however, both a response to disruption *and* the elite's attempt to hold onto its position of power.

Economics as a Determinant of Social Welfare Policy

All of the above theories share a number of common characteristics. Each theory suggests that social welfare policy is a consequence of historical events. Several identify a cyclical pattern, and all have an economic component. Industrialization changed the economy of this country, giving rise to our modern social welfare system. Social values changed as the acquisition of resources shifted—when private interests were not being met through sufficient growth in income, people looked to the government for remedy. Social welfare benefits expanded in response to social unrest. Often that social unrest was sparked by economic upheaval, such as the Great Depression.

Analysis of history and the evolution of social welfare policy suggests that economics is a driving force behind the policies and politics of social well-being (Segal, 1987). Our discussion in chapter 2 traced the historical ebb and flow between periods of economic growth and economic hardship. A pattern seems to emerge, demonstrating that social welfare policy changes in response to economic shifts: times of growth are marked by emphasis on individual responsibility, and times of economic belt-tightening are characterized by increased demands for the government to take responsibility for people's well-being.

As we have seen, the value placed on individual responsibility dates back to the earliest history of America. Rugged individualism meant that each person was responsible for his or her own welfare. This responsibility extended to the care of the individual's family and sometimes to the well-being of the immediate community. Throughout American history, however, there have been national upheavals, such as industrialization, urbanization, depressions, and wars, which have altered the marketplace. During these national upheavals, individuals could not adequately provide for their own well-being. At these times, government was called to step in and take over the responsibilities of individuals and families. Thus, in spite of the idealized image of the rugged individual, the reality of American life is that government has always stepped in to aid individuals (Dolgoff, Feldstein, & Skolnik, 1993). From the earliest history of this country to the present, government has helped to support medical care, economic credit, industrial development, and general social well-being.

The theory of economics as a determinant of social welfare policy focused on the public perception of government intervention. When the economy is strong, opportunity for economic gain appears limitless. If there are jobs and growth, and yet a person is not working, that person is viewed as lazy. Government assistance is seen as evidence that an individual is weak and not taking responsibility. When the economy is bad, however, the market system is blamed, rather than the individual. People turn to the government for assistance, and seeking help is not seen as a weakness. The Great Depression is the most significant illustration of this phenomenon. The rate of unemployment during the Great Depression exceeded 25%. With so many previously employed people out of work, public attention focused on the failures of the economic structure and people were open to government intervention. As discussed previously, this period resulted in the enactment of the Social Security Act and the birth of our modern social welfare system.

Public debate on national health insurance coverage is an example of how economic pressure can influence social welfare policy. For decades, advocates have been calling for a national health care program but have received little action from policy-makers. Following the election of Bill Clinton, however, there was a flurry of activity on health care reform. The federal government was considering the development of a comprehensive system. Although federal attention diminished, state governments are still struggling with the issue. Why? From the economic determinants theory, health care represents an area in which the marketplace has failed to adequately serve the needs of the individual. Many people today are employed and working full-time, yet do not have adequate health care coverage for themselves or their families. They are participating in the economy, yet they are not receiving what they need. When such an imbalance occurs, people look to the government to correct the inequity. The driving force behind the push for government intervention is not only economic inequality. It is a sense that those who participate fully in the marketplace are not reaping the rewards of their efforts. Thus, in response to public concern over the economic imbalance between working but not receiving health care coverage, social welfare policies are beginning to emerge through legislation.

Competing Ideologies and the Social Welfare System

Many concepts in social welfare policy represent competing ideologies or opposite ends of a spectrum. The design of the American social welfare system is in large part a result of pulls from competing values, often leading to a compromise that satisfies no one. Understanding competing ideologies helps to clarify some of the inconsistencies in social welfare policy and to explain why the system looks the way it does today.

Cause and Function

Early in the history of the social work profession, the role of human services was the focus of much debate. In 1929, the president of the first professional body of social workers, the National Conference on Social Work, addressed the issue. Porter Lee (1929) differentiated between two aspects of social work: cause and function. **Cause** represents standing behind a moral position to improve society. **Function** comprises day-to-day efforts to provide services. Lee called for embracing the cause while still carrying out the function of administering services.

The conflict between cause and function is ever-present in the social welfare system. To what extent do we take action and fight for a cause, and to what extent do we tend to the daily needs of those who are recipients of social services? Lee called for doing both: fighting to improve society while providing care to individuals. Some theorists argue that doing both is impossible and one must choose between the two. The War on Poverty of the 1960s demonstrated elements of this conflict. Some advocates felt that the public assistance system was punitive and treated people poorly. To labor in service of the system, or in Lee's terms to provide function, was to reinforce the continuation of a system that was bad. Instead, it was important to fight for the cause—better treatment of those who receive public assistance—and to move the program from a selective residual position to a more universal institutional system. Thus, the cause precluded continuing in the function role.

The struggle between cause and function is a part of our social welfare history, and social service providers face it today. For example, when a client lives in a dangerous neighborhood, should the social worker help him or her to move, or should the worker fight to change the neighborhood? Often, it is easier to change the individual's situation than to change entire communities.

"Worthy" Versus "Unworthy" Poor

Dating back to the earliest social welfare legislation in this country, which was modeled on the Elizabethan Poor Laws, the distinction between those who deserve help and those who do not deserve help has played an integral part in the development of social welfare policy. Social welfare recipients have always been categorized as falling into one of two groups, the worthy or unworthy poor. Other terms have been used, including Ronald Reagan's use of the term "truly needy" to distinguish those who were worthy from those who were not.

As discussed in chapter 2, the worthy poor have historically included the widow and her children, orphans, those with disabilities, and the elderly. Those considered unworthy were the able-bodied who were unemployed (predominantly single men and women without children) and unmarried women with children. Recent usage of the concept has maintained the distinction between those who cannot work and those who could work but do not. If a person appears healthy, little attention is paid to reasons why he or she does not work. The act of not working places a person in the category of those not deserving of government assistance.

The value of worthy versus unworthy is very apparent in current debate about our social welfare system. Many conservative analysts, such as Charles Murray (1984) and George Gilder (1981), argue persuasively that those who can work but do not should not receive any form of public assistance. These analyses ignore the reasons why people may not be working. The authors do not discuss the shortage of jobs that pay enough to support a person and that also provide adequate health insurance, nor the geographic imbalance between available jobs and potential workers, nor the lack of training available to prepare people for good jobs. The perspective of worthy versus unworthy poor considers the individual's capabilities only and does not take into account the environment or social circumstances.

Blaming the Victim

Individual responsibility is a key principle behind many of the values that shape our social welfare system. Holding each person responsible for his or her own circumstances is a significant part of American ideology. A variation of individual responsibility is the theory of **blaming the victim**.

The concept of blaming the victim was introduced by William Ryan (1971) to explain why poverty and other concerns are viewed as personal rather than social problems. Ryan argues that it is easier and more comfortable to blame the individual who is poor than to blame all of society. Social welfare in America has followed this philosophy, preferring "to treat what we call social problems, such as poverty, disease, and mental illness, in terms of the individual deviance of the special, unusual groups of persons who had those problems" (Ryan, 1971, p. 16). To identify defects in the community and the environment is to place responsibility on all members of society. Ryan argues that because of self-interest and class interest, the majority would prefer to see social problems as a result of individual defects than to attribute them to a social system that is unfair and exclusionary. If the individual is to blame, then the rest of society is not responsible to make changes or to offer help.

For example, if urban poverty is the fault of those who live in the poor parts of a city, then it is the residents' own responsibility to correct their behaviors and surroundings. On the other hand, if urban poverty is the result of the economic system, then social change through job creation is required to correct the problem.

Those who benefit from keeping society the way it is are reluctant to criticize a system that has been good to them. At the same time, there is genuine concern for those who are disadvantaged. The best way to reconcile the concern for the poor and maintain respect for the status quo is to put the responsibility for social problems on the individual—to blame the victim. Adherence to this perspective calls for social welfare services that focus on changing the individual rather than on changing society.

An extension of this theory is **second-order victim-blaming** (Dressel, Carter, & Balachandran, 1995). This theory refers to the reasons used to explain why social welfare programs fail. For example, a social problem, such as poverty, gives rise to social welfare programs such as AFDC. When critics claim these programs fail, the rationale given is that the recipients are at fault rather than the programs themselves. To clarify this point further, let us provide an illustration. If a client fails to show up for a scheduled appointment with the caseworker, the client is viewed as "non-compliant" as opposed to looking at the fact that the social service office may not be accessible to the client because public transportation is not available. This level of victim blaming is very important to social workers and their clients. If a client is not benefiting from a social service, workers should examine the program's design, funding, and implementation before considering the individual's motivation. Are the program components sound? If not, how can the program be changed? Too often, program failures are blamed on the individual recipients instead of faulty program design and implementation. This is second-order victim-blaming.

The Culture of Poverty and the Underclass

The idea of a **culture of poverty** goes hand-in-hand with the concept of blaming the victim. This ideology asserts that there are those who are born poor and are in turn socialized to remain poor. Poverty is their cultural destiny, and it is passed on from one generation to another. Poverty is viewed as a set of attitudes and behaviors, and the only solution is to help people to learn a new culture, that of the majority. This idea was prevalent in discussions of poverty in the 1960s, but it actually has elements that date back much earlier. For example, at the turn of the century, Charity Organization Society "friendly visitors" entered the homes of the poor to model ideal behaviors and thus change poor families.

In recent years, a newer version of the culture of poverty has surfaced. Many theorists, particularly William Julius Wilson (1987), have described the permanent underclass and the culture of the ghetto. Wilson cites both the individual and society as having responsibility for social conditions and specifically poverty. He argues that due to economic isolation and distress, urban ghettos of poverty do produce a unique culture that is antithetical to majority behaviors and values. As Wilson sees it, the solution to poverty and related problems is for both institutions and individuals to change. Social welfare programs and the economic system must become more sensitive to the needs of the individual, and each person must take responsibility for his or her personal behavior.

Biological Determinism

Many of the theories already discussed are related to the concept of biological heredity as the determinant of how people behave. This belief holds that one's heredity predetermines, or at least strongly influences, what social and economic position a person will achieve. The notion of **biological determinism** is not new. It has surfaced at numerous times throughout Western history. It gained early legitimacy through science by the application of Darwin's concept of "survival of the fittest" to humanity to explain poverty, racial differences, and gender differences (Shipman, 1994; Harvey & Reed, 1992; Duster, 1990). Supporters of this notion argue that those at the top economically and socially got there because of innate, inherited abilities. This approach ignores environment, social surroundings, and a person's access to opportunities such as education and employment.

The concept of biological determinism, which flourished during the 1920s and resurfaced during the 1970s, has again gained popularity. A recent book entitled *The Bell Curve* (Hernstein & Murray, 1994) claims educational ability is inherited and therefore predetermined. This belief, like all forms of biological determinism, is antithetical to the social work value that people are affected by their environment and have the ability to change. The development of social welfare policy is often a response to inequalities in the social and economic environment. The policies are public attempts to make changes in the social environment so that people may grow and change. Adherence to biological determinism blocks the development of social welfare policy.

Social Welfare Services as a Right

The last concept to be discussed here is the idea of social welfare services as a right. Most of the values behind our social welfare system reflect an emphasis on the individual. Focusing on the individual and his or her abilities or means ignores the larger social and economic structure. For example, viewing the failure to eradicate poverty during the War on Poverty as a result of badly planned programs or because poor people are unwilling to change ignores the reality of our economic system.

Theorists such as Richard M. Titmuss (1968) have argued that our private market system is plagued by problems of inequality, social injustice, and exclusion. Poorly educated, ill-clothed, homeless, disenfranchised individuals cannot participate fully in the market system because they are already outside the system. Their opportunities are limited as a result of where they were born, where they live, the color of their skin, their sex, their physical ability, their sexual orientation, or other factors. Individuals cannot control or change the discrimination and exclusion put upon them by others. Thus, the system and society as a whole must be held responsible for the social well-being of these individuals.

This value holds that social welfare programs should not be viewed as an afterthought provided selectively, but as a social right provided through a universal system. Health care is a good illustration of this view. Relying on the marketplace as the provider of health coverage has resulted in large groups of people not receiving insurance coverage for any health needs. Social welfare rights advocates support health care coverage as a right to which all people should be entitled, regardless of their own resources. The only way to achieve health care as a right is through universal coverage provided by the federal government. The concept of social welfare services as a right promotes public purpose over private interest.

The Effects of Conflicting Values on Our Social Welfare System

Social values, commonly held beliefs, and historically influenced ideals have played a major role in the development and maintenance of our social welfare system. Two key American social values, **social responsibility** and **personal responsibility**, have influenced the creation of our public policies. They are often contradictory and have been held by differing groups at various times. The contradictions, variations, and lack of agreement between those who believe in social responsibility and those who believe in personal responsibility have led to much of the controversy surrounding the provision of social welfare services in the United States.

Social Responsibility for Care of the Poor and Those in Need

This view holds that the public should help those who are less fortunate, but the recipients must be worthy of that assistance. This raises the question of the difference between help as assistance and help as maintenance. Many people believe that it is one thing to help people, but it is another to continually have to care for them. While this distinction may seem clear, one of the difficulties in policy-making and the use of public social services is differentiating between the two. When is a service assistance and when is it maintenance of a person in his or her position of need? The debates surrounding public assistance during both the political campaigns of 1992 and 1994 reflect this dilemma. Poverty programs are advocated by some as a way to provide a bare minimum of assistance to those who are poor, while others argue that these programs keep people dependent and therefore should be discontinued. While this specific question will be discussed in detail in chapter 5, it represents the struggle in American social welfare policy between the belief in helping citizens in need and the reluctance to continue that assistance beyond a certain point.

Personal Responsibility Through Self-Reliance

The values of independence and taking care of oneself are reflected by the high esteem attached to individualism in America. The idea that each person is responsible for his or her position in society permeates public policy debates. If we agree that we are each responsible for our own circumstances, then public intervention is not valued. What happens, however, when the pursuit of individual well-being is disrupted by occurrences not of our own doing? For example, if a person joins the military to serve national interests, and he or she is injured, shouldn't the nation intervene to assist the person in regaining independence and self-reliance? What if personal opportunities are hampered by outside conditions such as racism, sexism, or homophobia? Should the public intervene to ensure that all people have an opportunity to maximize the pursuit of their individual achievements? And how do we decide when there should be collective intervention, and when each person is responsible for challenging barriers to achieving self-reliance? How do we tell the difference between structural barriers and personal shortcomings? Is a person poor because economic or social barriers make it difficult to obtain gainful employment or because the person prefers not to work? With such a high value placed on individual achievement, it is difficult to promote social responsibility.

Conservative Versus Liberal Perspectives on Social Welfare

Conservative and liberal beliefs about social welfare policy represent opposite ends of a spectrum. Conservative ideology generally opposes government intervention because it regards such involvement as a waste of taxpayers' money. Social programs are viewed either as providing benefits to those who do not need them, or as creating a dependency that encourages people to stop trying to care for themselves. (This perspective is found in many of the previously discussed concepts.)

The liberal position supports active intervention by the federal government. Social welfare policies are regarded as being so important that they should be legislated by the government. Implicit in this view is the idea that the welfare of society cannot be left to freely operate without some controls. Liberal ideology views the government as both a referee to ensure fairness and a provider to correct imbalances and inequities.

Conservative and liberal views are often considered to be contradictory and exclusionary: a person can hold one belief or the other, but not both. The politics of the mid-1990s has demonstrated how polarizing this dichotomy can be. If the social welfare of all citizens is a high priority for policy-makers, then the debate between which perspective is better, conservative or liberal, needs to be changed to working together to discover what will be most beneficial for the most people.

Values of the Social Work Profession

In addition to social values, there are principles and ethics involved in the social work profession. Each social worker, when receiving a degree, agrees to abide by the profession's values. These values include fostering self-determination on the part of clients and promoting the general welfare of society (see Section 6 of the NASW *Code of Ethics*, reprinted on the next page). These professional values demonstrate that social workers are obligated to advocate for social welfare policies and programs that promote social justice, respect diversity, and improve social conditions.

Impact of Values on Social Welfare Policies

Taking a position on social welfare policy depends on one's values and beliefs. Because these values are often conflicting and contradictory, the development and acceptance of social welfare policies and programs are always filled with controversy. For example, there are essentially two positions on abortion: those who support a woman's "right to choose" and those who support a "right to life" for the fetus. These conflicting positions demonstrate how powerful the disagreement about social values and ideologies can be. Major conflicts between values are often at the root of disagreements over public policies. As we discussed in chapter 1, in spite of conflicting values, however, social welfare policies are developed and enacted. Usually, social welfare policies reflect some public consensus regarding social values. When those values change over time, however, policies seem outdated and become the subject of vigorous public debate.

Forms of Social Welfare Assistance

Understanding the values behind the development of social welfare policy and the theories of the evolution of our social welfare system is necessary preparation for analyzing current policies and influencing the creation of new policies. In this final section of chapter 3, we will define the terms used to describe the various types of social welfare services provided. Our social welfare system offers a combination of these forms of assistance, and they account for most of the social services provided. Which form of assistance is used is based on the values held by the persons responsible for shaping social welfare policy.

Cash Assistance

The most common form of public assistance is government transfer of money from taxpayers to those in need. Recipients of cash assistance re-

Section 6. The Social Worker's Ethical Responsibilities to the Broader Society

6.01 Social Welfare

Social workers should promote the general welfare of society, from local to global levels, and the development of people, their communities, and their environments. Social workers should advocate for living conditions conducive to the fulfillment of basic human needs and should promote social, economic, political, and cultural values and institutions that are compatible with the realization of social justice.

6.02 Public Participation

Social workers should facilitate informed participation by the public in shaping social policies and institutions.

6.03 Public Emergencies

Social workers should provide appropriate professional services in public emergencies to the greatest extent possible.

6.04 Social and Political Action

(a) Social workers should engage in social and political action that seeks to ensure that all people have equal access to the resources, employment, services, and opportunities they require to meet their basic human needs and to develop fully. Social workers should be aware of the impact of the political arena on practice and should advocate for changes in policy and legislation to improve social conditions in order to meet basic human needs and promote social justice.

(b) Social workers should act to expand choice and opportunity for all people, with special regard for vulnerable, disadvantaged, oppressed, and exploited people and groups.

(c) Social workers should promote conditions that encourage respect for cultural and social diversity within the United States and globally. Social workers should promote policies and practices that demonstrate respect for difference, support the expansion of cultural knowledge and resources, advocate for programs and institutions that demonstrate cultural competence, and promote policies that safeguard the rights of and confirm equity and social justice for all people.

(d) Social workers should act to prevent and eliminate domination of, exploitation of, and discrimination against any person, group, or class on the basis of race, ethnicity, national origin, color, sex, sexual orientation, age, marital status, political belief, religion, or mental or physical disability.

Source: National Association of Social Workers. (1997). *Code of Ethics*. Washington, DC: NASW Press.

ceive a check in the amount determined in accordance with the particular program rules and the individual's characteristics. The recipient is free to spend the money as he or she sees fit, although the money is intended to pay for basic necessities such as housing, food, and clothing. Often cash assistance raises the most resistance from the public because the recipient is in complete control of how the money is ultimately spent.

In-Kind Benefits

The distribution of in-kind benefits provides more limits on public assistance. In-kind benefits are services or commodities provided to eligible recipients. Medical care and public housing are examples of in-kind benefits. Rather than receiving cash, people receive the service directly. For example, instead of receiving money for rent, a person lives in an apartment that is paid for by the government. In place of choosing any doctor and paying for services, a person qualifies to receive medical treatment at a health clinic. These benefits (while costing the public to provide them) do not allow the individual any role in the exchange of resources and often limit choice in the provision of the service.

Vouchers

Vouchers represent a cross between in-kind benefits and cash assistance. Recipients receive a voucher earmarked specifically for a service or commodity, but they are free to use it as they see fit. Recent debate has centered around proposals for educational vouchers. Parents would receive a voucher valid for their child's school tuition, but the parent could choose which school the child would attend. The food stamp program operates in the same way. While food stamps are often considered in-kind benefits, they more closely resemble vouchers. A recipient of food stamps receives coupons that can be exchanged for food at grocery stores. The recipient can choose where and how to spend them. The coupons represent cash amounts, but they cannot be exchanged for money; they are strictly for food items.

Social Insurance

Social insurance benefits are provided like cash assistance, in the form of a transfer of money from government to the individual, but eligibility for benefits differs. Social insurance describes the system whereby individuals pay into a program over time in exchange for the promise of future coverage. The program commonly referred to as Social Security is the most prominent example of social insurance. In chapter 8, we will cover this program in detail. Simply stated, individuals who are employed in most jobs pay a prescribed amount into the system based on their earnings. They become eligible for benefits upon retirement or disability. Those who are dependent on a covered person, typically the wage-earner's spouse or children, become eligible to receive benefits if the worker dies. They are regarded as survivors and are entitled to certain benefits based on the employment history of the worker. The recipients receive a monthly cash payment based on the contributions made while working. This system allows the individual complete freedom to choose how the money is spent, and unlike cash assistance, a person's need does not affect what he or she receives. Benefits are based on a person's history of contributions made, regardless of his or her financial situation at the time benefits are paid.

The overriding concept behind social insurance is that because a person has paid in, he or she is entitled to receive benefits. In addition, there is a shared responsibility for the program. The social insurance system is not a personal savings account where benefits total exactly what a person paid in over the years. An individual may receive more in benefits than he or she paid in, just as it is possible that an individual will receive less than he or she paid into the system. The program is designed to insure society as a whole, not simply individuals.

The four types of assistance described above are the most widely used structures for the delivery of social welfare services. Each varies according to the degree of individual versus social choice and regulation, and who makes decisions for whom. In chapters 5 through 10, we describe the forms of assistance used to respond to various social problems and the values upon which the program decisions are made.

Final Thoughts on Theories and Values

The concepts and theories presented in this chapter reflect the overriding values that influence social welfare policy in America. At different times in history, different perspectives have held sway. At first reading they may seem complicated, but they are key ideas in understanding our social welfare system. These principles help to explain why and how our current social welfare policies came to be. Without understanding their evolution, it is impossible to intelligently evaluate them and make meaningful changes. Parts of all of them can be found in the patchwork we call our social welfare system. Throughout the rest of this book, these ideas will be called upon to explain social welfare policies, programs, and practice.

Key Concepts

social values

social control

personal responsibility

conservative ideology

cause and function

blaming the victim

second-order victim-blaming

culture of poverty

biological determinism

social responsibility

liberal ideology

cash assistance

in-kind benefits

vouchers

social insurance

Exercises

1. Make a list of services or benefits provided by a local social service agency. Can you identify whether the services are in-kind, cash assistance, vouchers, or social insurance?

2. Choose a social issue or problem. Choose a partner for debate, and take opposing positions based on the values presented in this chapter. After five minutes of debate, switch sides. Which perspective was easier for you to articulate? Why? How did your own feelings or values affect your arguments?

3. Obtain a copy of the mission statement of a social service organization in your community. Does it reflect the social worker's ethical responsibility to society as described in Section 6 of the NASW *Code of Ethics*?

References

Dolgoff, R., Feldstein, D., & Skolnik, L. (1993). *Understanding social welfare* (3rd ed.). New York: Longman.

Domhoff, C.W. (1990). *The power elite and the state: How policy is made in America*. New York: Aldine de Gruyter.

Dressel, P.L., Carter, V., & Balachandran, A. (1995). Second-order victim-blaming. *Journal of Sociology & Social Welfare, 21* (2), 107–123.

Duster, T. (1990). *Backdoor to eugenics*. New York: Routledge.

Gilder, G. (1981). *Wealth and poverty*. New York: Basic Books.

Harvey, D.L., & Reed, M. (1992). Paradigms of poverty: A critical assessment of contemporary perspectives. *International Journal of Politics, Culture, and Society, 6*, 269–297.

Hernstein, R.J., & Murray, C. (1994). *The bell curve: Intelligence and class structure in American life*. New York: The Free Press.

Lee, P. (1929). Social work as cause and function. *Proceedings of the National Conference of Social Work*. Chicago: University of Chicago Press.

Murray, C. (1984). *Losing ground: American social policy, 1950–1980*. New York: Basic Books.

Piven, F.F., & Cloward, R.A. (1971). *Regulating the poor: The functions of public welfare*. New York: Random House.

Ryan, W. (1971). *Blaming the victim*. New York: Pantheon Books.

Schlesinger, Jr., A.M. (1986). *The cycles of American history*. Boston: Houghton Mifflin.

Segal, E.A. (1987). *Social welfare policy in response to economic change: Fifty years of social security.* Doctoral dissertation, University of Illinois at Chicago.

Shipman, P. (1994). *The evolution of racism.* New York: Simon & Schuster.

Titmuss, R.M. (1968). *Commitment to welfare.* New York: Pantheon Books.

Wilensky, H.I., & Lebeaux, C.N. (1965). *Industrial society and social welfare.* New York: The Free Press.

Wilson, W.J. (1987). *The truly disadvantaged: The inner city, the underclass, and public policy.* Chicago: University of Chicago Press.

Chapter 4

Social Welfare Policy Analysis

Developing a working knowledge of the social welfare system includes learning how to analyze public policy. Social welfare policy analysis has often been thought of as the domain of political scientists, economists, or government officials, but social service professionals can bring a unique perspective to the critical analysis of social welfare policies: knowledge of the personal experiences of people who are affected by those policies. All too often, policy decisions have been made on the basis of economic and political considerations, while the experiences of those directly affected by those decisions have been given little attention.

Even though social welfare policy analysis seems to belong to the domain of other disciplines, social work practitioners are often called upon to provide insight into programs and policies. Because social work is involved in the delivery of social services, other professionals and the public often assume that social service practitioners can explain the purposes and rationales of social programs. For example, if a local zoning board is trying to decide whether to allow the placement of a children's group home in a residential neighborhood, the board members might ask a social worker who works in children's services to present testimony. The social worker might explain the needs of today's youth and describe what is involved in establishing a group home. Thus, in order to adequately explain the service needs of clients, it becomes a *professional requirement* for social workers to be capable of conducting some level of social welfare policy analysis (Gilbert, Specht, & Terrell, 1993).

In this chapter, we present theories concerning the development and implementation of public policy, approaches to policy analysis, and a model that can be used to analyze any social issue. Examples of the model's application are presented.

What Is Policy Analysis?

In a general sense, **social welfare policy analysis** is the investigation and inquiry into the causes and consequences of public policies (Dye, 1992). **Public policy** is the general term for decisions, laws, and regulations put forth by governing bodies. Typically, social welfare policy analysis is carried out to provide guidance and direction to policy-makers (Dobelstein, 1996) and to supply solutions to social problems (Dunn, 1994). The information gained through analysis of public policies can be used to develop policy alternatives for the future, to assess existing or previous policies, or to explain public problems and social phenomena.

To be better prepared to debate public policy–makers and to participate in the development and assessment of policies, social workers need to be versed in social welfare policy analysis. Before discussing how to analyze public policy, it is helpful to consider how public policy is created and put into operation.

Theories of Social Welfare Policy Development and Implementation

As discussed in the previous chapter, values and ideologies influence the content and structure of social welfare policy. Looking at values does not, however, explain how policy actually gets developed and put into place. Why did "welfare reform" become such an important issue in 1995? Why was health care a cornerstone of Bill Clinton's campaign in 1992, but four years later in his 1996 re-election campaign it was barely mentioned? How do we as social workers get policy-makers to pay attention to issues that are important to us? A number of theories attempt to explain how social problems receive recognition and then become the objects of policy debate and legislation. No one theory stands clearly as the best explanation of why and how certain public policies come to be. Taken together, however, these theories on the development of public policy provide a framework for analyzing the current social welfare system. They can also help social work practitioners to recognize opportunities for presenting positions and thereby influencing the social welfare policy decision-making process.

Rationalism

Generally, the most common assumption made by those who approach the study of social welfare policy is that public policy represents the culmination of a rational evaluation of a social problem and all possible solutions. Closer examination proves differently. **Rational policy-making** requires knowledge of the values of all segments of society, all possible policy alternatives, the consequences of those alternatives, and the costs and benefits—knowledge that is often hard to come by (Dye, 1992). While rational policy-making seems ideal, it is not realistic. Public policies reflect numerous values and competing interests. It is impossible to fully assess all values, alternatives, and consequences while adequately weighing the costs and benefits of each. Furthermore, rational policy analyses "often neglect the root causes of a problem" (Brewer & deLeon, 1983, p. 85). The deeper social conditions and structures that give rise to values are not explored. Also, most competing values cannot be weighed rationally without some degree of bias.

Newcomers to government positions are often warned that the policy process does not work the way they may have learned from a civics class. The making of public policy is usually messy, not logical or rational. Numerous factors interfere with rationality, such as competing values, interest groups with varying resources, lack of time to weigh all possibilities, and lack of adequate information. Instead, the development and implementation of social welfare policies reflect numerous influences and display different characteristics at different times in history.

As discussed in chapter 3, social issues are surrounded by competing values that impede rationality. The legislative and social fight over abortion exemplifies how difficult rational policy-making can be. Weighing the legislative options related to abortion includes consideration of varying religious beliefs, social mores, civil rights issues, and personal needs: those of the mother, father, and fetus. All these factors complicate the policy-making process.

Incrementalism

In 1959, Charles Lindblom published an article in which he attempted to explain how public policy is developed. He was writing in response to the prevailing theory that public policy decisions were made in a rational way, with policy-makers considering all available options and choosing the best course of action. Lindblom's seminal piece was titled "The Science of Muddling Through." In it he introduced the theory of **incrementalism**, which states that public policy is developed through small changes to existing policies.

Incrementalism in policy development suggests that there is never enough time to consider all information, that information on all possible choices is not readily available, and that it is easier to make small changes to existing policies than to create something entirely new. Often, great investments have been placed in current programs, and it is extremely difficult to dislodge systems that have been in existence for a long time.

Consider the attempts to diminish the Defense Department. Immediately following the fall of the Berlin Wall and the "end of the Cold War" came proclamations of the "peace dividend"—the anticipated savings from the newfound peace. Several years have passed, and only small decreases have been made in the Defense Department. Even attempting to close several military bases throughout the country has raised tremendous political disagreement. The results thus far have been small reductions that over time may add up to become significant. This process is incremental.

The Social Security Act is another example of incrementalism. It took twenty years of legislative activity before the Act became law in 1935. Through incremental change, the program gradually expanded. Initially it was designed to provide income for workers after retirement and coverage for family members if the worker died. In 1956, disability coverage was added. In 1965, health insurance through the Medicare program was added. In 1972, the Supplemental Security Income program was developed to consolidate and expand services to low-income seniors and low-income people with disabilities. In 1996, control of the AFDC program was shifted from the federal government to state governments and changed to the Temporary Assistance for Needy Families (TANF) program. In addition to these major programs, hundreds of amendments and legislative changes have occurred since the passage of the Act more than sixty years ago.

Window of Opportunity

Most policies that are part of today's social welfare system were being debated long before they actually became law. For example, the debate concerning national health insurance dates back more than one hundred years. Also, when this country began to consider social insurance during the Great Depression, it was already in place in most Western European countries. It was not a new idea, but an idea whose time had come. Why? What makes an idea unacceptable at one time and acceptable at another?

Kingdon (1984) refers to the timing of a public decision as the opening of a policy **window of opportunity**. Political and social events or a change in personnel can open the way for an opportunity, and advocates stand ready with their ideas. Policy windows do not stay open long. Events and personalities change, and public interest in a matter can be short-lived. The likelihood of an idea becoming a public policy relies on the timing and combination of factors. Three elements must be present for success: a compelling public problem, a solution, and political support. For an issue to get serious attention from policy-makers, these three elements must come together; when they do, the likelihood of public policy being developed is high.

The events of the 1930s demonstrate the three streams coming together to develop the Social Security Act. The timing was right, as the Great Depression brought significant attention to economic hardship. The solution of social insurance had been debated by political leaders and advocates for years, and the change in presidential leadership from Herbert Hoover to Franklin Delano Roosevelt represented political support for the idea both within government and from the voters. The window of opportunity for change is limited, however. Those who favored inclusion of medical coverage in the 1930s were not successful and had to wait for the policy window to open again thirty years later. This demonstrates the short-lived nature of the policy window opportunity.

Street-Level Bureaucrats

Not all developments in public policy occur on the political policy-making level. Michael Lipsky (1980) focuses what on happens *after* policy is implemented. He describes the power to shape policy that public service workers exercise. Service workers are described by Lipsky as "**street-level bureaucrats**." They occupy the lowest levels of the social welfare system but exert a tremendous amount of control over how public policy is implemented.

Street-level bureaucrats have significant control over people's lives. They make decisions that affect who gets what, how quickly, and under what circumstances. Because of the bureaucratic nature of social service agencies, workers tend to have discretion, and performance is difficult to measure. As long as certain regulations are followed, workers control the interactions with clients. Thus, policy-makers and public policy analysts must understand that what was designed as a general public policy may not be what is being delivered. Part of the challenge to policy-makers is to keep in mind the impact of street-level workers. Planners must recognize the role of those delivering the service; otherwise, implementation may alter the design of the intended policy.

Actions affecting policy can be as simple as how quickly applications are processed or whether phone calls are returned. For example, if the workers in an employment placement and training office are understaffed and feel overworked, they will not have sufficient time or energy to investigate job opportunities in the community. As a result, the support and information they can offer clients will be minimal. The intent of the policy—to place people in jobs—is compromised by the resources available to those assigned to carry it out. This brings into question the entire implementation process.

Implementation

What develops as a policy and what actually gets implemented as a program or service will often differ. **Implementation** of public policy is an evolutionary process, and policy changes when it is implemented (Pressman & Wildavsky, 1984). Policy-makers develop a policy, but this initial perception is seldom what is actually implemented. Often what is decided upon by politicians is vague and represents a general consensus, or is complicated because there were many differing views to be satisfied. Those who devise the policy are not the same people responsible for actually putting the ideas into practice. This leaves room for different interpretations and values; especially for social welfare programs. What may make political sense when passed by Congress, a state legislature, or a local board may not fit all communities or population groups. Thus, it is important to understand the difference between what was planned through public policy and what actually happened. For example, planners of public housing, while struggling to develop economical and efficient ways to house low-income people, never intended for public housing complexes to become dangerous, unpleasant places. Historical analysis reveals that a combination of poor program planning, misjudged social events, and restricted funding resulted in a social program very different from what the original planners had in mind.

Social Welfare Policy Analysis

Analyzing social welfare policy goes beyond applying one theory. It must encompass a realization that the policy arena is diverse, with numerous interests. Political scientist Aaron Wildavsky (1979) describes policy analysis as both an art and a craft. It requires creativity and technical skills. Numerous policy analysts posit models designed for assessing public policy. Some are prescriptive and culminate in suggested policy directions (Magill, 1986), while others provide explanation only (Dye, 1992; Gil, 1976). Our purpose in this book is to explain social welfare policy and to give direction for future policy proposals. Therefore, we have developed a model for social welfare policy analysis that includes both an explanation of what exists and guidance for suggested policy directives. This model is presented in this chapter and illustrated with examples throughout the book.

A Model for Analyzing Social Welfare Policy

In most instances, social welfare policy follows a linear flow. The model presented here is linear to reflect the common flow of policy and for purposes of explanation. The creation and operation of social welfare policies are dynamic, however, and the process is best viewed as a whole. Our model has multiple layers, reflecting the complexity of our social welfare system in

Figure 4.1
Model for Social Welfare Policy Analysis

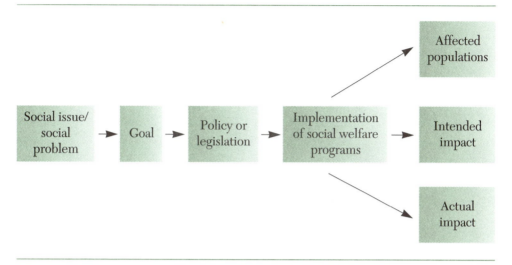

which policy is formulated. Figure 4.1 outlines the model. Applying the model requires the use of numerous questions to analyze the evolution and application of social welfare policy. The accompanying list of questions in Figure 4.2 will help you to structure your social welfare policy analysis.

The first component of the model requires the investigation of the social issue or problem. A number of questions should be posed to clarify the issue. For example, what is the definition of the problem? Are there competing and conflicting definitions, or is there general agreement? What is the extent of the problem? Who is defining it as a social concern at this time, and why? Often, social conditions are viewed as a problem by some, but not all, members of society. An issue gains acceptance as a social concern when more and more people, social groups, and policy-makers define it as a social problem. While there may be strong agreement in general, specific values and ideological leanings may color how the issue is viewed. For example, homelessness may be recognized by many as a social problem, but for some it may be defined as a problem of poverty, while for others it may be the discomfort of seeing people living on the street, and for others it may involve the lack of adequate treatment for people who are mentally ill.

If there is enough agreement that an issue warrants social concern and attention, then goals may begin to emerge. General goals to solve the problem may be formulated. These general goals, when shared by enough people, can gain momentum and draw the attention of policy-makers. General agreement on goals can lead to the development of social welfare policy. In this stage, however, goals are further analyzed and subgoals may emerge. The details of the subgoals may diverge greatly. Again, analyzing the issue of

Figure 4.2
Questions for Social Welfare Policy Analysis

Social problem	What is the problem?
	Definitions?
	Extent of problem?
	Who defines this as a problem?
	Who disagrees?
	Related social values?
	Competing social values?
	Underlying causes or factors?
Goal	What is the general goal?
	Are there subgoals?
	Do the subgoals conflict?
Policy/legislation	What is/are relevant public policies?
	If there are no public policies, why?
	What are the objectives of the policies?
	Are there hidden agendas?
	Who supports the policies?
	Who opposes the policies?
Implementation	What is/are the social programs implemented as a result of the policies?
	Are the programs effective?
	Strengths?
	Weaknesses?
Affected populations	Who is touched by the policy and programs?
	Are there positive effects?
	Are there negative effects?
Intended impact	What was supposed to be the result?
	Who was supposed to have been affected?
	How was the social problem supposed to have been changed?
Actual impact	Costs and benefits?
	Is the social problem changed?
	If so, how?
	Are there unintended results?

homelessness demonstrates this divergence. While there tends to be general agreement with the goal of ending homelessness, if it is viewed as a problem of poverty, subgoals may be to increase employment or expand public assistance. If the problem is viewed as individuals living on the streets, publicly mandating stays in shelters could be identified as the means of achieving the goal of ending homelessness. If the issue is mental illness, community mental health centers for treatment may be needed. Needless to say, these are very different approaches to the goal of ending homelessness.

While the entire policy process is influenced by values, this is particularly true with the identification and definition of social problems and the setting of goals. Social values and divergent views are played out in the policy-making process. Public policy–makers are charged with the role of making policies or legislation to carry out our social goals. They are individuals with their own value systems, while at the same time they occupy public positions in which they carry out the wishes of the citizens and groups who elect or appoint them. Conflict in values is frequently the reason why social welfare policy is difficult to develop. Social welfare policies that are passed usually include compromises and consist of numerous pieces that do not necessarily fit together. Most major public policy programs are not exactly what anyone wanted, but instead have something for a lot of different people. Gaining the consensus of so many different interests often creates vague legislation or policies that are very lengthy and complicated.

When analyzing a social problem, we may find that no social policy exists to address it. For example, as we discussed before, while AIDS was documented as a serious infectious disease throughout the 1980s, there was no federal legislation to address the issue until 1990. As mentioned in chapter 1, the absence of legislation can be seen as a form of public policy. In such instances, it is important to analyze why there has not been any public policy. Are those most directly affected by the social issue powerless or disenfranchised? Is there a lack of consensus about whether an issue is worthy of social concern and public policy? Are conflicting values keeping the issue from the agenda of policy-makers? These questions must be asked when analyzing a social problem which has not received any major public policy response.

Assuming that a social issue gains enough attention to warrant public concern and is dealt with through the development of policy, the policy must then be implemented. Program implementation, while outlined broadly through the public policy, is usually developed in detail within the agencies assigned management responsibility. During the implementation process, the programs authorized by the policies are likely to change. The programs that are actually implemented often do not look like what the planners and advocates envisioned. Social programs "frequently approach the problems they are meant to solve from an oblique angle, and provide only partial solutions. Valid and realistic standards for judging them are critically lacking. Implemented in an environment charged with emotional and political disagreement and subject to a number of uncontrollable variables, the programs defy careful and systematic evaluation" (Levitan & Wurzburg, 1979, p. 9).

There are occasions when, in spite of the passage of a social welfare policy, there is no implementation. In such cases, funding and economics may play a part. A policy plan may be endorsed, but when it comes time to fund the effort little or no money is allocated. The creation of social welfare policy may not be matched by economic commitment. Politics can also play a part. While a majority vote may pass a policy, there may not be a strong enough consensus to actually carry through on the implementation or development of programs. Timing also plays a role. For example, a Democratic Congress may pass legislation to be enacted, but before the process can begin, there is a change in leadership and a new Republican majority forms. The new majority may have different priorities and neglect to develop or implement the policies of the previous majority. Such was the case in the change of leadership after the 1994 election. The previous Congress of 1992 had been controlled by Democrats. Programs enacted did not receive funding when the next Congress, controlled by Republicans, took office in 1995. Thus, it is important to remember that passage of a public policy does not guarantee implementation.

Comprehensive policy analysis also includes consideration of the results of implementation. Once a program is implemented, some impact is made. A complete social welfare policy analysis examines three areas of impact: the intended impact, the actual impact, and examination of those who have been affected by the policy and its subsequent programs. It may seem clear who is affected by the implementation of a social welfare program, but over time those actually affected may not be those who were intended to be affected. For example, the deinstitutionalization of people with mental illness that occurred during the 1970s initially appeared to concern only those released from institutions and their families. Over time, however, the impact has been much greater. As we will see in chapter 6, without adequate community services to care for persons who were deinstitutionalized, social services were hard pressed to fill a void in services. Other instances of the unintended consequences of social welfare policy can be found throughout our social welfare system. Let us look at another example to emphasize this point.

Analysis of the high cost of medical care suggests that the expense may be an unintended outcome of public policy. When the federal government introduced Medicare in 1965, it became a funder of medical services. The initial structure of the program allowed medical providers, such as doctors and hospitals, to set the fee for service. The government would then reimburse the providers for the services rendered. Prices set by medical providers increased dramatically during the 1970s. Therefore, by 1983, the federal government passed legislation to regulate reimbursement. Some medical providers, feeling the government reimbursement was not enough, began to charge higher prices, which had the unintended consequence of implying that they were providing better services. Also, providers of new health procedures and technologies were frequently not covered immediately under government reimbursements. Private individuals with financial means were able to pay the higher prices and pay for new services, as were many private insurers. Over time, the public demanded access to these new and "better" services, so the government expanded coverage and increased reimbursements. The cycle of expanding reimbursement and limiting reimbursement continued, and the goal of cost containment for medical services has not been realized. One of the unintended impacts of public health care policies has been an inability to halt the escalating costs of medical services.

Ideally, if a social welfare policy is well conceived, after passage and implementation the actual impact will reflect the goal. If the actual outcomes are vastly different from the goal, then we may conclude that the policy, its implementation, or both were flawed. Such assessment of social programs is the primary purpose of social welfare policy analysis for social service practitioners.

Social Welfare Policy and the Political Arena

While social welfare policy reflects public input and the values and ideologies of the majority, the political process plays a crucial role. Most public policies are debated and subsequently developed in the political arena. Several key factors come into play when social welfare policy and politics are mixed. The political actors (presidents, elected officials, appointed personnel) and the political environment (timing of elections, interest groups, lobbying efforts) must be considered when analyzing social welfare policy. Chapters 12 and 13 provide greater detail on the political process and its relationship to social welfare policy. If we are to fully analyze a given policy, key political actors and important political events must be included in the assessment (Browning, 1986). Who supports public policy intervention? Who supported it in the past? Who opposes public policy intervention? Who did so in the past? How important is the timing of events? Is it during a campaign year? Is it late in a congressional cycle? Is it a time of recession or a period of economic expansion? These questions all should be part of a full social welfare policy analysis.

The Dynamics of Social Welfare Policy: Application of the Model

Social welfare policies exist at all levels of government as well as within social service settings. Social service providers are confronted by social welfare policies in their work all the time. While not all policies originate at the federal level, usually social welfare policy flows from the macro to the micro levels.

Typically, the federal government passes legislation that either mandates rules and regulations or offers funding that has attached requirements. State governments then are either required to follow those mandates or choose to apply for funds and agree to abide by certain rules if those funds are granted. In turn, state governments replay the federal role with local governments and communities who provide services. The localities are most

Figure 4.3
Example of a Social Welfare Policy Analysis:
The Family Support Act

Social problem	Public Assistance Dependency: • The belief and perception that too many able-bodied people are not working to support themselves and their families. • Values of individual responsibility and work ethic are key. • Belief by majority that the cost for public assistance is too great.
Goal	Economic Independence: • Subgoals vary from genuine desire to help the poor become self-sufficient to dislike of those who are poor and unwillingness to be responsible for the economic well-being of others. • Conflict between subgoals.
Policy/legislation	• Public Law 100–485, Title II. • Family Support Act of 1988. • Increase the numbers of adults who must participate in mandatory work/training efforts.
Implementation	• Programs to provide "job opportunities and basic skills training" for women with children 3–6 years old.
Affected populations	• AFDC recipients. • AFDC children younger than 6 years of age. • Employment training providers. • Taxpayers. • Existing child care systems.
Intended impact	• Self-sufficiency for public assistance recipients. • Dollar savings from decrease in public assistance funding.
Actual impact	• Lack of sufficient child care services to meet increased need. • Lack of adequate entry-level jobs to lift families to economic self-sufficiency.

likely to be the ones to actually implement the programs and directives of federal social welfare policies. Social service agencies, workers, and clients are those most closely involved with the application and impact of those policies.

In this section, we provide an example of the policy analysis model applied to a piece of social welfare legislation (see Figure 4.3). In 1988, Con-

Figure 4.4
Flow of Impact: Family Support Act of 1988, P.L. 100–485

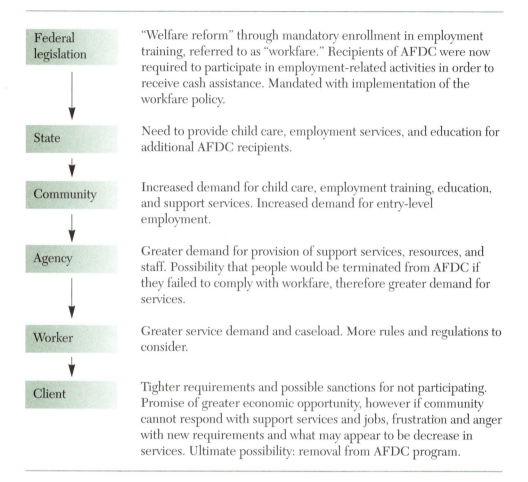

| Federal legislation | "Welfare reform" through mandatory enrollment in employment training, referred to as "workfare." Recipients of AFDC were now required to participate in employment-related activities in order to receive cash assistance. Mandated with implementation of the workfare policy. |

State — Need to provide child care, employment services, and education for additional AFDC recipients.

Community — Increased demand for child care, employment training, education, and support services. Increased demand for entry-level employment.

Agency — Greater demand for provision of support services, resources, and staff. Possibility that people would be terminated from AFDC if they failed to comply with workfare, therefore greater demand for services.

Worker — Greater service demand and caseload. More rules and regulations to consider.

Client — Tighter requirements and possible sanctions for not participating. Promise of greater economic opportunity, however if community cannot respond with support services and jobs, frustration and anger with new requirements and what may appear to be decrease in services. Ultimate possibility: removal from AFDC program.

gress passed the Family Support Act (P.L. 100–485) which made changes in the public assistance program AFDC. One change required AFDC adults with children between the ages of 3 and 6 to participate in a work training program. This change differed from previous legislation by changing the work participation requirement from adults with children older than 6 years of age to those with children between ages 3 and 6.

Figure 4.4 demonstrates how this social welfare policy change created a chain of events affecting local communities, workers, and clients. The changes made in the legislation meant that more adults with small children would be required to enroll in training or educational programs. It also meant that those participants would need additional child care, but states did not receive extra federal money nor spend additional state money to increase the supply of child care.

Figure 4.5

Flow of Impact: Stewart B. McKinney Homeless Assistance Act, P.L. 100–77

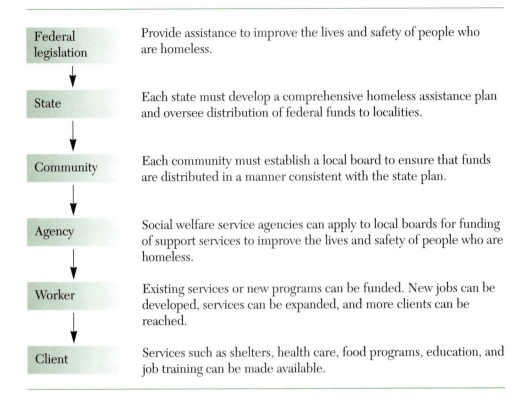

Federal legislation	Provide assistance to improve the lives and safety of people who are homeless.
State	Each state must develop a comprehensive homeless assistance plan and oversee distribution of federal funds to localities.
Community	Each community must establish a local board to ensure that funds are distributed in a manner consistent with the state plan.
Agency	Social welfare service agencies can apply to local boards for funding of support services to improve the lives and safety of people who are homeless.
Worker	Existing services or new programs can be funded. New jobs can be developed, services can be expanded, and more clients can be reached.
Client	Services such as shelters, health care, food programs, education, and job training can be made available.

Analysis of the proposed changes at the time of enactment revealed the flaws in the policy, including the fact that the needed child care never materialized (Segal, 1989). However, for policy-makers, the program represented an effort to change the AFDC program and fulfilled a political promise to reduce reliance on public assistance and promote employment. For a number of reasons, including the lack of available child care, lack of available employment, and insufficient funding to states to provide needed support services, the intended impact was never realized. Consequently, by 1994, Congress was once again discussing ways to change the public assistance system to promote economic self-sufficiency. Chapter 5 provides greater detail on the policy struggle to reform public assistance programs.

A second example of the impact of social welfare policy on localities, workers, and clients demonstrates the positive results of federal intervention (see Figure 4.5). The Stewart B. McKinney Act was enacted in 1987 to provide greater services for people who are homeless. Over the years, the federal funds have been routed through state and local administrations, and social service agencies have been able to apply for funds and enhance the services they offer.

While much legislation is national and passed through Congress, the impact ultimately can be very personal and local, as shown by the examples above. This is typical of the flow of public policy. Federal government mandates start a chain of events that ultimately affects individuals on a very personal level. While states accept the federal mandates or funds, community agencies often provide the actual services, thus involving social service workers and their clients. These examples demonstrate how national decisions affect all levels of social services.

Social Welfare Policy Research

Social welfare policy analysis is one form of social research. Because there is tremendous overlap, research and analysis are often regarded as the same process. Although the terms are often used interchangeably, social welfare policy analysis can be described as more theoretical in nature, while social welfare policy research is more applied. Social welfare policy research uses analysis "to provide policy-makers with pragmatic, action-oriented recommendations for alleviating the problem" (Majchrzak, 1984, p. 13). Thus, research prescribes directions for action, while analysis strives to present possibilities and consequences. Although the distinction is worth noting, typically social welfare policy analysis and social welfare policy research are used in much the same way.

Final Thoughts on Social Welfare Policy Analysis

The questions and guidelines for social welfare policy analysis that we have outlined in this chapter serve as a technical framework. These are the tools of the craft. The art of social welfare policy analysis comes in applying these techniques. Creativity comes into play as we focus on a social issue and analyze all the diverse components that have an impact on a social problem. The key is to ask many questions without losing one's focus on a particular social issue. Diagrams can help us visualize the multiple dimensions that influence the evolution of social welfare policy. Invariably, policy making is not a neat and precise process. All social welfare policies evolve through different ways and with different players. Advocates of one policy may be opponents on another. Thus, effective policy analysis requires staying focused on the issue and keeping the issue central to the analysis.

Key Concepts

social welfare policy analysis   public policy

rationalism   incrementalism

window of opportunity   street-level bureaucrats

implementation

Exercises

1. Identify a policy or rule within your school, job, or field practicum. Chart the flow of this policy. Where did it originate? On what or whose authority? What steps does it follow as it is applied? Are there unintended consequences of the policy? Who is directly affected? Who is indirectly affected? Does the actual impact reflect the original goal?

2. Using the same policy as in exercise 1, identify the key players involved in developing the policy. Are they still employed at the organization? If yes, would the policy still be in effect if they were gone? If they are no longer there, why has the policy endured? How much of a role did personalities play in the development and implementation of the policy?

References

Brewer, G.D., & deLeon, P. (1983). *The foundations of policy analysis*. Homewood, IL: Dorsey Press.

Browning, R.X. (1986). *Politics and social welfare policy in the United States*. Knoxville, TN: University of Tennessee Press.

Dobelstein, A.W. (1996). *Social welfare policy and analysis* (2nd ed.). Chicago: Nelson-Hall.

Dunn, W.N. (1994). *Public policy analysis* (2nd ed.). Englewood Cliffs, NJ: Prentice Hall.

Dye, T.R. (1992). *Understanding public policy* (7th ed.). Englewood Cliffs, NJ: Prentice Hall.

Gil, D. (1976). *Unraveling social policy*. Cambridge, MA: Schenkman.

Gilbert, N., Specht, H., & Terrell, P. (1993). *Dimensions of social welfare policy* (3rd ed.). Englewood Cliffs, NJ: Prentice Hall.

Kingdon, J.W. (1984). *Agendas, alternatives, and public policies*. Boston: Little, Brown.

Levitan, S.A., & Wurzburg, G. (1979). *Evaluating federal social programs: An uncertain art*. Washington, DC: The Brookings Institution.

Lindblom, C.E. (1959). The science of muddling through. *Public Administration Review, 19*, 79–88.

Lipsky, M. (1980). *Street-level bureaucracy*. New York: Russell Sage Foundation.

Magill, R.S. (1986). *Social policy in American society*. New York: Human Sciences Press.

Majchrzak, A. (1984). *Methods for policy research*. Newbury Park, CA: Sage Publications.

Pressman, J.L., & Wildavsky, A. (1984). *Implementation* (3rd ed.). Berkeley, CA: University of California Press.

Segal, E.A. (1989). Welfare reform: Help for poor women and children? *Affilia, 4* (3), 42–50.

Wildavsky, A. (1979). *The art and craft of policy analysis*. Boston: Little, Brown.

Part Two

Key Content Areas of Social Welfare Policy

Having explored the foundations of the social welfare system and outlined a model for analyzing policy, we will focus in part II on several critical areas of social welfare policy and the programs that have resulted from those policies. In chapter 5 we will look at poverty in America; asking who is poor and outlining the policies and programs designed to help those who are poor. In chapter 6 we will assess physical and mental health care in America. Our social welfare response to the health care needs of the nation and the current crisis in providing health care to all Americans are emphasized in this chapter. Our focus in chapter 7 will be on the social welfare policies affecting children and families, particularly our society's current and past responses to children and families and our lack of a clear social welfare vision for them. In chapter 8 we will explore the topic of aging and examine our social welfare policy response to the unique needs and issues of senior citizens in America. In chapter 9 we will look at civil rights in America and discuss how we guarantee the rights of individuals through our social welfare policy responses. We will explore the power of social welfare policy to prevent discrimination and examine how it has been used to institutionalize discrimination. Part two concludes with chapter 10, a discussion of economic factors and their impact on social welfare policy. Economics plays a crucial part in the stability of our nation. The material in this chapter provides a framework for understanding the relationship between societal well-being and economic concerns.

Ann Marie Rousseau/The Image Works

Chapter 5

Poverty

The United States is one of the wealthiest nations in the world, with abundant natural resources, land, and technology, yet it is also a country plagued by poverty. In 1994, more than 38 million people were officially categorized as living in poverty. This represented almost 15% of the American population. An additional 18 million people would be in poverty were it not for cash assistance from the government (U.S. Bureau of the Census, 1996b). More than one in five children—15.3 million youngsters under the age of 18—lived in poverty (Center on Budget and Policy Priorities, 1996).

While prosperity and wealth are widely proclaimed goals for all Americans, they are enjoyed only by part of our population. The majority of people struggle to make ends meet. Because of the extensiveness of poverty in America, and because so many social services are designed to address economic deprivation, those working in the social welfare service system must understand the dimensions and characteristics of poverty in the United States.

Defining Poverty

Poverty is a term used in many different ways. Within the realm of social welfare policy, **poverty** usually refers to the economic condition of being without enough basic resources. Defining exactly what is enough and what is basic are at the center of most controversy about poverty. What is enough depends on who is defining it and also on the group for whom the resources are intended.

Invariably, there are times in all people's lives when they feel they do not have enough. Self-definition of poverty, while valid in its own way, is not considered valid in the public policy arena. Instead, poverty is defined in a quantitative and concrete way, based on a commonly-agreed-upon definition that can be applied evenly to all situations. Such a specific definition uses an **absolute measure** of poverty. Measuring poverty with an absolute scale means that a dollar value is used as a cutoff above which people are not poor and below which people are poor. Once there is agreement on where the line should be drawn, it is clear who is and who is not poor.

Differing from an absolute measure of poverty is a **relative measure**. Relative poverty uses comparisons to an agreed-upon norm to determine if a person is poor or not. For example, let us say that if the average family in this country owns a home, then any household that does not own a home is below average and could be defined as being in poverty. A different view could advance the idea that compared to developing nations, there is no poverty here.

Needless to say, agreeing upon a relative level of poverty is very difficult. On any given day, many people feel impoverished, yet others would never recognize them as such. The simplest method for determining if a person is in poverty or not is an absolute measure. Once a dollar amount is set, it is easy to calculate how many people have incomes below that mark and are therefore in poverty. Within our social welfare policy system, poverty is defined using an absolute measure.

The Official Poverty Line

Since the 1960s, poverty has been measured using an official **poverty line**, sometimes referred to as the poverty threshold or poverty index. The poverty line is a set dollar amount of annual income below which a person or persons are determined to be poor. Table 5.1 outlines the official 1997 levels according to family size. Each year, the levels are adjusted to take into account inflation. The poverty line is used for calculating the number of people officially counted as poor, but it is not used to determine eligibility for all social welfare programs. Some social welfare programs for low-income people use an income level called a **standard of need**. This is a set dollar amount determined by each state, below which people must fall to become eligible

Table 5.1

1997 Federal Poverty Income Guidelines

Family of 1	$ 7,890
Family of 2	10,610
Family of 3	13,330
Family of 4	16,050
Family of 5	18,770
Family of 6	21,490

Source: Annual update of the HHS poverty guidelines (1997, March 10). *Federal Register, 62* (46), 10857.

to receive benefits or services. For example, the AFDC program was designed to provide cash assistance to poor families based on a standard of need determined by each state. Thus, standard-of-need levels can fall above or below the official poverty line, depending on the state. The median standard-of-need level for all states in 1994, however, was $507 per month for a family of three, less than half the official poverty line for that same year (House Committee on Ways and Means, 1994). The Food Stamp Program uses the official poverty line to determine who is eligible for benefits throughout the country. Thus, some people are poor enough according to federal guidelines to fall below the poverty line and receive food stamps but not poor enough by state standards to receive any cash assistance.

Origins of the Poverty Line

While the poverty line is absolute and can be applied uniformly and objectively, its development was not without subjective decisions. In 1963, Mollie Orshansky, Director of the Social Security Administration (SSA), developed the poverty line to assist the department in tracking poverty and determining eligibility for the early programs designed to address poverty. She and her staff gathered information concerning the costs involved in maintaining a base standard of living. Her own description at the time (Orshansky, 1965) sheds light on the dilemma the staff of the SSA faced in developing an official line for poverty.

Without any other standards to measure poverty, the SSA tried to put together a logical set of criteria upon which to base poverty. Logically, the measure had to be based on the needs of a typical family at the time. For Orshansky, the poverty line was useful, but certainly not perfect nor objective: "The standard itself is admittedly arbitrary, but not unreasonable. It is based essentially on the amount of income remaining after allowance for an adequate diet at minimum cost" (Orshansky, 1965, p. 4).

The adequate diet was the Department of Agriculture's "economy" food plan, which outlined the cost for food in temporary or emergency situations. The basis for the Department of Agriculture's plan was preparation for food needs in cases of war or natural disaster, not for long-term dietary use. In addition, while acceptable and adequate short-term diets could be provided through these plans, they required skills in food selection and preparation, as well as the availability of food items at reasonable prices.

In spite of its limitations, the economy food plan served as the basis of the poverty line. Using other Department of Agriculture research findings, it was found in 1955 that the average family used one-third of its after-tax income for food. Therefore, the developers of the poverty line reasoned that taking the economy food plan cost and multiplying it by three would give an income level below which a family would be poor.

As Orshansky (1965) stated,

> There is not, and indeed in a rapidly changing pluralistic society there cannot be, one standard universally accepted and uniformly applicable by which it can be decided who is poor.... And if it is not possible to state unequivocally "how much is enough," it should be possible to assert with confidence how much, on an average, is too little (p. 3).

Orshansky's view acknowledges the difficulty in setting an absolute measure of poverty when poverty is a relative condition. In spite of its limitations, the poverty line developed by the SSA in the early 1960s was used to identify the level below which people were poor. Even with its stringent levels, the poverty line has stood, with only minor changes, as the official index from which census data are drawn and program eligibilities are set.

How Accurate Is the Poverty Line?

Debate continues on whether the poverty line is adequate or should be changed to reflect the relative economic needs of people. Living conditions have changed since the early 1960s, making the measure even lower than it was at inception. Today, it is more likely that food costs are one-fifth of a family's expenses, not one-third as in 1955 (Haveman, 1992–1993). This is attributable to disproportionate increases in the cost of housing, child care, medical care, and other necessities. An example highlights how significant a difference this shift makes. Let us assume the current poverty line for a family of three is $12,000. If one-third of this amount is needed for food, the current economy food plan should cost $4,000 (three times the economy food plan equals the $12,000 poverty line). If the same economy food plan is used, but we assume that food represents one-fifth of overall family expenses, then the poverty line would be calculated as *five* times $4,000, which equals $20,000. This new definition would mean millions more people (all the people with household incomes between the old definition of $12,000 and the new definition of $20,000) would officially be in poverty.

Table 5.2

Poverty Rates by Income Definition, 1994

Number in poverty using official poverty rate	38.1 million	14.5%
Number in poverty after deducting payroll and income taxes and less government cash transfers	60.7 million	23.2%
Number in poverty after addition of all government benefits	29.0 million	11.1%

Source: U.S. Bureau of the Census (1996a).

Some observers argue that in order to truly measure the magnitude of poverty in this country, counting monetary income alone is not sufficient. What about all the other forms of assistance that people receive? What if we include all forms of assistance, including health care and food? Even using that measure, millions are still in poverty. A comparison of different measures in 1994 revealed that even if all forms of assistance, including cash, food, health care, and housing subsidies provided to the poor were taken into account, more than 29 million people, or 11% of the population, would officially be counted as poor. Table 5.2 outlines the comparisons between the official rate of poverty and after-tax poverty. If income is counted after taxes are paid and the Social Security payroll tax (FICA) is withheld, even more people have incomes below the poverty line. Almost one out of every four Americans have after-tax incomes that fall below the poverty line.

While the assumptions upon which the poverty line was developed raise questions and demonstrate the subjective values of the time, the poverty line still can be very useful. Although flawed as a perfect measure of true poverty, the line has been used consistently in gathering data over the years since its development. Consequently, the extent of poverty can be compared over time, giving a reliable departure point for discussion of how poverty has increased or decreased over the past thirty years. Using official poverty data, it is possible to develop a demographic picture of poverty in America.

Poverty in America: Who Are the Poor?

Since the late 1950s, shifts in demographics and in the composition of families, coupled with social welfare policies that unevenly provided assistance, have changed the face of poverty in this country. During the early 1960s poverty was most prevalent among the elderly, but today children and families headed by single women are disproportionately found among those officially counted as poor. People of color are also disproportionately

Table 5.3

Persons Below Poverty Level (in millions)

	All Persons		White		Black		Hispanic	
	Number	%	Number	%	Number	%	Number	%
1994	38.1	14.5	25.4	11.7	10.2	30.6	8.4	30.7
1993	39.3	15.1	26.2	12.2	10.9	33.1	8.1	30.6
1992	38.0	14.8	25.2	11.9	10.8	33.4	7.6	29.6
1991	35.7	14.2	23.7	11.3	10.2	32.7	6.3	28.7
1990	33.6	13.5	22.3	10.7	9.8	31.9	6.0	28.1

Sources: Center on Budget and Policy Priorities (1996); U.S. Bureau of the Census (1996b).

represented, reflecting economic patterns that historically have favored certain groups over others.

Table 5.3 provides an overview of the percentage of people in this country who are officially counted as poor in U.S. Bureau of the Census statistics. Two-thirds of the poor are white, but African-Americans and Hispanics are disproportionately represented. African-Americans are almost three times more likely to be poor than whites. While the difference was greater thirty years ago, with an almost four times greater likelihood of poverty for blacks as compared to whites (U.S. Bureau of the Census, 1993), the improvement still leaves a significant gap between the financial well-being of whites and African-Americans in this country. These numbers reflect decades of differing access to the economic system, dating back before the Civil War when African-Americans could not own property and did not have equal access to employment and financial security. The Hispanic population also fares poorly. While other groups recently experienced a small decrease, the poverty rate for the Hispanic population continues to grow. In 1994, Hispanics were almost three times more likely to be poor than whites.

Statistics on poverty among other minority populations are often listed separately from the rates for whites, African-Americans, and Hispanics. American Indian levels of poverty are often difficult to track down, reflecting the lack of official attention directed to American Indian concerns. In 1991, 30% of all American Indian households had incomes below the poverty line (Reddy, 1995). The Asian population fared better. In 1995, almost 10 million Asians and Pacific Islanders, or 14.6%, were below the poverty line (U.S. Bureau of the Census, 1996b).

The distribution of income and wealth in this country demonstrates a wide spectrum of inequality. Table 5.4 presents the distribution of annual income for all families. Those who earn the most, people in the highest fifth of the population, receive almost 47% of all income earned. The average family income for the top fifth was almost $116,000, compared to $10,400 for

Table 5.4

Distribution and Average of Aggregate Family Income by Quintile, 1994

Population Segment	Percent of Income°	Upper Income Limit
Highest fifth	46.9	no limit
Fourth fifth	23.3	$69,998
Third fifth	15.7	47,000
Second fifth	10.0	31,300
Lowest fifth	4.2	17,940

°Total is greater than 100% due to rounding.

Source: U.S. Bureau of the Census (1996b).

families in the lowest fifth in 1994 (Center on Budget and Policy Priorities, 1996). These measures of income do not take account of possessions, such as real estate holdings, nor do they reflect pensions, inheritance, or other sources of wealth. The data only reflect annual income. When considering family wealth, the disparity between those at the top and those at the bottom is even wider. The difference in net worth, which reflects all assets and debts, shows that the highest fifth claims 67% of the wealth, while the lowest fifth has no net worth (Oliver & Shapiro, 1990). In 1993, white households had a median measured net worth of almost $46,000, compared to $4,400 for African-American households and about $4,700 for Hispanic households (U.S. Bureau of the Census, 1995a).

Income and wealth in this country vary greatly. The economic system is not designed to promote equality. As discussed in chapter 2, the social welfare system tries to reduce some of the inequality, but in no way attempts any major redistribution of wealth. In fact, the gap between the top earners and the bottom earners has always been wide. What is worrisome now is the growing disparity. Since 1980, those at the bottom have seen their share of the national income decrease by 18%, while those at the top have seen theirs increase by almost 13% (calculations based on data from U.S. Bureau of the Census, 1996b). The 1980s Reagan plan for "trickle-down" economics, which promised redistribution of wealth from the top to the bottom, clearly did not work. Instead, we have seen a steady upward shift of income and wealth for those at the top, leaving those who were poor worse off than before.

Feminization of Poverty

Further analysis of poverty data indicates the historical lack of economic access for women. The average earnings for American workers in 1994 indicated that women earned only 66% of what men earned. Among people working year-round and full-time, men earned an average of $41,118, compared to $27,162 for women (U.S. Bureau of the Census, 1996b). What does this earning differential mean in terms of the poverty numbers? For women, poverty is a more likely occurrence than for men. There are at least two major reasons for this. The first has to do with the difference in average earnings for women versus men. The second reason is that women are more likely to have children for whom they are responsible, and this places an additional economic burden on them. This trend was described by sociologist Diana Pearce in 1978 as the **feminization of poverty** (Pearce, 1978).

The feminization of poverty reflects the phenomenon that poverty and gender are correlated, and that gender is a key factor in the likelihood of poverty (Pearce, 1989). This relationship is not new, but economic shifts and policy changes catapulted this trend to the attention of social scientists and policy-makers during the late 1970s. Policy changes, such as tightening of public assistance eligibility requirements under the Reagan administration, have deepened the impact of poverty on women (Sarri, 1985) as have social changes. Many argue that the transformation of the family has brought about increased poverty for women. The prevailing sentiment is that rising rates of divorce, separation, teenage pregnancies, and out-of-marriage births have resulted in greater numbers of poor, female-headed households.

The data do reflect an increase in the numbers of women heading households without a partner (U.S. Bureau of the Census, 1993). From 1959 to 1992, the percentage of families headed by a single woman increased from 10% of all families to 17.5%. Among families in poverty, the numbers changed significantly as well. In 1959, 23% of all poor families were headed by single women, while by 1992 that figure had increased to 52.4%. In 1960, 9.1% of all children lived with one parent, while by 1990 that had increased to 24.7% (House Committee on Ways and Means, 1992). For children whose fathers leave, the families' economic situation worsens. Research on change in family composition demonstrated that monthly family income dropped 37% following parental separation (U.S. Bureau of the Census, 1991).

Policy-makers across the political spectrum argue that changing family composition leads to poverty. Nevertheless, linking poverty with single motherhood ignores several realities of our social and economic systems. "Most poverty, even that of female-headed families, occurs because of income or job changes" (Bane, 1986, p. 231).

In the work force, women are at a disadvantage (Dabelko & Sheak, 1992). Family responsibilities, inequality in training, and lack of access to better-paying jobs all contribute toward women's underemployment and lack of employment. Working mothers frequently are relegated to lower-paying jobs, reflecting preferential hiring of men without family complications over women who may be distracted by the care of their children, and women are often closed out of higher-paying positions because of unequal access to the necessary education and training. These barriers have also curtailed the economic participation of minorities. Thus, combining gender and race leaves a distinct pattern in poverty status—women, particularly women of color, are disproportionately subject to poverty. In 1994, almost half of all African-American families headed by women were in poverty, compared to 29% of white female-headed families (Center on Budget and Policy Priorities, 1996). While not as great, the disparity among single-father households also reflects a racial difference. White single-father households had a poverty rate of 13.6% in 1992, compared to 24.7% of African-American single-father households. These rates compare with a national poverty rate of 6.2% for all two-parent families (U.S. Bureau of the Census, 1993). Single parenthood places a family at greater economic disadvantage than a two-parent family, and the difference is exacerbated by gender and race.

Juvenilization of Poverty

Growing numbers of single-parent families, coupled with the inability of families to prosper with only one adult working, have greatly affected the economic well-being of children in this country. The 1980s witnessed the **juvenilization of poverty**—the growing incidence of poverty among children (Segal, 1991; Wilson, 1985). Poverty among children, significant during the 1960s, abated somewhat as a result of the efforts of the War on Poverty. As a result of economic downturns and cutbacks in social programs, however, poverty among children worsened during the 1980s (see Table 5.5).

By 1994, almost 22% of all children younger than 18 were officially counted as poor: more than 15 million children. When examined by race, the difference is greater. In 1994, 43.8% of all African-American children and 41.5% of all Hispanic children lived in poverty, as compared to only 16.9% of white children (Center on Budget and Policy Priorities, 1996). Poverty seems to be inversely related to age, with younger children more likely to be poor. During the 1980s, the number of very young children in poverty rose by 26%. In some urban and rural areas, as many as 45% of all infants and toddlers were in poverty (U.S. General Accounting Office, 1994b). African-American children under the age of 6 are particularly vulnerable. In 1994, 49.1% of all these children were officially counted as living in poverty (Center on Budget and Policy Priorities, 1996).

American Indian children also experience high levels of poverty. In 1990, 38.6% of American Indian children (almost 800,000) lived below the poverty line. In the states of Arizona, Minnesota, Montana, Nebraska, New Mexico, and North and South Dakota, more than 50% of American Indian children fell below the poverty line (Reddy, 1995).

While there is no agreement on what causes poverty, or why families have changed and how this has affected the number of poor, it is clear that more children are living in poverty than in the past. Of all poor persons in this country, almost 40% of them are children (U.S. Bureau of the Census, 1996a). Child poverty, in addition to reflecting the feminization of poverty, also seems to be linked to the economic decline of young families. From

Table 5.5
Children Below Poverty Level (in millions)

	All Children		White		Black		Hispanic	
	Number	%	Number	%	Number	%	Number	%
1994	15.3	21.8	9.3	16.9	4.9	43.8	4.1	41.5
1993	15.7	22.7	9.8	17.8	5.1	46.1	3.9	40.9
1992	15.3	22.3	9.4	17.4	5.1	46.6	3.6	40.0
1991	14.3	21.8	8.8	16.8	4.8	45.9	3.1	40.4
1990	13.4	20.6	8.2	15.9	4.6	44.8	2.9	38.4

Percent of Children in Poverty

Period	Average %
1990–1994	21.8
1985–1989	20.1
1980–1984	20.8
1975–1979	16.3
1970–1974	15.1
1965–1969	17.0
1960–1964	24.7

Source: Calculations based on data from Center on Budget and Policy Priorities (1996).

1967 to 1986, families whose head of household was under 30 years of age saw their poverty rate increase from 12.1% to 21.6% (Grant Foundation, 1988). Even with the economic expansion of the 1980s, the financial well-being of young families did not greatly improve. By 1992, calculations of Census Bureau data (U.S. Bureau of the Census, 1995b) demonstrated that families with heads of households younger than 34 years of age had a poverty rate of 21.2%. In 1994, a family headed by someone between 15 and 24 years old was almost three times more likely to be in poverty than a household headed by someone between 35 and 44 years of age (Center on Budget and Policy Priorities, 1996).

It is understandable that economic need is greater in households with children. The care of children represents great financial costs for families, in addition to the demands on parents' time that can diminish their earning abilities. These costs have always existed, however. What is it that has changed over the past twenty years to make families, particularly those with young children and young heads of households, more vulnerable economically? The answer may lie in shifts in employment and the economy. Even if people are employed, more people are working at jobs that are part-time or pay inadequate wages. The result over the past fifteen years has been a growing rate of **subemployment** (Dabelko & Sheak, 1992). Subemployment means that people are finding work, but the majority of jobs provide wages and benefits that are below what is needed by a typical family. Subemployment disproportionately affects women and younger heads of households.

The Rise in Homelessness

The social phenomenon of people who lack permanent places of residence is not new, but it was rediscovered during the 1980s. The public, media, and policy-makers discuss homelessness as if it were a separate issue, but it is really a part of the larger problem of poverty in the United States. The recession of 1981–1983 highlighted the problem of homelessness as more people found themselves out of work and on the street, and the confluence of numerous factors directed the public's attention to people who are homeless.

The increase in homelessness can be traced to a combination of individual factors and social changes (Shinn & Weitzman, 1990). Poverty is a major contributor to the incidence of homelessness. Increased poverty among children and families, coupled with decreased availability of affordable housing, has led to rising rates of homelessness among children and families (Gustavsson & Segal, 1994).

Leaders of urban centers cited the lack of sufficient affordable housing as the most pressing social problem of the 1980s (U.S. Conference of Mayors, 1988). The supply of affordable housing declined due to urban development and a decrease in federal funding for low-income housing assistance (Children's Defense Fund, 1990). Many single people and some families in poverty rely on the rental of rooms designed to house one person, often referred to as Single Room Occupancies (SROs). Between 1960 and the mid-1980s, one-half of the SRO supply, about 1 million units, disappeared as a result of urban development and change, leaving a significant gap in available housing for people living in poverty (U.S. General Accounting Office, 1992b). Decreased availability of affordable housing hurts poor families as well as single adults. There are two low-income renters for every available low-rent unit. This shortage is exacerbated by the proportion of income required for housing. Typically, poor renters spend 60% of their income on housing (Center on Budget and Policy Priorities, 1995b).

Also during the 1980s, increasing rates of subemployment and unemployment among those on the margin of the economic system left more people in precarious situations. Confronted with a shortage of affordable housing and gloomier employment prospects, more and more people became homeless.

The number of people who are homeless is almost impossible to ascertain. The nature of homelessness itself—living without a permanent residence—means that census takers and researchers cannot accurately determine how many people are homeless at any given time. Often, analyses of how many people used social services or shelters are the basis for estimating the population of people who are homeless, and estimates vary widely. Early government statistics gathered by the Department of Housing and Urban Development (HUD) estimated that in 1983, 250,000 to 350,000 persons were homeless (U.S. Department of Housing and Urban Development, 1984). In 1987, the Urban Institute estimated that 600,000 people were homeless on any given night (Burt & Cohen, 1989). At the same time, advocates who worked with people who were homeless asserted that there were two million people who experienced periods of homelessness over the course of each year (Alliance Housing Council, 1988).

There is no way to be absolutely sure how many people are homeless and why. It has become clear, however, that more and more services are offered for people who are homeless, and there is still a growing need (U.S. General Accounting Office, 1992a). Surveys of services for people who are homeless reveal that there are more than 5,000 shelters for people who are homeless, a number that doubled between 1984 and 1988 (Weinreb & Rossi, 1995).

Cash Assistance and Social Programs to Aid the Poor

A mixture of changing demographics and shifting economics has affected the distribution of the population living in poverty. As we have discussed, the most significant trends of the past twenty years are the feminization of poverty, the juvenilization of poverty, and growing numbers of people who are homeless. Women, children, and those who are on the edge of the employment system are most directly affected by the economic downturns in our system and consequently are most likely to turn to public social welfare programs to cushion the impact. To fully comprehend what it means to be poor in America, it is necessary to understand the programs and services of the social welfare system that are designed to address poverty.

Public efforts to help the poor date back to the colonial period and the Elizabethan Poor Laws, but most of today's programs originated with the New Deal programs of the 1930s. Some programs to fight poverty were designed to be compatible and supportive of each other, but in reality the social welfare policy response to poverty has been patched together over the years. Coordination and a common sense of purpose are lacking. In general, social welfare programs designed to decrease poverty and ameliorate its impact are called **anti-poverty programs**.

The primary underlying goal of programs designed to aid the poor, particularly when women and children are involved, has been to support the American economic and social system, rather than redistribute resources or change the value structure (Piven & Cloward, 1993; Abramovitz, 1996). Contrary to what is often stated by opponents of the social welfare system, cash programs to the poor represent only a small portion of the federal budget. The cash outlays are less than 5% of the annual budget. As discussed in chapter 2, historically the various programs developed to aid the poor were designed to maintain the status quo. People were always encouraged to work and to participate fully in the economic system. Anti-poverty programs were meant to tide people over in times of downturn, not to redistribute wealth from the rich to the poor.

The array of federal public assistance efforts designed to aid those who are economically disadvantaged includes as many as seventy-five different programs (Jennings & Zank, 1993). Public services include distribution of cash, direct services such as health care, and vouchers that can be converted into commodities such as food. The administration of the programs also reflects a vast network, with operations covered at the federal, state, or local levels, or combinations of the three. The result of these differences is a collection of programs and services that operates under diverse regulations, is poorly linked, and serves varying goals and purposes. Consequently, it is difficult to develop a thorough and complete understanding of the anti-poverty programs offered. Nevertheless, providers and advocates of social welfare services should acquire a working knowledge of public assistance programs in America. A number of sources are available that explain the details of the various programs (Social Security Administration, 1993; House Committee on Ways and Means, 1994; Levitan, 1990; U.S. General Accounting Office, 1985). The following discussion provides a general overview of the major programs.

Before discussing each specific program, it is important to clarify some common values and perceptions of anti-poverty programs. As our historical analysis of social welfare policy revealed, the American public has been reluctant to provide assistance to people who are poor. The distinctions of worthy and unworthy helped to ensure that only people deemed "truly deserving" of assistance received it. The past ten years have witnessed increasing levels of public anger, frustration, and resentment directed toward anti-poverty programs and the poor themselves. The term most often used to describe efforts to assist the poor is *welfare*. As highlighted in the first chapter, the historical primary definition of welfare was good fortune, health, and happiness. That is no longer true. Today, "welfare" is used by opponents and supporters alike to mean the specific social welfare programs that provide cash or in-kind services to people in poverty. Welfare has now become a vague, over-reaching term that stigmatizes people and conjures up images of handouts given to people who are marginally deserving or not deserving at all.

In our discussions throughout this book, we attempt to avoid using the term "welfare" to refer to a group of anti-poverty programs. We have already identified the well-being perspective of welfare as used in the terms social welfare system, policies, and programs. When we refer to a poverty-related program, we try to use the actual program name. We hope you will finish this chapter with a clearer understanding of the major anti-poverty programs, their similarities and differences, and why mixing them all together does not contribute to sound social welfare policy analysis.

There are also practice implications. As social workers engaged in the delivery of anti-poverty services, our work is diminished when the variety of services in which we work are lumped together in one vague term such as "welfare." What becomes lost are the unique contributions and specialized accomplishments of programs that together provide an important safety-net for millions of children and families.

Aid to Families with Dependent Children/Temporary Assistance for Needy Families

The largest and most well-known public assistance program today is the Aid to Families with Dependent Children (AFDC) program, revised and re-named in 1996 as the Temporary Assistance for Needy Families (TANF) program. Originally passed as the Aid to Dependent Children program as part of the Social Security Act of 1935, the program was designed to provide cash assistance to families with dependent children in need. Need was rec-ognized as falling below a poverty standard of need and the incapacity, death, or continued absence of a parent, or in some cases the unemployment of both parents.

Until enactment of the Personal Responsibility and Work Opportunity Reconciliation Act of 1996, the federal government offered matching grants to states for their participation in AFDC. **Matching grants** means that for each federal dollar received, states were required to spend some pre-determined amount on the program. Thus, states match the federal spend-ing. Although the program was optional, every state chose to qualify for the matching funds and operated an AFDC program under federal guidelines. The federal rules included provisions guaranteeing that anyone who wished to apply could do so, that all eligible persons were guaranteed assistance for as long as they qualified, that the plan had to be operated throughout the entire state, and that the state government was responsible for administer-ing the program although localities could participate. The cost of AFDC was shared by federal, state, and local governments. The federal funds came out of general revenues and were available for all eligible recipients. The 1996 legislation significantly altered the sixty-one-year-old structure of AFDC. The new legislation replaced the AFDC program with TANF, which includes several provisions that are radical departures from the original de-sign of AFDC. Under TANF, there is no longer a guarantee that all eligible individuals will receive assistance; families who have received five cumula-tive years of assistance will no longer be eligible to receive cash aid; feder-al funding will be capped at a set amount and provided through a TANF block grant; and states must require families to work after two years on as-sistance (Department of Health and Human Services, 1996; Center on Bud-get and Policy Priorities, 1996). **Block grants** differ from matching grants in that states get a set amount of money through a block grant. The amount provided to a state each year is determined in advance by the federal gov-ernment and cannot be increased.

Eligibility, needs, and benefit levels continue to be set at the state level. Consequently, the AFDC or new TANF program varies greatly from state to state. Each state determines the minimum standard of need—the level of annual income below which a family must fall to qualify for aid. The standard of need is based on the minimum cost of living in a state, as determined by state officials and approved by the federal government through the Department of Health and Human Services. For example, in 1993 the monthly standard of need for a family of three was $577 in New York and $368 in Mississippi. In every state, the standard of need is lower than the poverty line. The state-by-state system of determining need allows states to offer monthly payments only to the poorest of the poor, those whose incomes fall far short of the poverty line.

Adult recipients of TANF are required to participate in work activities. Individuals are required to participate for at least twenty hours per week in unsubsidized or subsidized employment, on-the-job training, work experience, community service, or twelve months of vocational training, or to provide child care services to individuals who are participating in community service. The legislation does not provide child care, and only single parents with children under 6 years of age who cannot find child care will not be penalized for failure to engage in work activities. Penalties for failure to work are to be set by each state.

The TANF block grant program, although effective as of October 1, 1996, will not be completely implemented by all states for several years. Thus, it is still too early to assess the full impact of the changes imposed by the 1996 Act. Many national organizations and leaders are critical of the new law. An Urban Institute study concluded that the components of this legislation will push an additional 1.1 million children, and 2.6 million people in total, into poverty (Super, Parrott, Steinmetz, & Mann, 1996). The changes made to the AFDC program are likely to result in greater numbers of people looking for assistance from private social welfare services. Social workers will face new challenges to provide help to families in need.

Supplemental Security Income

The Supplemental Security Income (SSI) program provides cash assistance to any person aged (65 or older), blind, or with a disability whose income falls below the poverty line. Various components of SSI were originally outlined by the 1935 Social Security Act and eventually consolidated in 1972 under one program. The consolidation of two different programs—Aid to the Aged and Aid to the Blind and Disabled—coordinated eligibility and benefits under the federal government.

Unlike AFDC/TANF, funding for SSI comes solely from federal general revenues, and administration is through the Social Security Administration, a federal agency. Thus, eligibility and benefits are uniform across all states. A low-income person qualifies if he or she is unable to participate in paid employment due to a medically determined physical or mental impairment, or is over the age of 65. In 1994, the maximum income level for eligibility was $5,352.

Children with disabilities are also covered under SSI. The Personal Responsibility and Work Opportunity Reconciliation Act of 1996 tightened the definition of disability for children by excluding maladaptive behavior (such as Attention Deficit Disorder) as a medical criterion for disability. The result of this change will be the recategorization and termination of large numbers of poor children who previously qualified for cash assistance under SSI.

General Assistance or General Relief

No federal program exists to provide cash assistance to single able-bodied men or women under the age of 65 who are poor. This responsibility is left to the states and localities. The typical effort by states to provide economic assistance to this population is usually referred to as general assistance (GA) or general relief (GR). The lack of federal involvement is reflected in the variety and disparity of GA programs offered throughout the country.

Because there is no federal involvement, there is also no federal financial incentive to provide general assistance. Consequently, not all states offer the program, and eligibility requirements and benefits vary from program to program. In 1992, nine states had no GA programs at all, and ten other states had only partial programs (Center on Budget and Policy Priorities, 1995a). Over the past few years, GA programs have come under attack from those who are opposed to providing any economic assistance to people who do not fit into the centuries-old categories of worthy poor. The result has been severe cutbacks and even cancellation of GA programs. For example, in 1991, Ohio decreased the program from a year-round assistance to only six months of coverage in a calendar year. For the other six months, even if eligible persons still had economic need, they were on their own.

Earned-Income Tax Credit

In 1975, the Earned-Income Tax Credit (EITC) was established to aid families who fell into poverty in spite of having working family members. The program is designed to supplement the income of low-wage workers. For families with dependent children in which a family member works, if their income is below a certain level, they qualify to receive an income tax credit. The credit is based on family income and the number of children. For example, in 1996, a family with one child and income up to $25,000 would receive a tax credit. The EITC is a federal program administered by the Internal Revenue Service. Participation is done through the filing of a federal tax return and therefore involves only the same bureaucratic procedures as paying one's taxes.

The general goal of the federal EITC program and state enhancements of the program is to allow low-wage workers to keep more of their earnings. Thus, the program acts as a wage supplement for people in low-wage jobs and can decrease poverty for working poor families.

Medicaid

Federal matching funds are provided to states to cover the cost of medical care and services for low-income individuals under the Medicaid Program. Added to the Social Security Act in 1965 as Title XIX, Medicaid covers all AFDC/TANF recipients and most SSI recipients. Medicaid programs, like AFDC/TANF, vary from state to state. Each state designs and administers the program following federal guidelines. Medicaid programs are required to provide physician services, inpatient and outpatient hospital care, home health services, nursing home care, and some preventive services. States may choose to offer additional services such as dental care, eyeglasses, or drugs and receive federal matching dollars for providing these additional services. Details of the Medicaid Program will be provided in chapter 6.

Food Stamps

Social welfare policies for food distribution, developed as part of the New Deal, were originally designed to utilize surplus agricultural commodities. Support for government involvement in the purchase of food came from agricultural groups as a way to guarantee price support. With government subsidies through food distribution programs, people were able to purchase needed foods and farmers received price supports during periods of over-production. The agricultural support of surplus food distribution programs resulted in their administration by the Department of Agriculture. Legislative changes to government food distribution programs in later years changed the emphasis to an anti-poverty program (Finegold, 1988).

In response to the War on Poverty and the push for anti-poverty programs, the Food Stamp Program was enacted in 1964 as a way to assist poor individuals and families to purchase food. The program distributes coupons to those who fall below a federally determined level of need. This system allows recipients to choose what food items they want to buy, but coupons may *not* be used for alcoholic beverages, tobacco, paper products, diapers, personal care products, or ready-to-eat foods. The Food Stamp Program is administered through the Department of Agriculture, with local public aid offices responsible for determining eligibility and allotment of coupons. The Food Stamp Program is funded from federal general revenues for the full value of the coupons, with administrative costs shared by the states and federal government. The social welfare policy analysis example in this chapter assesses the Food Stamp Act of 1964 (see Figure 5.1).

Figure 5.1

Social Welfare Policy Analysis Model:
The Food Stamp Act of 1964

Social Issue

- Hunger, malnutrition
- Agricultural food surpluses

Goal

- Feed people in need
- Use and distribute food surplus

Policy or Legislation

- Food Stamp Act of 1964 (P.L. 88–525) as amended over the past 30 years
- Eligibility based on income
- Eligible individuals and households receive coupons redeemable for food
- Value of coupons depends on household size and income

Implementation

- Develop federal program, implemented by states, to provide vouchers for the purchase of food
- Administer program through the Department of Agriculture
- Operate program through local public assistance offices

Affected Populations

- Poor families and single adults
- Grocers
- Farmers

Actual Impact

- Provide basic food necessities for people who are poor
- Guarantee transfer of $20 billion a year for agricultural products

Intended Impact

- Provide for basic food necessities
- Reduce food surpluses
- Support agricultural prices

Supplemental Food Program for Women, Infants, and Children

The Supplemental Food Program for Women, Infants, and Children (WIC) is a federal program designed to provide nutrition and health assistance to pregnant and postpartum women, infants, and children up to the age of 5. To be eligible, women and their children must be at nutritional risk and have income below the standards consistent with measuring need in the state. Administered by the Department of Agriculture with the assistance of local clinics, the program provides participants with vouchers that can be redeemed for nutritious foods such as milk and eggs. Participants also qualify to receive nutrition education and health services aimed at improving the health of newborn babies and young children.

Public Housing

A number of housing programs are administered by federal, state, and local governments. Almost all are funded with federal money through HUD. Low-rent public housing projects, originally developed under 1937 legislation, are federally funded programs managed and administered by local Public Housing Authorities. Families, elderly persons, and people with disabilities usually qualify if their income is less than 50% of the median income for the area. Rental charges, set by the federal government, are about 30% of the recipient's monthly after-tax income.

The Department of Housing and Urban Development also provides rental assistance to poor families through what is commonly referred to as the Section 8 program. The federal government provides rental certificates and vouchers that can be used to subsidize the lease of a privately owned rental unit. Participants pay 30% of their income toward rent, and a government voucher pays the rest. For a unit to qualify, its monthly rent cannot exceed a specific amount set by the government.

Since the late 1980s, the federal government has developed additional housing support programs specifically for people who are homeless. The Stewart B. McKinney Homeless Assistance Act of 1987 (P.L. 100–77) was the first comprehensive federal effort to aid people who are homeless. The housing programs covered by the legislation include grants and funds for emergency shelter and monies to support transitional and permanent housing. From 1987 to 1993, however, the Congress never fully funded the McKinney Act programs, spending only 75% of the funds authorized (U.S. General Accounting Office, 1994a).

Other Anti-Poverty Efforts

The programs described above represent the major provisions and structures of our social welfare efforts designed to aid people who are poor. The array of programs differs widely with regard to who is eligible, how much is provided through benefits, who pays for the program, and who is responsible for its administration. As stated earlier in this chapter, our anti-poverty efforts are a patchwork of programs and services largely dependent on federal funds and regulated by numerous federal departments. These programs are usually adopted by states and administered locally.

Other programs, falling primarily under social insurance or federal tax exemptions, help to keep some people from falling into poverty. This has been especially true for the elderly over the past twenty years. Social insurance, unemployment insurance, workers' compensation, survivors' benefits, and disability insurance are examples of other cash assistance programs. Unlike the programs discussed here, however, they do not require poverty as a prerequisite for eligibility. These programs are discussed in greater detail in chapter 8. It is important to remember that although they may keep people from poverty, they are not regarded as anti-poverty programs. Consequently, the negative attitudes toward social welfare programs and close scrutiny of whether or not a person is deserving of assistance are most often attached to the income-tested anti-poverty programs presented in this chapter, not the social insurance programs introduced in chapter 2 and discussed in detail later.

Clearly, a comprehensive and unified institutional approach to provision of services for the poor is lacking in this country. There can be both positives and negatives to our residual approach. On the positive side, local administration can allow programs to be tailored to meet the unique needs of each community. Federal guidelines can create national minimums so that each citizen is entitled to an equal baseline of services. Federal funding can equalize the differing financial means of states, thereby not penalizing poorer states and their residents. On the negative side, a piecemeal approach can leave gaps in services and a lack of coordination, leaving many without needed assistance. Funding may be inadequate because states are reluctant to contribute, preferring to rely on federal funds instead. Our reliance on a residual approach often results in programs that are inadequate in coverage, funding, and support services. In the next section we will look at the array of programs and their effectiveness in fighting poverty.

How Effective Are Existing Programs in Fighting Poverty?

Recent public debate has highlighted disagreements over public assistance in America. Many argue that too much is given without enough personal effort on the part of recipients. This argument is not new. Historically, public policy–makers have struggled to find the right amount of assistance to provide for basic necessities while maintaining people's desire and commitment to work. This dilemma was addressed in the Elizabethan Poor Laws

Table 5.6

Average Monthly Payments for Income Support Programs, 1994

AFDC

Family—$378
Individual—$135

SSI

Overall average—$351
Aged—$243
Blind—$264
Disabled—$384

Source: U.S. Bureau of the Census (1996b).

and is still evident in discussions of "welfare reform" today. Before we can explore how to simultaneously help people and encourage them to provide for themselves, we need to ask whether existing public efforts at ameliorating poverty have been adequate.

Table 5.6 lists the average monthly benefits provided through AFDC and SSI in 1994. Simple arithmetic reveals that on an annual basis, none of the programs pay enough to lift a person or a family past the official poverty line. General assistance programs provide even less. For example, remember from our previous discussion that eight states offer absolutely no general assistance, while fourteen states offer programs only in selected counties (Nichols, Dunlap, & Barkan, 1992).

The AFDC program has been the most frequently discussed public assistance program. In 1993, the AFDC program served more than 4.9 million households, comprising 14.3 million individuals. Of these, almost 68% were children, 28% were women, and 4% were men (Administration for Children and Families, 1995). Comparing these statistics to the number of children officially counted in poverty makes it clear that AFDC has not reached many of the families in poverty. In 1990, less than half the population in poverty received AFDC, and only 60% of poor children were covered (House Committee on Ways and Means, 1992). By 1994, the situation had improved slightly; almost 65% of children in poverty were covered by AFDC (calculations based on data from U.S. Bureau of the Census, 1996b).

Even when AFDC benefits are combined with food stamps, it is not enough to lift a family above the poverty line. The median combined benefit for a family of three was about $7,900 in 1993, or about two-thirds of the poverty threshold (House Committee on Ways and Means, 1994). From 1980 to 1988, the number of poor young families increased while the percentage receiving public assistance decreased. Almost 25% of all poor young families, in spite of need, received no public assistance in 1988, and even after all forms of assistance were combined, less than one out of five families were lifted above the poverty level (U.S. General Accounting Office, 1992c).

Cash assistance programs do not reach all poor Americans. Of those they do reach, the programs provide only a minimum level of subsistence, not enough to lift an individual or a family above the official poverty level. It is impossible for the average family on public assistance to cover all necessities. In spite of the minimum support, public assistance does provide something that most low-paying jobs do not: health care coverage. For a woman with children, a full-time job paying minimum wage would not bring in enough money to lift her family out of poverty and would not provide her with the health benefits she can receive through the Medicaid program. While many critics argue that laziness or lack of commitment to work keeps people on "welfare," for many parents it has been the only way to guarantee health care for their families.

The publicly shared image of "welfare families" is often distorted. The typical family who received services through the former AFDC program did so for less than three years. Public assistance usually serves to assist a family after a change in family circumstances such as divorce or economic hardship such as loss of a job. Families who receive public assistance are not really different from most other families, except for the fact that they are poor and often lack the skills to acquire better-paying jobs. According to the Administration for Children and Families (1995), in 1994:

- The average AFDC family consisted of one adult and two children, with 90% of the families having three or fewer children.

- Sixty-six percent of AFDC families received subsidies for three years or less.

- Only 23% received housing assistance through public housing or rent subsidies.

- Forty-seven percent of the children were five years old or younger, and the average age among all children was just over seven years old.

- Less than 5% received any direct child support.

- 99.3% of AFDC recipients were U.S. citizens or legal residents of the United States.

- Only 1.7% of female adult recipients were younger than 18 years of age.

- The average monthly payment for a family of three was $381 in 1994.

Public assistance programs are doing what they were established to do following the Great Depression: providing a safety net of minimal resources to keep people from total economic destitution. There is no way a person can live well under our public assistance programs. In spite of this, public perception views these "welfare" programs as creating a dependent and unmotivated population. Consequently, debate rages on about how to get people off public assistance and into work. In the next section we will examine efforts to combine employment with public assistance.

Work and "Welfare"

The center of debate around poverty and social welfare programs is the issue of work. While there are many correlates of poverty, lack of earnings is the largest reason why people are poor. The most likely factor to raise a family out of poverty is a rise in earnings. Thus, the most pressing policy question is why people who are poor are not working or are not earning enough to lift themselves out of poverty.

The reasons offered to explain unemployment among the poor span the ideological spectrum. Conservative ideology posits that the poor are lazy or uninterested in working because the public assistance system provides enough income to deter them from seeking work. This perspective focuses entirely on individual motivations. Liberal ideology suggests that structural barriers such as not enough jobs, low wages, lack of education, unequal opportunity, racism, and sexism prevent people who are poor from getting adequate employment. The emphasis is placed on the structure of the social and economic system. In support of this perspective, a number of significant trends reveal the difficulty of acquiring work that is adequate to lift a family out of poverty.

It is important to consider work and public assistance in the context of what we already know about the composition of the poverty population. As already discussed, poverty disproportionately affects children, families headed by single women, and young families. It is not difficult to conclude that single mothers and young parents are more likely to encounter barriers to adequate employment, in spite of wanting to work.

Research conducted during the 1980s indicated that while poverty is concentrated among these populations, family changes are not necessarily the cause of poverty. Rather, the problem of poverty rests with the availability of employment, the wages paid, and the skills of those looking for work (Bane, 1986). Because of employment differences between men and women, older and younger workers, and those with differing levels of education, however, poverty disproportionately affects women and children. The employment market tends to be very ineffective in providing adequate opportunities for single mothers. Increases in rates of employment do not seem to help single women raising children (Segal, 1997).

Divorce has contributed greatly to the increase in poverty among women. For example, almost three-fourths of single mothers are divorced (Arendell, 1987). In addition, because of family composition, acquiring and maintaining adequate employment is difficult for single mothers. In a study of AFDC recipients during a period of economic prosperity, Osterman (1993) found that family considerations created obstacles to full-time employment, particularly for single women raising children. Many of the poor persons interviewed had worked, but family problems such as unreliable or nonexistent child care and absence from work because of children's illnesses had forced many women to leave jobs. Other studies come to the same conclusion: "The structure of female-headed families puts them at economic disadvantage" (Rank, 1988, p. 191).

In addition to family demands, the kinds of employment available make it difficult for those in poverty to work their way out. In 1990, almost 40% of men and 48% of women aged 18 to 24 who worked year-round and full-time had insufficient income to keep a family above the poverty line (U.S. Bureau of the Census, 1992). These figures are significantly higher than those in 1979, when only 18% of men and 29% of women had below-poverty annual earnings. One-fourth of all American workers, or 30 million employees, have earnings which place them below or just above the poverty line (McDermott, 1994). Low wages, coupled with underemployment, have left workers with lower incomes and less employment stability.

The combination of family demands and lower-wage jobs makes it difficult for people to earn enough to remain out of poverty. As outlined in this chapter, the 1980s and early 1990s were years when the distribution of income shifted to favor those in the highest brackets, wages of lower-paying jobs did not keep pace with inflation and changes in the economy, and more families were headed by single women who are at a disadvantage in competing in the marketplace. In addition, levels of support available through public assistance declined after cutbacks in eligibility and benefits. These reasons have contributed significantly to the increase in poverty over the past ten years.

Efforts to Achieve "Welfare Reform"

Despite a lack of agreement on what to do, there is strong public support for change. Frustration with providing public assistance is not new. Since the inception of the AFDC program and other antipoverty programs, efforts to change the system have received tremendous public policy attention.

From ADC to AFDC

The first major policy shift after the inception of the Aid to Dependent Children (ADC) program in 1935 took place in 1962. The original structure of the program treated dependent children as separate from their families by designing aid and services solely around the children. Amendments in 1962 expanded the support services for families, expanded the AFDC-Unemployed Parent program that had been instituted the previous year as a temporary effort to support two-parent families, and changed the name to Aid to Families with Dependent Children (Abramovitz, 1996). The program's goal of providing services to help people leave public assistance was never truly embraced by policy-makers. Achieving this goal would have required developing or expanding programs for job creation, child care, and vocational education. Without this level of support, social services could not counteract the employment discrimination women faced in the job market (Miller, 1992).

From "Worthy" to "Unworthy" Poor

Since 1967, Congress has passed numerous pieces of legislation either linking AFDC to work requirements or tightening eligibility, or both. Amendments in 1967 created the Work Incentive Program (WIN), which required AFDC mothers to work or to participate in training, departing from the previous thirty years of supporting mothers to stay at home (Abramovitz, 1996). This legislation signaled a major shift in public perception toward poor women. Historically, poor women with children were considered part of the worthy poor, but typically these women were widows and were supported to stay at home and care for their children. By the 1960s, the majority of poor women with children were divorced or had never married. Perceptions and attitudes about providing public support shifted with the change in the make-up of poor families. From 1967 until the present, women on AFDC have no longer been perceived as worthy. Work requirements make that clear. If a woman is poor and she is receiving public assistance, she is no longer permitted to stay at home with her children but must go to work.

This attitude was particularly evident in legislative changes to AFDC in 1981. Policy-makers of the 1960s and 1970s had viewed the poor as inexperienced and needing government guidance to learn the value of work, but during the Reagan years the perception of the poor "as flawed, as lacking in civility, and as victims of government benevolence" (Berkowitz & McQuaid, 1988, p. 209) took firm hold. The changes of 1981, as part of the Omnibus Budget Reconciliation Act (OBRA), restricted eligibility and reduced federal subsidies. These limits paved the way for the 1988 Family Support Act (FSA), which was regarded as major "welfare reform." The FSA further restricted eligibility for assistance by placing stronger work requirements on recipients and eliminating the exemption from work for mothers of children under the age of 6. In total, the changes from the FSA were punitive toward poor women (Segal, 1989). The changes of the 1980s, taken together, were responsible for reinforcing the conservative ideology that people who are poor are to blame for their own condition and that society has minimal responsibility for changing the employment market to make it more accessible to the poor.

Focus on Individual Responsibility

Debate on "welfare reform" raged again during the 1994 presidential election and during the 1995 and 1996 congressional sessions. The measures introduced and the legislation actually passed, the Personal Responsibility and Work Opportunity Reconciliation Act of 1996 (P.L. 104–193) promoted by the new Republican majority in both the House of Representatives and the Senate, were even more restrictive and punitive than the efforts of the 1980s. These recent legislative changes to public assistance for poor women and children, through enactment of TANF, not only end sixty years of guaranteed government support but demonstrate a complete shift from the values of the New Deal era. Americans no longer feel socially responsible for the poor. The belief in individual responsibility dominates the 1996 "welfare reform" strategies enacted into law.

Even before Congress agreed on how to limit public assistance and passed TANF, the emphasis on individual responsibility was already being implemented on the state level. In 1995, President Clinton and Congress granted a number of states permission to modify their AFDC program without losing federal financial support. For example, on November 1, 1995, the state of Arizona implemented the EMPOWER program (Employing and Moving People Off Welfare and Encouraging Responsibility). This program was designed to limit AFDC cash assistance for adults to twenty-four months within a five-year period. An extension could be granted for the adult (1) to complete an education or training program; or (2) when the person is unable to find a job and proof is given that a "good-faith effort" to find employment has been made. Other states made similar changes. State legislatures are responsible for making the necessary changes to conform to the 1996 TANF block grants. After these dramatic changes, will more AFDC/TANF adults be employed, or will former AFDC families find themselves without any means of support? Only time will tell. What can be seen is that the focus on individual responsibility with minimal regard for structural barriers to economic self-sufficiency dominated the "welfare reform" efforts of 1996.

This discussion on "welfare reform" has centered on the AFDC/TANF program to the exclusion of other public assistance programs. The reason for this emphasis is that public attention and policy efforts historically have focused primarily on AFDC, usually creating the impression that public assistance and AFDC are one and the same. During recent years, however, there has been a quieter revolt against the poor through state-by-state cuts in GA. Because of the decentralized and smaller nature of GA, less publicity has accompanied these cuts. To date, at least a dozen states have reduced or discontinued their GA programs, including limiting the months a person can receive benefits and cutting the benefit amounts (Halter, 1992).

Final Thoughts on Poverty

Poverty is not a new phenomenon in our country, but it continues to evoke strong responses from policy-makers and the public. The debate surrounding what to do about poverty reflects the dilemma of reconciling the level of wealth in the United States with the persistence of poverty among millions of people. To acknowledge that the structure of our economic system results in poverty would demand large-scale changes in our market and labor systems. If one holds that the individual is responsible for his or her poverty, then the emphasis is on changing people's behaviors. Thus far in American history, neither approach has been implemented effectively. The current trend toward holding individuals completely responsible for their economic conditions means that millions of people, particularly children, will lack proper shelter, sufficient nutrition, adequate education, or access to opportunities. Over time, that approach guarantees the perpetuation of poverty and its consequences in this country.

Key Concepts

poverty

absolute measure of poverty

relative measure of poverty

poverty line

standard of need

feminization of poverty

juvenilization of poverty

subemployment

anti-poverty programs

matching grants

block grants

Aid to Families with Dependent Children (AFDC)

Temporary Assistance for Needy Families (TANF)

Supplemental Security Income (SSI)

general assistance (GA)

Earned-Income Tax Credit (EITC)

Medicaid

food stamps

Supplemental Food Program for Women, Infants, and Children (WIC)

public housing

Exercises

1. Find the local public assistance office in your community. Spend some time sitting in the waiting room. What does it look like? How many people are there? Can you find information on its programs? How was this waiting room different or the same as other public offices or private offices, such as doctors' or motor vehicle registration offices? After you leave, write down your observations and impressions. Compare your experience with those of your classmates.

2. Apply for an entry-level job at a local business. How much does the job pay? How does the annual salary compare to the poverty level? Does the employer provide health care coverage? What about other benefits, such as sick leave or vacations? Are there other costs involved, such as transportation or uniforms? Could you care for children with the schedule of this job?

3. Call a local public assistance office and identify yourself as a student. Ask for an application for TANF or food stamps. What information does the application require? Does it seem extensive or minimal? Is it like other applications you have filled out? Why or why not?

4. For one month, record all your living expenses. How much is your monthly budget? What percentage do you spend on food? On housing? How does your budget compare with the poverty line?

References

Abramovitz, M. (1996). *Regulating the lives of women* (rev. ed.). Boston: South End Press.

Administration for Children and Families. (1995). *Characteristics and financial circumstances of AFDC recipients FY 1993.* Washington, DC: U.S. Government Printing Office.

Alliance Housing Council. (1988). *Housing and homelessness.* Washington, DC: National Alliance to End Homelessness.

Annual update of the HHS poverty guidelines. (1997, March 10). *Federal Register, 62* (46), 10857.

Arendell, T.J. (1987). Women and the economics of divorce in the contemporary United States. *Signs: Journal of Women in Culture and Society, 13* (1), 121–135.

Bane, M.J. (1986). Household composition and poverty. In Danziger, S.H., & Weinberg, D.H. (eds.), *Fighting poverty: What works and what doesn't* (pp. 209–231). Cambridge, MA: Harvard University Press.

Berkowitz, E., & McQuaid, K. (1988). *Creating the welfare state.* New York: Praeger.

Burt, M.R., & Cohen, B.S. (1989). *America's homeless: Numbers, characteristics, and programs that serve them.* Washington, DC: The Urban Institute.

Center on Budget and Policy Priorities. (1995a). *General assistance programs: Gaps in the safety net.* Washington, DC: Author.

Center on Budget and Policy Priorities. (1995b). *In short supply: The growing affordable housing gap.* Washington, DC: Author.

Center on Budget and Policy Priorities. (1996). *Poverty and income trends: 1994.* Washington, DC: Author.

Children's Defense Fund. (1990). *SOS America: A children's defense budget.* Washington, DC: Author.

Dabelko, D.D., & Sheak, R.J. (1992). Employment, subemployment and the feminization of poverty. *Sociological Viewpoints, 8,* 31–66.

Department of Health and Human Services. (1996). *Summary of provisions: Personal Responsibility and Work Opportunity Reconciliation Act of 1996.* Washington, DC: Author.

Finegold, K. (1988). Agriculture and the politics of U.S. social provisions: Social insurance and food stamps. In Weir, M., Orloff, A.S., & Skocpol, T. (eds.), *The politics of social policy in the United States.* Princeton, NJ: Princeton University Press.

Grant Foundation. (1988). *The forgotten half: Pathways to success for America's youth and young families.* Washington, DC: Author.

Gustavsson, N.S., & Segal, E.A. (1994). *Critical issues in child welfare.* Thousand Oaks, CA: Sage Publications.

Halter, A.P. (1992). Decimating general assistance: Its impact on the relationships of the poor. *Arete, 17* (2), 28–37.

Haveman, R. (1992–1993). Changing the poverty measure: Pitfalls and potential gains. *Focus, 14* (3), 24–29.

House Committee on Ways and Means. (1992). *Background material and data on programs within the jurisdiction of the Committee on Ways and Means—Green book.* (WMCP 102-44). Washington, DC: U.S. Government Printing Office.

House Committee on Ways and Means. (1994). *Background material and data on programs within the jurisdiction of the Committee on Ways and Means—Green book.* (WMCP 103–27). Washington, DC: U.S. Government Printing Office.

Jennings, E.T., Jr., & Zank, N.S. (1993). The coordination challenge. In Jennings, E.T., Jr., & Zank, N.S. (eds.), *Welfare system reform: Coordinating federal, state, and local public assistance programs* (pp. 3–19). Westport, CT: Greenwood Press.

Levitan, S.A. (1990). *Programs in aid of the poor* (6th ed.). Baltimore, MD: Johns Hopkins University Press.

McDermott, J. (1994). And the poor get poorer. *The Nation, 259* (16), 576–580.

Miller, D.C. (1992). *Women and social welfare.* New York: Praeger.

Nichols, M., Dunlap, J., & Barkan, S. (1992). *National general assistance survey, 1992.* Washington, DC: Center on Budget and Policy Priorities & National Conference of State Legislatures.

Oliver, M.L., & Shapiro, T.M. (1990). Wealth of a nation: A reassessment of asset inequality in America shows at least one–third of households are asset-poor. *The American Journal of Economics and Sociology, 49* (2), 129–151.

Orshansky, M. (1965). Counting the poor: Another look at the poverty profile. *Social Security Bulletin, 28* (1), 3–29.

Osterman, P. (1993). Why don't "they" work? Employment patterns in a high-pressure economy. *Social Science Research, 22* (2), 115–130.

Pearce, D. (1978). The feminization of poverty: Women, work, and welfare. *Urban and Social Change Review, 11* (1–2), 28–36.

Pearce, D. (1989). The feminization of poverty: A second look. Paper presented at the American Sociological Association Meetings. Washington, DC: Institute for Women's Policy Research.

Piven, F.F., & Cloward, R.A. (1993). *Regulating the poor: The functions of public welfare.* New York: Vintage Books.

Rank, M.R. (1988). The dynamics of welfare use: How long and how often? In Tomaskovic-Devey, D. (ed.), *Poverty and social welfare in the United States* (pp. 177–193). Boulder, CO: Westview Press.

Reddy, M.S. (ed.). (1995). *Statistical record of native North Americans* (2nd ed.). New York: Gale Research Inc.

Sarri, R.C. (1985). Federal policy changes and the feminization of poverty. *Child Welfare, 64* (3), 235–247.

Segal, E.A. (1989). Welfare reform: Help for poor women and children? *Affilia, 4* (3), 42–50.

Segal, E.A. (1991). The juvenilization of poverty in the 1980s. *Social Work, 36* (5), 454–457.

Segal, E.A. (1997). Welfare reform and the myth of the marketplace. *Journal of Poverty, 1* (1), 5–18.

Shinn, M., & Weitzman, B.C. (1990). Research on homelessness: An introduction. *Journal of Social Issues, 46* (4), 1–12.

Social Security Administration. (1993). *Social security programs in the United States.* SSA publication 13–11758. Washington, DC: U.S. Department of Health and Human Services.

Super, D.A., Parrott, S., Steinmetz, S., & Mann, C. (1996). *The new welfare law.* Washington, DC: Center on Budget and Policy Priorities.

U.S. Bureau of the Census. (1991). *The economics of family disruption.* SB/91–10. Washington, DC: U.S. Government Printing Office.

U.S. Bureau of the Census. (1992). *Workers with low earnings: 1964 to 1990.* Current Population Reports, Series P60, No. 178. Washington, DC: U.S. Government Printing Office.

U.S. Bureau of the Census. (1993). *Poverty in the United States: 1992.* Current Population Reports, Series P60–185. Washington, DC: U.S. Government Printing Office.

U.S. Bureau of the Census. (1995a). *Asset ownership of households: 1993.* Washington, DC: U.S. Government Printing Office.

U.S. Bureau of the Census. (1995b). *Statistical abstract of the United States: 1995* (115th ed.). Washington, DC: U.S. Government Printing Office.

U.S. Bureau of the Census. (1996a). *Income, poverty, and valuation of noncash benefits: 1994.* Washington, DC: U.S. Government Printing Office.

U.S. Bureau of the Census. (1996b). *Statistical abstract of the United States: 1996* (116th ed.). Washington, DC: U.S. Government Printing Office.

U.S. Conference of Mayors. (1988). *A status report on children in America's cities.* Washington, DC: Author.

U.S. Department of Housing and Urban Development. (1984). *A report to the Secretary on homelessness and emergency shelters.* Washington, DC: Author.

U.S. General Accounting Office. (1985). *Federal benefits programs: A profile.* GAO/HRD 86–14. Washington, DC: Author.

U.S. General Accounting Office. (1992a). *Homelessness: McKinney Act programs and funding through fiscal year 1991.* GAO/RCED–93–39. Washington, DC: Author.

U.S. General Accounting Office. (1992b). *Homelessness: Single-room-occupancy program achieves goal, but HUD can increase impact.* GAO/RCED–92–215. Washington, DC: Author.

U.S. General Accounting Office. (1992c). *Poverty trends, 1980–1988: Changes in family composition and income sources among the poor.* GAO/PEMD–92–34. Washington, DC: Author.

U.S. General Accounting Office. (1994a). *Homelessness: McKinney Act program and funding through fiscal year 1993.* GAO/RCED–94–107. Washington, DC: Author.

U.S. General Accounting Office. (1994b). *Infants and toddlers: Dramatic increases in numbers living in poverty.* GAO/HEHS–94–74. Washington, DC: Author.

Weinreb, L., & Rossi, P. H. (1995). The American homeless family shelter "system." *Social Service Review, 69* (1), 86–107.

Wilson, G. (1985). The juvenilization of poverty. *Public Administration Review, 45,* 880–884.

Michael Newman/PhotoEdit

Chapter 6

Health Care Policy

One of the most important aspects of people's lives is their physical and mental well-being. Poor health impairs every aspect of daily living. It affects one's social and economic participation in society, including involvement in one's work place, education, and family life. Thus, the health of our population is an issue of national concern. In this chapter, we will explore the policies and programs through which our country has attempted to care for people's physical and mental welfare.

Overview of Health Care Policy in the United States

Like so many of today's social issues, health and well-being were historically personal and family concerns. It was not until the mid-1800s that public involvement in health care began. The few hospitals that existed in that era were charities for the poor, often attached to almshouses (Katz, 1986). Medical care of the time was harsh and not very effective. Home remedies were often just as effective as medical treatments, or more so.

With industrialization, immigration, and urbanization, cities of the 1800s became overcrowded, and people lived in very unhealthy environments. Filthy conditions favored the rapid spread of disease within cities, leading to recognition that organized efforts for public sanitation were necessary. What really changed the state of health in this country, however, was the introduction of scientific techniques into medicine. When science broadened the understanding of how diseases were spread, significant medical advances were accomplished. Science helped to "establish the cultural authority of medicine" (Starr, 1982, p. 59). From 1890 to 1910, public health efforts expanded through enactment of hygiene laws, inoculations, and segregation of those who were carriers of disease (Trattner, 1994). Public awareness grew, and the professions of health care and medicine gained recognition.

While public health was an important part of the social reform agenda at the turn of the century, most social welfare policies reflected local intervention. Cities developed public sanitation services in response to pressure from groups such as settlement workers who knew first hand the problems associated with urban living. These services included the establishment of public trash collection and sewage systems and emphasized public sanitation more than health care.

Federal legislation addressing health care was first developed in 1921 with passage of the Sheppard-Towner Act. The legislation was passed to provide resources for improving maternal and infant health care. The bill promoted public health education through public health workers. It was opposed by private physicians and the American Medical Association (AMA) who felt health care belonged to medical specialists (Starr, 1982). The legislation lasted only eight years, after which the care of mothers and young children was returned to states and localities (Axinn & Levin 1992).

Even through the Great Depression when social welfare policies were expanded and institutional efforts gained support, health care remained focused on individual curative care. Health care concerns were addressed primarily under the domain of private practice, with an emphasis on curing illness rather than preventing poor health (Starr, 1982). The emphasis reflects the trend in social welfare policy toward a residual response and an individual focus. Advocates of a national health insurance system that would have taken an institutional approach to health care pushed very hard for national legislation during the New Deal but were not successful. Although the Social Security Act of 1935 did contain the Maternal and Child Health Services program, it was one of the smallest components of the legislation and received limited funds.

It took an additional thirty years to achieve federal health care legislation. For some population groups, national health insurance legislation was successfully adopted in 1965 with amendments to the Social Security Act.

Medicare (Title XVIII) health insurance for the elderly and **Medicaid** (Title XIX) health coverage for the poor were added to the Social Security Act. These programs followed the structure of income support policy already implemented through the Act. Medicare, which is part of the social insurance program, is available to people who have worked in covered employment and paid in over their working years. Medicaid is for people without a work history who are too poor to afford health care coverage on their own.

Medicare and Medicaid had met with stiff opposition from organized medical groups, such as the AMA, and organized insurance groups. After World War II, most coverage for health care was included through group insurance policies at places of employment. Government involvement was perceived as interference. In reality, however, millions of people were not covered because of the limitations of the private insurance system. If a person was not in a job with health care benefits, or was too old to work, or could not afford an individual health insurance policy, there were no provisions for health care. The enactment of legislation to provide national health insurance for the elderly and medical assistance for low-income people was the last major social welfare policy initiative added to the Social Security Act.

Medicare and Medicaid provide medical coverage for millions of people. In 1994, almost 37 million people were enrolled in Medicare and more than 35 million people received services through Medicaid (U.S. Bureau of the Census, 1996b). Despite public and private insurance, however, there are many others who are not covered by any form of health insurance. More than 40 million people had no health insurance at all during 1995 (U.S. Bureau of the Census 1996a). Included in this group were more than 10 million children who were uninsured (U.S. General Accounting Office, 1996). These uninsured people represent a major social welfare policy concern.

In 1985, Congress addressed the issue of working persons maintaining health insurance coverage after losing or quitting a job through passage of the Consolidated Omnibus Reconciliation Act (COBRA, P.L. 99–272). The COBRA program allows a person to continue group coverage for up to eighteen months after leaving her or his employment. The person must pay the entire cost, including the portion previously paid by the employer, but is guaranteed the same coverage for up to eighteen months. The COBRA program provides some protection for already insured workers, but it does nothing for people who are uninsured.

During the 1992 presidential election and during President Clinton's first two years in office, proposals for **national health insurance** were hotly debated. Political infighting and interest group pressures blocked passage of any legislative initiatives for health care reform. Republican control of Congress in 1995 and 1996 shifted the focus from consideration of national health care coverage to incremental adjustments and cost containment of existing programs. Congress and the president came to agreement on an adjustment to current health insurance legislation with the Health Insurance Portability and Accountability Act of 1996 (P.L. 104–191).

Workers who lose or leave a job can now qualify to purchase individual coverage from their previous insurer. If the worker was originally covered for at least eighteen months while working, is not eligible for coverage under any other group plan, and has exhausted COBRA coverage, she or he is entitled to purchase an individual policy through the insurer. In addition, the legislation limits to twelve months the period during which insurers can refuse to limit coverage of a new enrollee for a previously treated or diagnosed condition for which the enrollee has sought treatment in the last six months, and insurers cannot refuse coverage or renewal because of an employee's health status (Langdon, 1996). These changes, like COBRA, are primarily directed toward persons who are already insured. The issue of health insurance coverage for the 40 million people without any health care benefits remains unresolved.

Overview of Mental Health Care Policy in the United States

The history of mental health care policy parallels the movement of public health care in general. Until the mid-1800s, care of mentally ill persons was done at home or in almshouses. Mental health treatment was nonexistent. People with mental illnesses were tolerated at best, and punished and treated poorly at worst. Health care advocate Dorothea Dix (1802–1887) is credited with bringing national attention to the needs and concerns of people with mental illness (Stroup, 1986). Her goal was federal funding of hospitals to care for persons with mental illness. Dix believed that government had an ethical, legal, and medical obligation to care for people with mental illnesses. Dix's advocacy led to the establishment of more than thirty state hospitals by the mid-1800s (Fellin, 1996). Although she and other advocates were not successful in gaining national support, they were able to gain early state support. By the late 1800s, however, funds to maintain the institutions were minimal and state mental hospitals were perceived as places for economically destitute people with mental illness (Jansson, 1997).

Although inadequate state funding led to overcrowding and custodial care at some institutions, the continued development of state institutions for the mentally ill was supported by the growing belief that people with mental problems could be treated, cured, and released, rather than locked away (Starr, 1982). This belief, coupled with creation of state institutions, led to the development of professional mental health specialists. Following World War I, the mental hygiene movement emerged. Emphasis was placed on psychology and local community care. Thus, although state hospitals continued to be the major providers of mental health care, the scope of mental health services expanded to include community care (Fellin, 1996). The impact of World Wars I and II furthered the development of mental health care as veterans returned from war in need of psychological intervention (Trattner, 1994).

In 1946, the federal government became involved in the delivery of mental health services through the National Mental Health Act, which provided minimal funds to states to develop community mental health centers and created the National Institute of Mental Health (Axinn & Levin, 1992). While some efforts were made to provide community-based care, most mental health services continued to be provided through state institutions. With the advent of medications that could help people to function outside of institutions, Congress passed the Community Mental Health Centers Act of 1963. This legislation provided federal funds for communities to build mental health centers and thereby provide outpatient services. (Jansson, 1997).

The development of mental health centers was never fully funded, but public awareness of institutional life and the cost savings of treating people outside of institutions led to the **deinstitutionalization** of thousands of people with mental illness during the 1970s. While in theory deinstitutionalization promised freedom and community integration for people newly released from state hospitals, the reality was different. Without adequate resources and community mental health centers, many people were left with little or no mental health care. From 1955 to 1980, the number of people in state mental institutions dropped from 559,000 to 138,000, a 75% decrease. The system of community mental health centers that was to have been established in conjunction with deinstitutionalization never fully materialized, falling short by more than half of the anticipated need (U.S. General Accounting Office, 1985). The result of this shift has been countless persons in need of mental health services who are not receiving adequate care. For many, the outcome has been reinstitutionalization not in mental health facilities but in substandard nursing homes, or release to a precarious existence in tenements, homeless shelters, or on the streets (Trattner, 1994).

In spite of insufficient funding and limited availability, community mental health centers are vital in providing many people with mental health services they could not obtain otherwise. For people who are not covered through private insurance or cannot pay for services out-of-pocket, these centers are their only source of mental health care. The creation of community mental health centers provided greater access to mental health services for many people.

Major Health Programs

Medicare

Medicare provides health insurance for individuals eligible to receive benefits from the program commonly referred to as Social Security. Basic coverage is provided for inpatient hospital services and related post-hospital care. The Medicare program consists of two separate plans: Hospital Insurance, or Part A, and Supplementary Medical Insurance, or Part B. Hospital Insurance is a social insurance program that covers inpatient hospital services, post-hospital skilled nursing facility services, home health services, and hospice care.

Supplementary Medical Insurance is a voluntary insurance program subsidized by the government. It is designed to cover health needs that Hospital Insurance does not, such as physician services, outpatient services, physical and outpatient therapy, and diagnostic tests. Participants pay a monthly premium ($54.70 in 1996), an annual deductible, and copayments for services. Generally, Medicare pays 80% of the cost of services under Part B, and the participant is responsible for the remaining 20%.

Taxation for Part A Hospital Insurance is applied in the same manner as for the Old-Age, Survivors, and Disability Insurance (OASDI) program (commonly referred to as Social Security). The tax is paid based on workers' earnings in covered employment and matched by their employers. Part B is optional, and those who elect its coverage must pay the monthly premium.

The overall administrative responsibility for Medicare rests with the Department of Health and Human Services (HHS). The Health Care Financing Administration (HCFA), which is an agency within HHS, handles the direct management. Currently HCFA contracts with carriers such as Blue Cross/Blue Shield and other insurers to handle the processing of claims, but Medicare recipients can choose to receive their care through managed care providers instead.

Medicare, while comprehensive, does not cover all medical costs. For example, coverage for long-term care is not included. While stays of up to 100 days in skilled nursing facilities are paid for, Medicare does not pay beyond that period. Many older people elect to purchase additional health coverage through Medigap insurance. Medigap is private insurance that pays for health services not covered by Medicare. Although it is private, in 1990 the federal government passed legislation to regulate it, including provisions that prohibit companies from denying coverage, discriminating, or overpricing. (Sources on Medicare: Social Security Administration, 1993a and 1993b; Social Security Administration, 1994; House Committee on Ways and Means, 1994.)

Medicaid

Federal matching funds are provided to states to cover the cost of medical care and services for low-income individuals under Medicaid. Medical coverage under Medicaid includes physician care, inpatient hospitalization, outpatient services, diagnostic tests, home health services, nursing home care including long-term care, and early and periodic screening and diagnostic treatment for those under 21 years of age. States may elect to offer additional medical services such as dental care, pharmaceuticals, and eyeglasses, and receive federal matching grants for those services. The program covers all AFDC/TANF recipients, most SSI recipients, and some children in foster care.

States can also choose to extend Medicaid coverage to people who are "medically needy." If medical costs would deplete so much of the financial resources of a person or family that they would then be impoverished, many states elect to provide coverage under the Medicaid program. Typically, people "spend down," using their own money to pay for medical care until their finances reach a prescribed level at which Medicaid covers the rest of the costs.

Medicaid payments are usually made directly to the provider of services rather than the recipient. This format reflects the nature of public assistance, where the low-income recipient receives in-kind benefits.

Medicaid is administered by the HCFA under the HHS, but each state designs and administers its program in keeping with federal standards. States establish standards; set the type, amount, and duration of services; and establish the rate of payment for services. Thus, unlike Medicare, the Medicaid program varies from state to state. (Sources on Medicaid: Congressional Research Service, 1988; Social Security Administration, 1993a and 1993b; Social Security Administration, 1994; House Committee on Ways and Means, 1994.)

Medicaid coverage is extremely important for low-income people, but it does not cover all people in need. Many people who are poor and uninsured do not qualify for Medicaid. About 43% of the poor are covered by Medicaid (Wolfe, 1996). Even with Medicaid coverage, medical care is not always available. Many physicians and medical care facilities choose not to serve Medicaid patients. For example, in 1990, 85% of physicians in New York State did not participate in Medicaid (Morgan, 1994). The reasons for not participating included low reimbursement rates and bureaucratic red tape.

Medicaid is often thought of as a program for poor, young families. More than 70% of the participants in Medicaid are also covered by AFDC. Although less than 12% of Medicaid recipients are 65 years of age or older and about 15% are people with disabilities, the majority of medical costs paid under Medicaid cover services provided to the elderly and people with disabilities. About 29% of Medicaid costs cover AFDC families, while 31% are used for the elderly and 39% for people with disabilities (U.S. Bureau of the Census, 1996b). Thus, Medicaid serves as an important safety net for the poor elderly and people with disabilities. The result of the differences between Medicaid and private insurance is that we have a two-tiered medical care system: one level is for those who can afford to pay, and the other is for those who cannot.

Immunization

One of the most effective preventive health measures for children has been routine immunization. It has proven effective in guarding children against preventable diseases such as measles, mumps, pertussis, rubella, and polio.

Keeping children healthy results in lower costs for health care over the years of childhood. Although immunizations are cost-effective, the United States lacks a comprehensive program.

Because of school regulations, almost all children are immunized against most preventable childhood diseases by the age of 5 (Public Health Service, 1990), but many infants and toddlers are not fully immunized. Many health insurance programs do not cover the cost of preventive measures such as immunizations. People lacking health care coverage cannot afford to pay for childhood immunizations. In many urban areas less than half of all young children are immunized. The decrease in immunizations is showing up in higher disease rates for children. For example, cases of measles increased more than 500% from 1983 to 1991 (Children's Defense Fund, 1992). Free vaccines are available through Medicaid or public health clinics, yet lack of awareness, inadequate resources such as insufficient clinic staff, and inaccessible clinic locations contribute to under-immunization of children at risk of disease (U.S. General Accounting Office, 1995b). Prevention of childhood illnesses through immunization was a major breakthrough for modern medicine, but these illnesses cannot be held at bay unless the needed resources for immunization programs are maintained.

Disability Insurance

The **Old-Age, Survivors, and Disability Insurance (OASDI)** program (commonly referred to as Social Security) includes coverage for people who must stop working because of a disability. Added to the Social Security Act in 1956, the program provides monthly cash benefits for eligible workers. It is part of the social insurance provisions of the Social Security Act. The program pays monthly benefits to disabled workers under 65 years of age equal to what a worker would receive in retirement. In order to qualify, the person with a disability must have acquired at least twenty quarters (five years) of coverage paid in during the previous forty quarters (ten years) (Social Security Administration, 1993a and 1993b).

The **Disability Insurance (DI)** component of OASDI also includes medical care through the Medicare program, but Medicare coverage does not begin until after twenty-four months of receiving benefits. There were 5.2 million recipients of DI in 1993, with disabled workers receiving an average of $642 per month (House Committee on Ways and Means, 1994).

Supplemental Security Income

As discussed in chapter 5, Congress developed the **Supplemental Security Income (SSI)** program, Title XVI of the Social Security Act, in 1972. SSI replaced the previous categorical federal/state programs Old-Age Assistance and Aid to the Blind that had originally been provided through the

1935 Act, and Aid to the Disabled that had been added in 1956. These three programs had a multiplicity of eligibility requirements and benefit payment systems. The SSI program consolidated them and created a unified federal operation.

The SSI program is a means-tested program that provides cash payments to people who are 65 or older, blind, or disabled and whose income places them below the poverty line. The payments are reduced by any other income received, including wages or other program benefits. The Social Security Administration administers SSI, and the program is funded by the federal government (Social Security Administration, 1993a and 1993b).

It is important to understand that SSI is different from OASDI, the program commonly referred to as Social Security. There is often confusion between these two programs but they are radically different. While both programs serve people with disabilities and people over 65 years of age, the funding and eligibility criteria differ greatly. SSI is an anti-poverty program that provides cash assistance to seniors and people with disabilities if they fall below the poverty line. It is residual in its approach. OASDI is social insurance, and people who have previously worked and paid into the program receive monthly benefits when they reach retirement age or become disabled. Thus, OASDI takes an institutional approach. SSI is funded through general tax revenues, and OASDI is funded through FICA payroll taxes.

While SSI is not directly a health care program, it is significant to the financial well-being of many medically needy individuals. Disability at any age and illness in old age can cause severe financial stress. For persons who are not covered through the disability coverage of OASDI, particularly young workers who do not have a long enough work history to provide adequate social disability insurance, this program offers the only source of economic support.

Community Mental Health Centers

Care of people with mental illness is provided through both inpatient and outpatient treatment. Federal support of mental health care is provided predominately through funding of the Community Mental Health Centers Act of 1963 (P.L. 88–164). The original intent of the legislation was to support the construction of **community mental health centers** throughout the country to provide inpatient and outpatient care, emergency services, some hospitalization, consultation, and education (Johnson & Schwartz, 1994). The goal of the Act was to return to their communities people who had been hospitalized for mental illness. It was hoped that through mental health centers, institutional care would be replaced by community care, prevention would be emphasized, and a continuity of care would develop with the centers offering the least restrictive mental health care environment (Fellin, 1996).

Today, more than 5,000 public and private facilities offer inpatient and outpatient mental health services, of which about 15% are community mental health centers (U.S. Bureau of the Census, 1996b). Thirty years after passage of the Act, mental health services still fall short of treating the multiplicity of needs among the general population (Lin, 1995). The social welfare policy analysis in Figure 6.1 details the goals and outcomes of the Community Mental Health Centers Act of 1963. This example demonstrates both the shortfalls of the policy and its positive impact. Although inadequate funding left a shortage of needed services, the policy made mental health services readily accessible to the public for the first time.

Current Needs and Policy Issues

America's changing health care needs present new challenges with each generation. We have seen success over the public health problems of sanitation and hygiene during the 1800s, followed by awareness and sensitivity to mental illness and medical technological breakthroughs during the 1900s. Yet there are still serious social concerns related to health care in this country. Our social welfare system is confronted by millions of people without health care coverage, as well as escalating costs, new diseases, and increases in existing social health problems. These emerging issues must be addressed through social welfare policies and programs.

Lack of Health Insurance Coverage

The most pressing health issue of the 1990s is the lack of health insurance coverage for millions of Americans. In 1995, 40.6 million people lacked any form of health insurance coverage. In spite of the existence of public health care programs, 11 million people with incomes below the poverty line lacked any health insurance during 1995 (U.S. Bureau of the Census, 1996a). Young adults and part-time workers were most likely to lack health insurance coverage (U.S. Bureau of the Census, 1996b). This problem has been growing in recent years. The number of people who are without health insurance increased by 28% from 1987 to 1993 (Summer & Shapiro, 1994). These numbers may understate the extent of the problem. The statistics reflect people who lacked insurance for the entire year. Many more people may have been uninsured for some amount of time during the year, and they are not counted in the total.

Lack of health insurance means a person is less likely to receive needed medical care. Without coverage, people do not receive preventive services, they tend to wait longer to seek medical treatment, and when they do it is most likely as emergency care through hospitals. This process is more costly than preventive care or immediate medical attention for a health problem.

Figure 6.1
Social Welfare Policy Analysis Model: Community Mental Health Centers Act

Social Issue

- Inhumane treatment of institutionalized people with chronic mental illness
- High expense of custodial care in state mental hospitals

Goal

- Reduce number of patients in state mental hospitals
- Develop a system of community mental health centers to provide services

Policy or Legislation

- Community Mental Health Centers Act of 1963 (P.L. 88–164)

Implementation

- Federal block grant
- State-local oversight and monitoring through regional boards
- Services delivered through local agencies

Affected Populations	Actual Impact	Intended Impact
• Patients • Family members • Local communities	• Insufficient funding, resulting in development of fewer centers and inadequate staffing • Pressure on families to provide care beyond their means • Inability of community centers to monitor chronic and severe patients • Increased homelessness of people with mental illness • Greater local access to mental health services	• To provide care for formerly institutionalized people in the least restrictive and most natural setting—in the community and with family

High Cost of Medical Care

The problem of the cost for health care is another pressing concern. In 1994, a total of $949 billion was spent for health care. This represented 13.7% of the gross domestic product, a 170% increase over the past thirty years (U.S. Bureau of the Census, 1996b). Per capita expenses for health care are higher in the United States than in any other country (Aaron, 1992). The increase in expenditures was due in part to the development of new technology as well as the expanded coverage of the elderly and low-income people through Medicare and Medicaid. Federal and state governments were not prepared for the escalating costs of health care. Methods to reduce costs through regulating the supply of services and freezing fees have not been successful at keeping the cost of health care down (Anderson, 1989).

The containment of costs for health care is further complicated by the mixture of public and private health coverage. Health coverage is based primarily on a market system, and those who are covered or can afford care receive treatment, while people without coverage are relegated to public medical facilities. With diminished public resources, care is more difficult to come by for the uninsured. In a 1991 survey, 40% of public hospitals reported having turned away ambulances because they had no room (Sherrill, 1995). Medical facilities that are for-profit can pick and choose who they want to serve, leaving those who are uninsured to be served by government-supported institutions. This practice has further fueled the cost of medical care by inflating the cost for those who can pay. Health care providers prefer to treat privately insured people because they can receive higher fees than if they treat publicly funded individuals.

Trend Toward Managed Care

The movement toward "managed care" is affecting the entire health care field. **Managed care** is the term used to describe a system in which a person's medical care is controlled by the insurer. The goal of managed care is to minimize unnecessary and questionable health care services and maximize procedures known to be effective. Managed care is usually provided through group plans and administered by for-profit organizations, typically health maintenance organizations (HMOs) and preferred provider organizations (PPOs). The number of managed care plans is on the rise. In 1988, 29% of employed Americans were enrolled in managed care plans, and by 1995 that number had increased to 51% of workers (Landers, 1995).

Each insured person in a managed care program receives regulated care as determined by administrators of the plan. For example, until recently, women covered by some HMOs were released from the hospital twelve hours after childbirth because it saved $2,000 over a customary stay of one to two days (Sherrill, 1995). While early discharge saves money, whether it is good health care is questionable. Thus, in response to this practice, Congress in September of 1996 enacted federal legislation that mandates insurance coverage for a minimum hospital stay of two days for a normal delivery and at least a ninety-six-hour stay after a Cesarean section (Pear, 1996). This is precisely the concern with managed care—is the final decision concerning medical care based on the cost or on the adequacy of the treatment?

Even state governments are turning to managed care for their public health care programs. In an effort to cut costs, state governments are reorganizing their Medicaid programs to follow the managed care model. Arizona was the first state to do so back in 1982. The state redesigned its Medicaid program and created the Arizona Health Care Cost Containment System (AHCCCS). The AHCCCS program, which is state-operated and regulated, delivers services through health plans selected on a county-by-county basis. The state calculates the funding for each plan according to the number of patients and adjusts the yearly fees to reflect a county's population. Thus, if a plan serves more people with higher-cost procedures, the next year's insurance amount is refigured to provide for those greater expenses. Evaluations of the program have been positive, citing cost savings and care within expected Medicaid standards (Balaban, McCall, & Bauer, 1994).

Managed care is also being used to contain public costs in the state of Tennessee. The TennCare program, begun in 1994, is administered by the state, but services are provided through private companies that contract with medical personnel to provide treatment. The companies receive a fixed amount of money, called a capitation, for each person covered. If the program is to be financially sound, the cost of care must not exceed the capitation rate. After one year the TennCare program seemed to be working: state spending on health care had been stabilized; coverage for the uninsured had increased; and health care for the poor seemed to have improved (Brown, 1996). Whether managed care can be beneficial to states over time remains to be seen.

Concern over whether health care decisions are being made by medical personnel or by insurance administrators continues to be a hotly debated issue. These issues contribute to the debate surrounding national health insurance. The policy push for national health insurance dates back to the early 1900s. Groups have advocated for a system of health care that is provided by the federal government and equally covers all Americans, regardless of their income, employment status, or age. Opposition to such a system has been very strong, with groups such as the AMA and the insurance industry fighting such legislation. The most recent attempt to change the health care system was in 1993 when Clinton presented his proposed legislation. It, like previous proposals, was defeated. The current trend is toward managed care. With more state Medicaid systems and employers adopting managed care programs, it would seem that this is the future of medical care in America.

Emerging Health Concerns

There are numerous health concerns that require the attention of policy-makers and the public. For social work practitioners, the growth in the incidence of Acquired Immune Deficiency Syndrome (AIDS) and the Human Immunodeficiency Virus (HIV), and the pervasiveness of problems with alcohol and drug use present challenges to the social welfare system. The following discussion highlights the social welfare policy implications of these health concerns.

HIV/AIDS

Until the 1980s, no one had heard of AIDS or HIV. Today, AIDS and HIV are common terms, representing a disease that has deeply touched the social welfare of our country. AIDS and HIV are first and foremost health concerns, but they are also related to economics and social values. The social welfare policy response to HIV/AIDS has been slow, reluctant, and at times hostile. Addressing the problem on a social welfare policy level has not been easily accepted by the United States government. Randy Shilts (1988) documents the disdain and reluctance of federal government officials toward taking public action to prevent the spread of HIV/AIDS. He wrote:

> The bitter truth was that AIDS did not just happen to America—it was allowed to happen by an array of institutions, all of which failed to perform their appropriate tasks to safeguard the public health. This failure of the system leaves a legacy of unnecessary suffering that will haunt the Western world for decades to come (p. xxii).

In those early years, the federal government viewed AIDS as a budget problem, local public health officials saw it as a political problem, gay leaders considered AIDS a public relations problem, and the news media regarded it as a homosexual problem that would not interest anyone else. Consequently, few confronted AIDS for what it was, a profoundly threatening medical crisis (Shilts, p. xxiii). Before discussing related policies and programs, we need to examine the extent of HIV/AIDS.

Incidence of HIV and AIDS.   The Worldwatch Institute estimates that between 15 and 23 million people are infected with HIV worldwide (Lee, 1994). In 1981, the Centers for Disease Control and Prevention (CDC) had documented 189 cases of AIDS in the United States. By June of 1996 that number had risen to 548,102 cases of AIDS (CDC, 1996). At least 343,000 of these people, more than 60%, are now dead. These numbers are more than likely lower than the actual incidence of AIDS. For social, political, and personal reasons, many illnesses and deaths related to AIDS go unreported. Therefore, there is little doubt that the official numbers of the CDC are less than the real incidence and extent. HIV/AIDS is not limited to any one group. The implications for social welfare policy are clear: the more pervasive the disease, the more likely any and all members of society will be faced with dealing with the needs and fallout of the disease.

It has been more than fifteen years since AIDS was identified as a global health concern, and most people are reluctant to believe that HIV/AIDS has anything to do with their lives. The implication is that AIDS is a disease that affects only people who are gay and people who are intravenous drug users. HIV and AIDS are health concerns for all Americans, however. AIDS is now the leading cause of death among young men and women between the ages of 25 and 44 in the United States, and the fastest growing group of people with AIDS is women (CDC, 1996).

AIDS is often referred to as a **pandemic** as opposed to an epidemic. In medical terms, a pandemic is an epidemic that is occurring across a large geographic region. Pandemic is an accurate description of AIDS because of its worldwide impact and spread.

Social Policy Efforts.   The only federal policy implemented as a direct response to the AIDS pandemic has been the Ryan White Comprehensive AIDS Resources Emergency (CARE) Act of 1990. This legislation was passed after years of pressure from advocacy groups for some government response. The law authorizes federal funds to support health care services for people who have AIDS or are HIV-positive. Services include home- and community-based care, provisions for early intervention, prevention, research, and education. In 1994, thirty-four metropolitan areas and all states shared in $483 million appropriated to carry out the Ryan White CARE Act (U.S. General Accounting Office, 1995a).

Critics argue that the federal response was slow in coming until people other than gay men and intravenous drug users contracted the disease. The bill was named after a young boy with hemophilia who contracted AIDS through a blood transfusion. His case highlighted the divisiveness surrounding social welfare policy and AIDS. Because marginalized groups were initially predominant among those infected, public opinion and federal policies viewed people with AIDS as responsible for their illness. This differs from the view of children like Ryan White as innocent victims. With no other life-threatening disease do we make such a clear distinction. This social value has delayed public response to a growing health problem. The conflict between social policy and social values has hampered the legislative response to health care interventions and the HIV/AIDS pandemic.

Social Service Programs for People Affected by HIV/AIDS.   With scientists reporting in 1993 at the Ninth International Conference on AIDS that a cure is not soon to be found, we must continue the only method available to us for slowing the spread of this disease: prevention. As social work professionals and members of American society, we are and will be involved in the lives of those who are infected, those who are sick, and the families of those who have died. Half of all social work clients may be directly or indirectly affected by AIDS (Miller & Dane, 1990). This percentage will only continue to grow.

We need a broader policy response to HIV/AIDS. In 1988, the New York City AIDS Task Force estimated that by the early 1990s a minimum of 60,000 children would experience the death of at least one parent from AIDS (Levine, 1991). Of these, about 10,000 would lose both parents to AIDS. Statistics have not been kept on the number of children orphaned by the AIDS pandemic, but with deaths numbered in the hundreds of thousands, many families have been (or will be) devastated by AIDS. Housing, drug treatment programs, counseling, case management services, and proper medical care are in constant shortage and the result is unnecessary suffering for families. In addition, direct service programs throughout the country are feeling a great deal of strain to meet the needs in their communities. Many programs operate through the heavy use of volunteers and cannot provide services without such support. For example, a full-service AIDS organization in Ohio uses more than 400 volunteers to provide services to its caseload. Volunteer efforts are crucial because caseloads are high. Funding for these organizations is precarious, and under-funding is a constant problem.

To add to these already difficult administrative situations, homophobia, fear, and stigma make service delivery even more problematic. Nursing homes, for example, will claim they have a long waiting list when they discover that a patient who is in need of services has AIDS. One result of the reluctance of nursing homes to serve people with AIDS is that hospital stays have been extended because patients have nowhere else to go. This in turn places unnecessary stress and cost on our medical care system, particularly our public health institutions.

The spread of HIV in the United States has disproportionately affected populations who are poor and oppressed. Groups who lack civil rights protection and are continually discriminated against in our society are disproportionately found among those people who live with HIV and AIDS. People who are stigmatized by color, drug use, poverty, and sexual orientation lack strong political and economic advocates in this country.

HIV and AIDS continue to spread through our population. The cost in dollars and lost human lives grows greater each year. HIV/AIDS represents a social problem that must be addressed by policy-makers, however difficult that may be.

Alcohol and Illegal Drugs

The use of illegal drugs and alcohol is not a new social concern. Federal involvement has increased, however, in response to shifts in public attitudes and what appears to be greater use of substances. The early 1900s was the first period of federal involvement in control of illegal drugs. Laws were enacted in 1914 to regulate the sale and use of narcotics. In 1937, legislation was passed that controlled the use and distribution of marijuana (Hogan & Doyle, 1989). Alcohol was officially regarded as an illegal substance with legislation prohibiting the manufacture and sale of liquor in 1919. This law of prohibition was extremely difficult to enforce and was repealed fourteen years later (Axinn & Levin, 1992). Since the 1930s, American attitudes toward alcohol have become more and more tolerant and alcohol continues to be a legal substance, yet ambivalence towards the use of alcohol still exists today. The policy issue is whether to treat alcohol as a drug to be legislatively controlled in the same manner as narcotics and marijuana, or to allow individuals to decide. It is clear that alcohol use is a major part of our society: more than 90% of adults reported having used alcohol, while 64% of people between the ages of 18 and 25 reported that they were current users of alcohol in 1994 (U.S. Bureau of the Census, 1996b). Currently, alcohol is viewed as a legal substance and therefore its use is prohibited only for people younger than age 21. Nevertheless, underage drinkers gain access to alcohol and are at great risk of addiction at a young age.

The sale, possession, and use of other drugs such as heroin, cocaine, and marijuana are illegal. Differentiation between legal and illegal drugs was codified through the Controlled Substances Act of 1970. This legislation controls and regulates drugs and identifies levels of enforcement (Gray, 1995). Further efforts to use public policy to control behavior related to drug use took place in 1973. Congress created the U.S. Drug Enforcement Administration (DEA) as part of the Department of Justice. The DEA was empowered to enforce federal drug laws (Dye, 1992).

Federal control of illegal substances peaked with passage of the Anti-Drug-Abuse Act of 1988 (P.L. 100–690). Much of the legislation involved control strategies, rather than treatment. Although there are laws against drug use, in 1994, almost 45% of people between the ages of 18 and 25 reported having tried marijuana, with 12% having tried hallucinogens (U.S. Bureau of the Census, 1996b). The social welfare policy struggle in **substance abuse** is between two ideologies. Is the use and abuse of drugs to be controlled through punishment and law enforcement, or is it a health care concern that should be treated through medical and mental health interventions? There are more than 11,000 treatment centers for drug and alcohol abuse. These service agencies reported almost a million clients in 1993 (U.S. Bureau of the Census, 1996b). The debate between enforcement and treatment has yet to be resolved. Until it is, social welfare policies related to drug use and abuse will reflect these two conflicting philosophies.

Final Thoughts on Health Care Policy

Health care and medical services are significant issues at the forefront of social welfare policy debate. The need for national health insurance has been debated for decades and will continue to be at the center of social welfare policy proposals. Emerging health concerns such as HIV/AIDS and substance abuse present major challenges to policy-makers and providers of social welfare services. With rising costs, more people facing medical problems, and the aging of the population, social welfare policy will need to adapt to meet the challenges facing health care in America in the coming years.

Key Concepts

Medicare	Medicaid
national health insurance	deinstitutionalization
community mental health centers	managed care
Old-Age, Survivors, and Disability Insurance (OASDI)	Disability Insurance (DI)
	pandemic
Supplemental Security Income (SSI)	substance abuse

Exercises

1. Find out if there is a community mental health center in your city. If none exists, find out why not. Where do people go for mental health services? If there is a community mental health center, visit it. What services does the center offer? How accessible and affordable are the services?

2. As you may have done for exercise 2 in chapter 5, apply again for an entry-level job or return to the same place. Ask about health care benefits. Are they available? Is the coverage affordable? Can dependents also be covered?

3. In class, identify several managed care companies in your community. Divide into groups by company. Call and ask for information on their services. Is it a private or public agency? Non-profit or for-profit? What services are covered? What services are not? What is the cost? Who decides what treatments are provided: a primary care physician or a case manager? Do doctors get bonuses for keeping costs down? Compare your group's findings with those of the other groups. How are the services different or similar? Which company would you prefer for your own health care coverage? Why?

References

Aaron, H.J. (1992). Health care financing. In Aaron, H.J., & Schultze, C.L. (eds.), *Setting domestic priorities: What can government do?* (pp. 23–61). Washington, DC: Brookings Institution.

Anderson, O.W. (1989). Issues in the health services of the United States. In Field, M.G. (ed.), *Success and crisis in national health systems* (pp. 49–71). New York: Routledge.

Axinn, J., & Levin, H. (1992). *Social welfare: A history of the American response to need* (3rd ed.). New York: Longman.

Balaban, D., McCall, N., & Bauer, E.J. (1994). *Quality of Medicaid managed care: An evaluation of the Arizona health care cost containment system (AHCCCS).* Discussion Paper #94–2. San Francisco: Laguna Research Associates.

Brown, D. (1996, July 15–21). Mixing medicine and money. *The Washington Post National Weekly Edition*, pp. 6–10.

Centers for Disease Control and Prevention. (1996). *HIV/AIDS surveillance report*, 8 (1). Atlanta, GA: Author.

Children's Defense Fund. (1992). *The state of America's children*. Washington, DC: Author.

Congressional Research Service. (1988). *Medicaid source book: Background data and analysis*. Committee Print 100–AA. Washington, DC: U.S. Government Printing Office.

Dye, T.R. (1992). *Understanding public policy* (7th ed.). Englewood Cliffs, NJ: Prentice Hall.

Fellin, P. (1996). *Mental health and mental illness: Policies, programs, and services*. Itasca, IL: F.E. Peacock.

Gray, M.C. (1995). Drug Abuse. In *Encyclopedia of Social Work* (19th ed.) (pp. 795–803). Washington, DC: NASW.

Hogan, H., & Doyle, C. (1989). The drug problem and the federal response: A growing problem. *CRS Review, 10* (10), 11–13

House Committee on Ways and Means. (1994). *Overview of entitlement programs: 1994 Green book*. Washington, DC: U.S. Government Printing Office.

Jansson, B.S. (1997). *The reluctant welfare state* (3rd ed.). Pacific Grove, CA: Brooks/Cole.

Johnson, L.C., & Schwartz, C.L. (1994). *Social welfare: A response to human need* (3rd ed.). Needham Heights, MA: Allyn & Bacon.

Katz, M.B. (1986). *In the shadow of the poorhouse: A social history of welfare in America*. New York: Basic Books.

Landers, S. (1995). "Spinning dry" with managed care. *NASW News, 40* (10), 3.

Langdon, S. (1996). Health insurance. *CQ Weekly Report, 54* (31), 2197–2200.

Lee, G. (1994). For most of the world, lives are getting longer. *The Washington Post Weekly Edition, 11* (40), 32.

Levine, C. (1991). The special needs of women, children, and adolescents. In McKenzie, N. (ed.), *The AIDS reader: Social, political, ethical issues* (pp. 200–212). New York: Meridian.

Lin, A.M.P. (1995). Mental health overview. In *Encyclopedia of social work* (19th ed.) (pp. 1705–1711). Washington, DC: NASW.

Miller, S.O., & Dane, B.O. (1990). AIDS and social work: Curricula development in an epidemic. *Journal of Social Work Education, 26* (2), 177–185.

Morgan, D. (1994). Even Medicaid misses many. *Washington Post Weekly Edition, 11* (17), 12.

Pear, R. (1996, September 20). In Congress, leaders agree on insurance plans. *The New York Times*, p. A11.

Public Health Service. (1990). *Child health USA '90*. HRS-M-CH 90–1. Washington, DC: U.S. Department of Health and Human Services.

Sherrill, R. (1995). The madness of the market. *The Nation, 260* (2), 45–72.

Shilts, R. (1988). *And the band played on.* New York: Penguin.

Social Security Administration. (1993a). *Social security handbook, 1993* (11th ed.). SSA No. 65–008. Washington, DC: U.S. Department of Health and Human Services.

Social Security Administration. (1993b). *Social security programs in the United States*. SSA No. 13–11758. Washington, DC: U.S. Department of Health and Human Services.

Social Security Administration. (1994). *Social security bulletin: Annual statistical supplement*. Washington, DC: U.S. Department of Health and Human Services.

Starr, P. (1982). *The social transformation of American medicine.* New York: Basic Books.

Stroup, H. (1986). *Social welfare pioneers.* Chicago: Nelson-Hall.

Summer, L., & Shapiro, I. (1994). *Trends in health insurance coverage, 1987 to 1993.* Washington, DC: Center on Budget and Policy Priorities.

Trattner, W.I. (1994). *From poor law to welfare state* (5th ed.). New York: The Free Press.

U.S. Bureau of the Census. (1996a). *Health insurance coverage, 1995.* Cat. No. P60–195. Washington, DC: U.S. Government Printing Office.

U.S. Bureau of the Census. (1996b). *Statistical abstract of the United States, 1996.* (116th ed.). Washington, DC: U.S. Government Printing Office.

U.S. Bureau of the Census. (1995). *Health insurance coverage 1994.* Cat. No. P60–190. Washington, DC: U.S. Government Printing Office.

U.S. General Accounting Office. (1985). *Homelessness: A complex problem and the federal response.* GAO/HRD–85–40. Washington, DC: U.S. Government Printing Office.

U.S. General Accounting Office. (1995a). *Ryan White CARE Act.* GAO/HEHS–95–49. Washington, DC: U.S. Government Printing Office.

U.S. General Accounting Office. (1995b). *Vaccines for children.* GAO/PEMD–95–22. Washington, DC: U.S. Government Printing Office.

U.S. General Accounting Office. (1996). *Health insurance for children.* GAO/HEHS–96–129. Washington, DC: U.S. Government Printing Office.

Wolfe, B. (1996). A Medicaid primer. *Focus, 17* (3), 1–6.

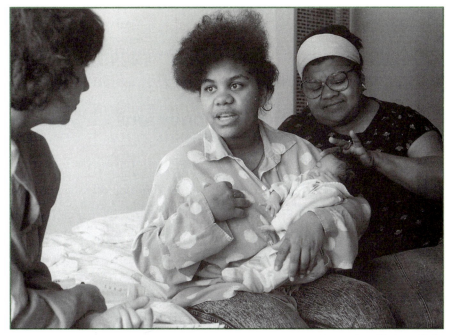

Chapter 7

Social Welfare Policies Affecting Children and Families

People's experiences in life differ, yet being a child is an experience we all share. All of us have been children, yet our childhood experiences vary greatly. For some, childhood includes times of stress and family breakdown. It is during difficult times that families may turn to outsiders for help and guidance.

Traditionally, the guiding principle in caring for children has been to leave that responsibility to the family. Over the past fifty years, however, there has been a shift in focus. In spite of the belief that the family is the central place to care for children, public intervention has occurred in numerous ways. When the family has been deemed incapable of care or dangerous to a child's well-being, for example, the government has intervened. Public intervention in relation to children and families has been mandated and guided by social welfare policies. Those rules and guidelines are generally referred to as child welfare policy. In this chapter we will look at the development, focus, and extent of child and family social welfare policies and the social and political values that have shaped them.

Overview of Current Conditions

There are more than 72 million children (infants to age 18) in this country out of a population of 263 million people. Children represent 27% of our total population (U.S. Bureau of the Census, 1996). Table 7.1 presents demographic characteristics of children in America. Thirty-four million households include children under 18 years of age. Table 7.2 provides a breakdown of family composition by race and head of household. Overall, in 1995, 26% of all households with children and youth were headed by a single parent. Among African-American families, the proportion was twice as high, at 59%, and for Hispanic families it was 30%. These demographics demonstrate some of the unique concerns for families today. More children will spend part or all of their childhoods living with only one parent. This is particularly true for African-American children. As discussed elsewhere, more and more parents are working, both in two-parent and single-parent households. These phenomena mean that the services and support of child welfare programs will become increasingly important to families.

It would seem that a group this large and diverse would be among our greatest social welfare concerns. While we speak strongly about the well-being of children and families in this country, however, our social welfare policy response demonstrates a very different picture. The United States lacks a coherent and comprehensive social welfare system for the care and protection of children. The existing child welfare system is a collection of

Table 7.1

Demographics of Children and Youth, 1995 (newborn to age 18)

	Total Number of Children and Youth	Children 9 Years Old or Younger	
Total	72.2 million	38.8 million	54%
White	57.3 million	30.7 million	54%
Black	11.3 million	6.1 million	54%
Hispanic°	10.1 million	5.9 million	58%
Asian	2.9 million	1.6 million	55%
American Indian	0.8 million	0.4 million	50%

°Persons of Hispanic origin may be of any race.

Sources: U.S. Bureau of the Census (1996), p. 22, and author calculations.

Table 7.2

Household Composition, 1995: Households with Children Under 18 Years of Age (in millions)

	Total	Two-Parent	Female-Headed	Male-Headed
Total	34.3	25.2 (73%)	7.6 (22%)	1.4 (4%)
White	28.0	22.0 (79%)	4.8 (17%)	1.1 (4%)
Black	4.7	1.9 (40%)	2.5 (53%)	0.3 (6%)
Hispanic°	4.0	2.7 (68%)	1.0 (25%)	0.2 (5%)

°Persons of Hispanic origin may be of any race.

Source: U.S. Bureau of the Census (1996).

programs and policies that evolved incrementally, with little planning or co-ordination. Social problems such as poverty and inequality of access to re-sources and opportunities have contributed to poor coordination of services. Racism further exacerbates the problems of the system. The service treat-ment of minority children has historically been inadequate and insufficient (Hogan & Siu, 1988). Families of color often receive inferior services or are held to different standards because of their race and the stereotypes associated with race. Although child welfare services are an integral part of social welfare policy, there are problems that need attention if families and children are to be served adequately.

More than eighty federal programs affect children, and countless additional programs exist on the state and local levels (U.S. General Accounting Office, 1988). Services a family receives in one state are often very different or unavailable in another state. Levels of assistance and gaps in services also vary across the county. This variability and complexity make our child welfare system difficult to understand.

Almost all public social services for children and families are targeted and categorical, not preventive. Most evolved out of publicly recognized need or breakdown. This residual approach has resulted in a patchwork of services, sometimes overlapping, and sometimes leaving needs unmet. For the majority of programs, the rules and regulations are federally mandated and state administered. Examination of the main programs reveals the variability and residual nature of child welfare policy.

Historical Development of Child and Family Policy

As outlined in chapter 2, the historical foundation of social welfare policy in this country rests on the philosophy that needs and problems should be

Figure 7.1
Timeline for Child Welfare Legislation and Organizations

		Source of Action	
Year	State	Federal	Private
1824	House of Refuge, NY— first state funded institution for juvenile delinquents		
1836	Child labor law enacted in Massachusetts		
1853			Children's Aid Society founded
1867	County homes for children authorized in Ohio		
1868	Foster homes for orphans funded by Massachusetts		
1875			Society for the Prevention of Cruelty to Children established
1899	First juvenile court— Chicago		
1900	32 states have compulsory education		
1904			National Child Labor Committee formed
1909		White House Conference on Children & Youth	
1911	First mothers' aid law enacted by Illinois		
1912		Establishment of U.S. Children's Bureau in Department of Labor	
1916		Congress passes Child Labor Bill	
1920			Child Welfare League of America organized
1921		Maternity & Infancy Act passed (Sheppard-Towner)	
1929		Defeat of Sheppard-Towner	
1935		Aid to Dependent Children	
		Maternal & Child Health Services	

Figure 7.1

Timeline for Child Welfare Legislation and Organizations

		Source of Action	
Year	State	Federal	Private
1961		Juvenile Delinquency & Youth Offenses Control Act	
1964		Food Stamp Act	
		Head Start	
1965		Medicaid	
		Elementary & Secondary Education Act	
1966		Child Nutrition Act	
		WIC—Supplemental Food Program for Women, Infants, and Children	
1967		Child Health Act	
1973			Children's Defense Fund
1974		Title XX—Social Services Block Grant	
		Child Abuse Prevention & Treatment Act	
		Juvenile Justice & Delinquency Prevention Act	
1975		Education for All Handicapped Children Act	
1978		Indian Child Welfare Act	
1980		Adoption Assistance & Child Welfare Act	
1983		Creation of House Select Committee on Children, Youth, & Families	
1984		Child Support Enforcement Amendments	
1988		Family Support Act	
1993		Family & Medical Leave Act	
		Child welfare amendments —Family preservation	
1996		Temporary Assistance for Needy Families Block Grant (TANF)	

Sources: Axinn & Levin, 1992; Katz, 1986; Kimmich, 1985; Stein, 1991; Trattner, 1994; House Committee on Ways and Means, 1994.

dealt with privately and that the family should be the key social resource. Only in the most significant times of need should the public intervene. The role of the federal government in child welfare was nonexistent until the early 1900s. The first major congressional policy initiative did not occur until 1916, when Congress pursued legislation to protect children from labor abuses (see Figure 7.1). Instead of federal involvement, the earliest efforts at public intervention took place at the state level. Policies and programs as diverse as juvenile justice, public education, foster care, child labor regulation, and cash assistance all began with state legislation. Often the push for these efforts came from private groups.

The Progressive Era

As indicated in Figure 7.1, by 1920 most major private organizations developed to protect and advocate for children had been founded. As early as 1853, the Children's Aid Society (CAS) was founded in New York to care for children who were orphaned, whose families were too poor to care for them, or who had left their families. The goal of CAS was to remove children from urban slums and place them with rural families (Hasci, 1995). This paralleled the general efforts of social reform of the period, which were concerned with care for people through institutions outside the family. As the Progressive Era took hold around the turn of the century, child welfare advocates were successful in securing a number of key policy initiatives. Recognition of youths as being different from adults spurred the development of the juvenile court system. For the first time, children were tried for crimes with sensitivity to their young age. Compulsory education, first passed into law in Massachusetts in 1852, was commonplace by the early 1900s (Katz, 1986). Also during this period, child abuse gained limited recognition as a social concern.

Four key periods firmly established the role of government in child and family welfare. The first wave came during the early 1900s. Awareness of the need to care for children on a national level grew during the Progressive Era. The exploitive and unhealthy treatment of children as economic entities—laborers—was targeted by reformers. A growing middle class and social reform movement served as the impetus for change. Children were no longer thought of only as economic entities, but as family members with sentimental value (Zelizer, 1985).

Social reformers advocated to end child labor through the National Child Labor Committee. The first formal federal effort toward recognizing child welfare occurred in 1909 with the White House Conference on Children and Youth. The first federal agency for child welfare was established in 1912 as the Children's Bureau in the Department of Labor. Congress regulated child labor in 1916 with the passage of the Child Labor Bill. Although it was deemed unconstitutional by the Supreme Court, it set the stage for state regulations, which covered all jurisdictions by the 1930s.

The opposition to child labor demonstrates the conflict inherent in public intervention in private family matters and the resistance of the private marketplace. While protection of children was viewed as a worthy goal, removing children from the labor market had a negative impact on poor families (Stadum, 1995). Many families relied on the economic contributions of their children. Furthermore, private industry was strongly opposed to any government regulation that was perceived to interfere in the free market.

The Great Depression and the New Deal

The next period of permanent federal involvement came with the Great Depression. The Maternity and Infancy Act (commonly referred to as the Sheppard-Towner Act), passed in 1921, provided for health care and assistance to pregnant women, mothers, and their children. After meager funding and support, however, it was repealed eight years later. The legislation was terminated because it was viewed as federal interference with the rights of states (Jansson, 1997). Despite its brief existence, the legislation did succeed in setting the stage for permanent federal intervention on behalf of mothers and children. The Great Depression cemented the role of the federal government in child and family welfare policy. As discussed in chapter 5, the Aid to Dependent Children cash assistance program was enacted in 1935 as part of the Social Security Act. The Social Security Act also included the Maternal and Child Health Act. Together, these pieces of legislation and subsequent amendments to the Social Security Act represent the core of today's child welfare assistance and preventive social service programs (see Figure 7.2).

Figure 7.2
Current Child Welfare Components of the Social Security Act

AFDC/TANF	Title IV (A)
Child Welfare Services	Title IV (B)
Child Support Enforcement	Title IV (C)
Foster Care and Adoption Assistance	Title IV (E)
Maternal and Child Health	Title V
Medicaid	Title XIX
Social Services Block Grant	Title XX

War on Poverty

The period of the 1960s and the War on Poverty was the third period of key federal involvement in child welfare. During the 1960s, the Food Stamp Program, child nutrition services, and Supplemental Food Program for Women, Infants, and Children (WIC) were enacted. Health needs were met through the development of Medicaid and the Child Health Act. Social opportunities were expanded through the Head Start program and the Elementary and Secondary Education Act (discussed later in this chapter).

The 1970s

The fourth, and to date last, period of federal expansion of child welfare legislation came during the 1970s. Recognition of the problem of **child abuse and neglect** grew during the 1960s following the medical "discovery" of the phenomenon. The legislative response came with the Child Abuse Prevention and Treatment Act of 1974. This legislation provides for federal assistance to states to enable the development of prevention and treatment programs for abuse and neglect. The Act also established the national Center on Child Abuse, which serves as a clearinghouse for current data and information on child abuse and neglect.

Also in 1974, the Social Services Block Grants were developed as Title XX of the Social Security Act. Title XX legislation provides funds for a variety of social services. About half the funds are spent on children's services (Stein, 1991). The services include abuse and neglect prevention programs and efforts to prevent or reduce unnecessary institutional care.

In 1978, the federal government passed the Indian Child Welfare Act. This bill was enacted in response to concerns that American Indian children were being taken out of their homes and placed with non-Indian families. At the time, up to 35% of all American Indian children were removed and placed in foster care (McMahon & Gullerud, 1995). The goal of the legislation is to protect American Indian children from removal from their homes, and in cases where it is necessary, to create alternatives that maintain a link to tribal culture (Mannes, 1995).

The problem of children being removed from their homes and placed in substitute care became a major concern during the 1970s. In response to that growing concern, the Congress passed the Adoption Assistance and Child Welfare Act of 1980 (P.L. 96–272). This legislation serves as the foundation to all protective services today. The goals of the legislation are first of all, to prevent the unnecessary removal of children from their homes; and second, if a child must be removed, to develop a permanent solution through reunification with the family, or when not possible, through adoption (Stein, 1991). The policy analysis example in Figure 7.3 outlines the impact of this legislation.

Figure 7.3

Social Welfare Policy Analysis Model:
Adoption Assistance and Child Welfare Act of 1980

Social Issue

- Too many children in foster care for long periods of time

Goal

- Decrease numbers in foster care
- Prevent unnecessary removal of children from their homes
- Establish a program of adoption assistance to encourage permanent solutions

Policy or Legislation

- Adoption Assistance and Child Welfare Act of 1980 (P.L. 96–272)

Implementation

Mandate states to:
- Review cases at least once every six months
- Examine cases after 18 months to determine plan for permanent solution
- Expand jurisdiction of courts
- Increase funding for state programs of child welfare services, foster care, and adoption

Affected Populations

- Children identified as abused or neglected
- Children in foster care
- Families of these children
- State and local child welfare and protective service agencies

Actual Impact

- Initial decrease in foster care numbers
- Greater awareness of state and local agency personnel of child abuse and neglect
- Increase in number of reported abuse and neglect cases
- Tighter state regulations

Intended Impact

- Fewer children in foster care
- Emphasis on finding permanent solutions for care of children in need

The 1980s and Beyond

Legislation during the 1980s was primarily concerned with the economic efficiency of public assistance. Efforts to amend the AFDC program during the early 1980s were punitive and designed to cut people off from public assistance. Both the Child Support Enforcement Amendments of 1984 and the Family Support Act of 1988 amended the AFDC program to find ways to get non-custodial parents to pay child support and custodial parents to work and become economically self-sufficient.

One piece of recent legislation has shifted slightly to a more preventive tone. Advocates had tried for almost ten years to get legislation guaranteeing job protection for employees who needed to take time off to care for children or sick dependents. Although business interests were strongly opposed to the legislation and George Bush had twice vetoed it during his presidency, the election of Bill Clinton opened the door. The Family and Medical Leave Act was passed in January 1993. The law represents one of the few times the federal government has taken a preventive approach to child and family welfare. The legislation allows workers to take up to 12 weeks of unpaid leave to care for a newborn or newly adopted child, or to care for a sick dependent, without losing their jobs.

Another recent policy effort was the addition of new preventive services for child welfare. Funds for **family preservation** and family support services—programs that emphasize permanency or keeping families together—were included in federal budgetary legislation (P.L. 103–66) in 1993 (House Committee on Ways and Means, 1994). It is too soon to know if these services, which attempt to take a more preventive approach, will improve the child welfare system. Following the 1900s' wave of growing awareness, the 1930s' establishment of federal intervention on behalf of children, the 1960s' War on Poverty for children, and the 1970s' recognition of child abuse and neglect, the 1990s' family leave and family preservation initiatives may mark the beginning of a fifth wave of federal involvement in caring for families.

Overall, government intervention in the family still remains an extremely controversial issue. This struggle characterizes most child welfare policy and has affected the development of the child welfare system. For example, in recent years courts have become more reluctant to remove children from their homes and have returned children to their biological families. Two highly publicized cases of disrupted adoptions, one in Michigan and one in Illinois, demonstrate the trend of courts to return children to their biological parents. In both cases, adoptive families were mandated through court decisions to relinquish care of the children. In the Illinois case, the biological father claimed he had not known about the existence of the child, known to the public as "Baby Richard." In spite of the fact that the baby had been legally adopted and had lived with his adoptive family from birth to age four, in April 1995 the courts negated the adoption and returned him to the biological parents he had never known. Emphasis on keeping a child with his or her birth family reflects the belief that the family of origin is the primary place for a child.

Major Federal Programs Providing Aid and Services to Children and Families

The constellation of social welfare policies outlined above serves as the legislative foundation for the majority of programs and services for children and families. Like other areas of social welfare policy, child welfare programs are mandated by the federal government and implemented on the state level. The consequence of this duality is that child welfare programs vary from state to state. In addition, statutory laws, regulations, and court decisions have played key roles in shaping child welfare policy. While the state variations are too voluminous to cover here, the main federal provisions are discussed below.

The key areas of child welfare services cover income assistance, health, food and nutrition, education, employment, corrections, and social services. The conceptualization of child welfare services can be organized into three areas: **supportive**—to help families cope with problems; **supplementary**—to provide needed resources; or **substitutive**—to take the place of family (Kadushin & Martin, 1988). Supportive services include family preservation, child care, and training in parenting skills. Supplementary services include cash assistance, health care, and nutrition services. Substitutive services refer primarily to foster care and adoption programs. These three domains broadly define child welfare services. In the following sections we will outline the major child welfare programs and policies behind them.

Income Maintenance

The AFDC program has most often been thought of as a poverty program, as discussed in chapter 5, yet it has also been a significant child welfare program. In 1994, 14 million people received benefits through AFDC, of which 9.5 million, or 68%, were children (U.S. Bureau of the Census, 1996). More than three out of four children on AFDC were younger than age 12 (Administration for Children and Families, 1995). The average AFDC family comprised a mother and two children. Thus, AFDC was primarily a program for young children living with a mother. This made AFDC a crucial source of economic support for needy children and their families. While the program was extremely important for the financial well-being of families, benefits were set at a level that kept a family below the poverty threshold. In 1993, the average family payment through AFDC was $381 per month, with the majority of families receiving benefits for two years or less (Administration for Children and Families, 1995).

The AFDC program was not designed to be a permanent part of the social welfare system. When it was enacted in 1935 as part of the Social Security Act, it was seen as a temporary program until all workers were covered by the Social Security system. It was built on demographic assumptions of the 1930s: children will live with two parents, and the father will work in a good job covered by Social Security. As discussed in chapter 5, however, families and economic conditions have changed over the past sixty years. The number of single-parent families has grown. More women head households and were never married, making them ineligible to be survivors of workers who participated in Social Security. As we will see in chapter 10, the employment market does not provide the economic support needed by all families. Consequently, the AFDC program, despite the low levels of cash assistance provided, represented a much-needed safety net for poor children and their families.

The future of cash assistance for poor children is now in question. Passage of the Personal Responsibility and Work Opportunity Reconciliation Act of 1996 (PRWOR) (P.L. 104–193) eliminated the guarantee of cash assistance and turned control of the program over to state governments through the TANF block grant program. The extent of protection for children in poverty will most likely vary greatly from state to state with implementation of this policy.

Another program designed to provide economic support is the Child Support Enforcement program. Created as part of the AFDC program, it was established in 1975 as Title IV–D of the Social Security Act to enforce the payment of court-mandated child support by non-custodial parents (U.S. General Accounting Office, 1996a). The program was expanded in 1984, 1988, and again in 1996. Eligibility for AFDC, and now TANF, rests on the enforcement of child support through state and local Child Support Enforcement agencies. The program assists custodial parents in receiving payments from non-custodial parents. The program is designed to assist non-TANF individuals as well. Money collected on behalf of TANF families is used to offset the costs of the program, while money collected on behalf of non-TANF families goes to the non-TANF family. In 1992, more than 15 million AFDC and non-AFDC cases were handled, and support collections were made in 18% of the cases (U.S. General Accounting Office, 1994a). Efforts to expand the program and increase the collection of child support were addressed in the PRWOR Act in 1996. The goal is to establish paternity and enforce payments of child support.

Health Care

In chapter 6 we discussed in detail the Medicaid program, which serves financially needy persons. For poor children, Medicaid serves as the only public medical insurance program. In 1993, about 14 million dependent children under the age of 21 received Medicaid services. These children and youth represented 49% of all recipients, yet were responsible for only 16% of the program expenses (U.S. General Accounting Office, 1995b). As we discussed in chapter 6, most of the money paid out under Medicaid is used to assist the aged, blind, and disabled population. Nevertheless, the Medicaid program is the most important health service for poor children. While employment-based health insurance has declined for children, Medicaid coverage has increased. From 1989 to 1993, the number of children enrolled in Medicaid increased from 8.9 to 13.7 million. This increase raised the proportion of children covered by Medicaid from 13.6% to 19.9% (U.S. General Accounting Office, 1995b).

Infant mortality is a major health concern and it is used as a measure of the well-being of a nation's children. In the 1930s, the infant mortality rate in the United States was one of the highest among industrialized nations. In addition, significant numbers of children were born with severe physical disabilities. These phenomena prompted Congress to develop legislation to provide health care for all mothers and children (National Commission to Prevent Infant Mortality, 1988). The Maternal and Child Health Act was included in the original 1935 Social Security Act. Amended to become a block grant program, the Maternal and Child Health Services Block Grant (Title V, Social Security Act) provides health services for low-income mothers and children. The program is designed to reduce the incidence of infant mortality, to treat and prevent communicable diseases, and to provide prenatal and postpartum care. Services today include immunizations, genetic disease testing, and treatment for children with physical disabilities. Unlike many other social services, this legislation mandates a number of preventive programs. Regrettably, funding has been limited. In 1993, the federal spending totaled only $650 million.

Foster Care and Adoption Services

Although historically there has been a public hesitancy to interfere with the rights of parents to raise their children as they see fit, government intervention is a central part of child welfare services. Until the 1870s, families raised their children with complete autonomy. The first officially documented case of child abuse occurred in 1874 (Watkins, 1990; Tower, 1989). Legend has it that the case of "Little Mary Ellen" was publicized through the efforts of the New York Society for the Prevention of Cruelty to Animals (SPCA). Neighbors found Mary Ellen physically and emotionally abused by her foster parents. Concerned about her welfare, they approached the only organization protecting the rights of animals. The SPCA had never handled a case concerning a child. In response to this gap in service, coupled with the growing recognition that children were vulnerable and deserved protection, the Society for the Prevention of Cruelty to Children was founded. Although this version of the story is found in many accounts of child welfare history, it is most likely embellished. The Mary Ellen case received public action because of other factors including journalistic attention from a strong women's rights movement, and the growing strength of the judiciary system (Costin, 1991). These factors led to organized efforts to protect children. For the next several decades, most efforts to protect children centered on the efforts of private organizations.

The impetus behind today's policies stems from publicized documentation of the vulnerability of children in the 1960s. In 1962, a medical doctor, C. Henry Kempe, documented the impact of abuse and neglect, developing the term "battered child syndrome" (Kempe et al., 1962). The battered child syndrome was based on the growing medical evidence of physical abuse toward children. Professional and public attention to this report and related research began to raise awareness that many children were abused and neglected within their families.

The 1974 Child Abuse Prevention and Treatment Act (P.L. 93–247) elevated the protection of children from abuse and neglect to the federal level. It provided grants to states on the condition that recipient states had a mandatory reporting law that required health care professionals to report suspected cases. It also required the establishment of immunity for those who reported suspected incidents of child abuse and neglect (Costin, Bell, & Downs, 1991). Today, all states have such provisions. The development of mandatory reporting gave rise to the collection of statistics documenting the incidence of child abuse and neglect.

It is difficult to accurately assess the number of abusive or neglectful acts committed. Statistics represent cases that are actually reported to authorities. While many cases go unreported, the numbers are revealing. From 1980 to 1986, the incidence of reported cases of child maltreatment increased 65%, from 650,000 to more than 1.5 million annually (Gustavsson & Segal, 1994). In 1994, more than 1.9 million reports alleging abuse and neglect were filed with state children's services agencies, and about 40% were substantiated following investigation (U.S. Bureau of the Census, 1996).

While preventive efforts have sporadically been funded and supported, the main public response to abuse and neglect is to document the abuse and remove the child from the dangerous environment. Removal can be temporary through foster care, or permanent through adoption. Foster care and adoption are the major social program interventions. The number of children in foster care has fluctuated over the years. During the 1970s, as many as 500,000 children were in foster care (Gustavsson & Segal, 1994). Exact numbers are not available because there is no national tracking or census kept on foster care placements. Estimates are based on state-by-state reports. According to the American Public Welfare Association's Voluntary Cooperative Information System, 449,000 children were in foster care in 1993, up from 340,000 in 1988 (U.S. General Accounting Office, 1995a). In 1986, Congress mandated the HHS to establish a system for collecting national data on foster care, but it took seven years for the agency to issue regulations. The system finally became operational in mid-1995 (U.S. General Accounting Office, 1994b).

During the 1960s and 1970s, child welfare advocates noted with concern that more and more children were spending greater amounts of time in foster care. Some children remained in foster care on a permanent basis, often drifting from one placement to another. Little effort was made to keep children in their own homes. Disproportionate numbers of minority children were placed in foster care, and poverty was often a precursor to foster care placement. Furthermore, awareness was growing about the negative consequences of children growing up separated from their families (Pecora, Whittaker, & Maluccio, 1992). These trends prompted child welfare advocates to push for changes. The result was the Adoption Assistance and Child Welfare Act of 1980 (P.L. 96–272).

Advocates regarded the legislation as a new era in foster care and adoption. The law implemented a number of services and guidelines designed to correct the imbalances in the system. Foremost was the goal of **permanency planning**. Permanency planning stressed the concept that foster care was a temporary service, and that children either be returned to their family or placed for adoption in the shortest time possible (Lindsey, 1994). Components of the Adoption Assistance and Child Welfare Act required case review of each child at least once every six months; a mandatory hearing after eighteen months to promote the achievement of a permanent placement; expanding the role of the courts by requiring a judicial finding that all reasonable efforts had been made to keep the child in the family; expanding Title IV (B) of the Social Security Act to provide greater child welfare services; and creation of Title IV (E) of the Social Security Act to develop a state-federal partnership in funding services related to foster care and adoption.

Title IV (E) provides federal funding for foster care and adoption services for children who, if not in out-of-home care, would live in an AFDC/TANF-eligible household. Compared to public assistance, the cost of caring for a child in foster care is greater. The median AFDC benefit for a parent with two children was $377 in 1992, compared to $604 for two children in foster care (Center for Law and Social Policy, 1994). Foster care costs were 60% more than AFDC. Nevertheless, some policy-makers have suggested that if poor families cannot become self-sufficient, the state should provide care for their children. This suggestion raises numerous developmental and ethical questions, as well as economic concerns.

The initial impact of the legislation on foster care was evident in the numbers of children in placements. From 1980 to 1985, the number of children in foster care dropped by about 10%, from over 300,000 to 269,000. Since that time, however, the numbers have grown. By 1992, more than 440,000 children were placed in foster care and 43% had been in continuous care for more than two years (House Committee on Ways and Means, 1994). These numbers and the growing lengths of stay raised concern about the effectiveness and quality of foster care. The structure of the child welfare system did not promote family preservation:

> The current federal system for financing child welfare programs offers little incentive for states to provide services designed to achieve the 1980 legislative

goals of keeping families together and averting the need for foster care (U.S. General Accounting Office, 1993).

Child welfare advocates engaged in efforts to pass new legislation that would revise the 1980 legislation and emphasize ways to keep families together.

Emphasis on prevention and treatment in child welfare services is expanding. In response to the growth in foster care placements, services promoting family preservation have evolved. The federal government supported those efforts by including family preservation and support provisions as part of the Omnibus Reconciliation Act of 1993 (P.L. 103–66). "Family preservation services are typically designed to help families alleviate crises that, left unaddressed, might lead to the out-of-home placement of children" (U.S. General Accounting Office, 1995a, p. 4). Five-year plans were developed by states in 1994 and implemented that year. The impact of these federally funded family preservation efforts remains to be seen.

While new legislation may improve services, the evidence over the past fifteen years suggests that the impact of the legislation will be short-term. The system of removing children from their homes is entirely residual in nature and has been resistant to preventive efforts. The need for improving the social environment and providing support for families also should be addressed when developing policies to protect children. How can families be better equipped to care for children? For legislation to be effective over a longer time, policies must be developed that support families socially and economically and help families develop the skills and resources to care for children in the home.

Education

As a result of compulsory education laws, access to schooling is considered an opportunity available to all children. Education has proven to be an effective way to increase earning potential and provide a means to economic self-sufficiency. In general, the greater a person's education, the higher his or her earnings. Survey data from 1990 showed significant variation in earnings:

Educational Level	Average Monthly Earnings
No high school diploma	$ 492
High school degree	1,077
Associate degree	1,672
Bachelor's degree	2,116
Master's degree	2,822
Doctorate	3,855
Professional degree	4,961

Source: U.S. Bureau of the Census, 1993.

These numbers demonstrate that the higher the degree, the higher the earnings.

While public education is available, it varies widely. Jonathan Kozol (1991), a journalist who investigates social issues, visited a number of public schools across the country. He compared schools in wealthy communities with schools in poor communities, and he discovered incredible disparity. He found almost total racial segregation, huge differences in per-pupil spending, and classroom resources ranging from non-existent to state of the art. In Chicago, the suburban schools spent 78% more per pupil than did the city schools; in New York City, the difference was more than 100%; and in New Jersey, the difference was almost 120%. Kozol's assessment of the state of children's education was that "in public schooling, social policy has been turned back almost one hundred years" (p. 4), and "I often wondered why we would agree to let our children go to school in places where no politician, school board president, or business CEO would dream of working" (p. 5). Research on the state of school facilities concluded that the majority of students attend schools with inadequate building or environmental conditions. Those schools with the most problems were located in central cities, had student populations that were more than 50% minority, and 70% or more of the students were poor (U.S. General Accounting Office, 1996b).

The disparity in schools reflects the dependence on local authority and local funding raised through property taxes. Because public schools rely heavily on funding from their surrounding communities, those in wealthy areas receive more money than do schools in poorer communities. The role of the federal government has been to provide funding only in those cases where there are special needs.

The major policies intended to provide education to all children include the Elementary and Secondary Education Act of 1965 and the Education for All Handicapped Children Act of 1975 (Gustavsson & Segal, 1994). The 1965 legislation provided federal funds to support education for severely handicapped children. The 1975 legislation expanded coverage of the program. States administer the program and determine eligibility. Over the years, the definition of "severe handicap" has been expanded to include learning disabilities and speech impairment. Although the Education for All Handicapped Children Act has not been applied uniformly and there are differences in expenditures and services, it has been successful in providing education for children with disabilities who without the legislation would have received little or no schooling.

The **Head Start Program** is both an education and anti-poverty program. Established in 1964 as part of the Economic Opportunity Act, it serves low-income preschool children. The program provides funds to states for education, socialization, and on-site nutrition at Head Start preschools. The goal is to help economically disadvantaged children be better prepared for school and thus have an equal start with more advantaged children. In spite of research documenting the success of Head Start, funding has never been enough to reach all eligible children. Only about 20% of the low-income children who are eligible receive Head Start services (Cooper, 1990).

Final Thoughts on Child Welfare Policy

The policies described in this chapter represent the key areas of child welfare policy. Almost all of them share a number of characteristics. The vast majority of child and family social welfare policies have only been concerned with pressing social problems. Foster care and adoption are responses to family breakdown, abuse and neglect services identify children after the maltreatment has occurred, and cash assistance programs are available to families only after all resources have been exhausted. The challenge confronting policy-makers is to create social welfare policies that address the current needs of children and families, while also redressing the structural inequalities and obstacles that place children at risk. Preventive approaches to caring for children and their families are both socially responsible and cost-effective. For example, immunization can save thousands of dollars in costly care for preventable childhood diseases; early childhood education and compensatory learning can save the cost of a high school dropout; job creation and training can employ a parent who can therefore afford to provide healthy and safe care of children (Segal and Gustavsson, 1990). Dealing with today's social problems through preventive measures will not only alleviate the immediacy of the problems but may help to solve them.

Key Concepts

child abuse and neglect

family preservation

supportive, supplementary, and
  substitutive services

infant mortality

permanency planning

Head Start Program

Exercises

1. Each state sets laws that mandate who must report suspected cases of child abuse and neglect. What are the laws in your state? Who is mandated? Are you, as a social work student, mandated? Are professionals, such as social workers, teachers, lawyers, and doctors, mandated?

2. You are interested in providing foster care. What are the requirements for becoming a foster parent in your community? Can anyone become a foster parent? What about single adults, gay adults? Why or why not?

3. Call your local office for child protective services (CPS). Ask if you can meet with a CPS worker to learn more about his or her job. What duties are involved? How does the CPS worker feel about serving as a state intermediary in families' lives? How large is a typical caseload? Does the worker feel able to serve each family adequately? Why or why not?

4. Visit a local elementary school. What are the facilities like? What type of student is served? Is the school different from or similar to the school you attended? Are social work services provided at the school?

References

Administration for Children and Families. (1995). *Characteristics and financial circumstances of AFDC recipients, FY 1993.* Washington, DC: U.S. Department of Health and Human Services.

Axinn, J., & Levin, H. (1992). *Social welfare: A history of the American response to need* (3rd ed.). New York: Longman.

Center for Law and Social Policy. (1994). AFDC versus foster care monthly payments, 1992. *Family Matters, 6* (1), 12–13.

Cooper, K.J. (1990). 25 years of giving kids a Head Start. *The Washington Post National Weekly Edition, 7* (26), 9.

Costin, L.B. (1991). Unraveling the Mary Ellen legend: Origins of the "cruelty" movement. *Social Service Review, 65* (2), 203–223.

Costin, L.B., Bell, C.J., & Downs, S.W. (1991). *Child welfare: Policies and practice* (4th ed.). New York: Longman

Gustavsson, N.S., & Segal, E.A. (1994). *Critical issues in child welfare.* Thousand Oaks, CA: Sage Publications.

Hasci, T. (1995). From indenture to foster care: A brief history of child placing. *Child Welfare, LXXIV* (1), 162–180.

Hogan, P.T., & Siu, S.F. (1988). Minority children and the child welfare system: An historical perspective. *Social Work, 33* (6), 493–498.

House Committee on Ways and Means. (1994). *Overview of entitlement programs—1994 Green book.* WMCP: 103–27. Washington, DC: U.S. Government Printing Office.

Jansson, B.S. (1997). *The reluctant welfare state: A history of American social welfare policies* (3rd ed.). Pacific Grove, CA: Brooks/Cole.

Kadushin, A., & Martin, J.A. (1988). *Child welfare services* (4th ed.). New York: Macmillan.

Katz, M.B. (1986). *In the shadow of the poorhouse: A social history of welfare in America.* New York: Basic Books.

Kempe, C.H., Silverman, F., Steele, B., Droegmueller, W., & Silver, H. (1962). The battered-child syndrome. *Journal of the American Medical Association, 181,* 17–24.

Kimmich, M.H. (1985). *America's children: Who cares?* Washington, DC: Urban Institute Press.

Kozol, J. (1991). *Savage inequalities: Children in America's schools.* New York: Crown Publishers.

Lindsey, D. (1994). *The welfare of children.* New York: Oxford University Press.

Mannes, M. (1995). Factors and events leading to the passage of the Indian Child Welfare Act. *Child Welfare, LXXIV* (1), 264–282.

McMahon, A., & Gullerud, E.N. (1995). Native American agencies for Native American children: Fulfilling the promise of the Indian Child Welfare Act. *Journal of Sociology and Social Welfare, XXII* (1), 87–98.

National Commission to Prevent Infant Mortality. (1988). *A historic day for children.* Washington, DC: Authors.

Pecora, P.J., Whittaker, J.K., & Maluccio, A.N. (1992). *The child welfare challenge.* New York: Aldine de Gruyter.

Segal, E.A., & Gustavsson, N.S. (1990). The high cost of neglecting children: The need for a preventive policy agenda. *Child and Adolescent Social Work, 7* (6), 475–485.

Stadum, B. (1995). The dilemma in saving children from child labor: Reform and casework at odds with families' needs. *Child Welfare, LXXIV* (1), 33–55.

Stein, T.J. (1991). *Child welfare and the law.* New York: Longman.

Tower, C.C. (1989). *Understanding child abuse and neglect.* Boston: Allyn & Bacon.

Trattner, W.I. (1994). *From poor law to welfare state* (5th ed.). New York: The Free Press.

U.S. Bureau of the Census. (1993). *Education: The ticket to higher earnings.* SB/93–7. Washington, DC: U.S. Government Printing Office.

U.S. Bureau of the Census. (1996). *Statistical Abstract of the United States* (116th ed.). Washington, DC: U.S. Government Printing Office.

U.S. General Accounting Office. (1988). *Children's programs.* Washington, DC: U.S. Government Printing Office.

U.S. General Accounting Office. (1993). *Foster care: Services to prevent out-of-home placements are limited by funding barriers.* GAO/HRD–93–76. Washington, DC: U.S. Government Printing Office.

U.S. General Accounting Office. (1994a). *Automated welfare systems.* GAO/AIMD–94–52FS. Washington, DC: U.S. Government Printing Office.

U.S. General Accounting Office. (1994b). *Child welfare: HHS begins to assume leadership to implement national and state systems.* GAO/AIMD–94–37. Washington, DC: U.S. Government Printing Office.

U.S. General Accounting Office. (1995a). *Child welfare.* GAO/HEHS–95–112. Washington, DC: U.S. Government Printing Office.

U.S. General Accounting Office. (1995b). *Health insurance for children.* GAO/HEHS–95–175. Washington, DC: U.S. Government Printing Office.

U.S. General Accounting Office. (1996a). *Child support enforcement.* GAO/HEHS–97–11. Washington, DC: U.S. Government Printing Office.

U.S. General Accounting Office. (1996b). *School facilities: America's schools report differing conditions.* GAO/HEHS–96–103. Washington, DC: U.S. Government Printing Office.

Watkins, S.A. (1990). The Mary Ellen myth: Correcting child welfare history. *Social Work, 35* (6), 500–505.

Zelizer, V.A. (1985). *Pricing the priceless child.* New York: Basic Books.

© Joel Gordon

Chapter 8

Aging and Social Welfare Policy

Aging, like childhood, is part of the human condition. With good health and care, most people in our society are likely to live into their seventies, and many will live ten or even twenty years longer. Life expectancy has risen gradually over the years, from about 50 years at the turn of the century (House Committee on Ways and Means, 1994) to almost 76 for someone born in 1994 (U.S. Bureau of the Census, 1996a, 1996b). From 1900 to 1994, there was an eleven-fold increase in the elderly population (U.S. Bureau of the Census, 1996a, 1996b). In 1995, more than 33 million people were 65 years of age or older, representing 12.8% of the total population. From 1980 to 1995, the population of people older than 85 grew by almost 1.4 million (U.S. Bureau of the Census, 1996a, 1996b). One of the results of this longer lifespan has been a need to consider social welfare policies that provide care and support for people as they age.

Historically, care for the elderly was handled within the family. The percentage of older people in the general population was relatively small, so there were more people to share in the care and support of the elderly. Because of the increasing proportion of elderly people in the population, families are no longer able to provide all the necessary care for their aging members. As a result, families increasingly look to government to help care for and support the older generation. In this chapter, we will examine the social welfare policies and programs that have been developed to assist aging Americans.

History of Social Welfare Policies Related to Aging

During the nineteenth century, most people worked throughout their lives. In fact, the concept of retirement is relatively new (Richardson, 1993). The idea of leaving the work force at a specific age began to receive public support after the 1930s and was formalized with policies and programs that evolved over the years from the Great Depression into the 1960s.

The Great Depression hit older people particularly hard. Most lost their life savings and their homes, and families were dispersed. These events gave rise to a political movement of elderly citizens. During the 1930s, thousands of older people organized to push for the creation of federal old-age pensions (Torres-Gil, 1992). This was the first time that older adults had organized and supported legislation as a voting bloc. The result of the economic devastation of the Great Depression and the organized political pressure of older people was the passage of the Social Security Act of 1935. The major social welfare policy created by this legislation was the Old-Age, Survivors, and Disability Insurance program (OASDI), commonly referred to as Social Security. This program is the foundation of today's Social Security coverage and serves as the largest social welfare program in the nation. During the 1930s there was significant resistance to such a broad social welfare effort by the federal government, but the social insurance system established by the Social Security Act is now strongly supported.

It took another thirty years after the enactment of the Social Security Act to establish the other major public program to aid the elderly—Medicare. Although advocates had tried repeatedly to gain legislation that would provide federal support for health care insurance for older people, it was not until 1965 that the Social Security Act was amended to include Title XVIII, Health Insurance for the Aged and Disabled, as discussed in chapter 6 (Social Security Administration, 1993b). When Medicare is included, the entire program is sometimes referred to as Old-Age, Survivors, Disability, and Health Insurance (OASDHI). In this book, to maintain clarity, Medicare and OASDI are discussed separately.

Also in 1965, the Older Americans Act was passed. Although not as significant and comprehensive as OASDI and Medicare, this legislation furthered the policy gains made by older adults. The Act provided federal

Figure 8.1
Social Welfare Policy Analysis Model:
The Older Americans of 1965

Social Issue

- Lack of organization of social welfare services for the elderly
- Need to generate additional resources for older people

Goal

- Provide government coordination of public resources and services for older people

Policy or Legislation

- Older Americans Act of 1965 (P.L. 89–73)

Implementation

- States develop and monitor service areas through Area Agencies on Aging (AAAs)
- Local agencies qualify for federal funds through the AAAs and provide direct services

Affected Populations

- People 60 years of age and older
- Providers of social services to seniors

Actual Impact

- Increased availability of services for elderly persons, targeted to low-income seniors
- Greater coordination of services

Intended Impact

- Increased services to seniors
- Greater coordination of services

financial support for programs and services for older citizens. These programs, implemented and administered on state and local levels, are coordinated through a network of Area Agencies on Aging (AAAs) established by the Older Americans Act (Trattner, 1994). The social welfare policy analysis example in Figure 8.1 outlines this Act.

Major Social Welfare Policies and Programs for the Elderly

The three pieces of legislation discussed above—OASDI, Medicare, and the Older Americans Act—provide a full spectrum of national social welfare policies to support the elderly. The enactment of these programs demonstrated the growing political strength of senior citizens. Although older adults constitute a minority of all eligible voters, their political power is very strong. Voting and voter registration are highest among those who are 65 years of age and older (U.S. Bureau of the Census, 1993). The voting strength of older citizens keeps policy-makers politically tied to support of senior citizen programs and very sensitive to the wishes of this substantial voting group.

Social Security

The most well-known program for older Americans is the **Old-Age, Survivors, and Disability Insurance Program (OASDI)**, commonly referred to as Social Security. As discussed previously, the Great Depression left the elderly extremely vulnerable. Without work, people quickly exhausted their savings. Although there had been some movement toward worker protection in a few states, there was no national system to protect workers from the economic consequences of job loss or old age. In 1935, passage of the Social Security Act created financial protection for workers as they age.

The initial legislation provided for old-age benefits for retired workers who would have paid taxes into the system while employed in industry and commerce. The program was to begin collecting taxes in 1937 and pay out benefits starting in 1942. Before full enactment of the law, it was expanded in 1939 to cover, in addition to the retired worker, his or her survivors and dependents. Survivors provisions meant that if a worker died, dependent family members would continue to receive benefits. Disability insurance was added in 1956 to provide cash benefits for disabled workers. Although there have been incremental changes throughout the years, retirement, survivor, and disability coverages reflect the major provisions of the OASDI program today.

Public Perceptions of Social Security.   From the beginning, the social insurance provisions of the Social Security Act have been viewed differently from the public assistance programs created by the Act. In order to maintain public support, the administrators and supporters of Social Security publicized the insurance aspect of the program:

> Because insurance implied a return for work and investment, it preserved the self-respect of the beneficiaries; because it implied a return in proportion to in-

vestment, it satisfied a widely held conception of fairness; and because it implied the existence of a contract, it appeared sound and certain (Derthick, 1979, p. 199).

These aspects, which are firmly ingrained in the popular perception of the program, have solidified public acceptance and made the Social Security program the most widely supported social welfare policy in our country. Nevertheless, closer examination reveals that the design of the program, while more institutional than other social welfare programs, is not as fair as it is perceived.

How the Program Works.   The structure of the OASDI program requires that while people are young and working, they pay into the system. The amount paid in is a set percent of income, 7.65% (as of 1996) for OASDI and Medicare together, up to a certain amount of overall salary. In 1996, Social Security taxes had to be paid on all income up to $62,700. Any income exceeding that amount was taxed only for the Medicare portion (1.45%). Thus, because of the cap, as salary rises, a decreasing percentage of income is withheld. Some argue that this is unfair because people with lower incomes pay a larger percentage of their salary. For example, in 1996 a person who earned $30,000 paid $2,295 in Social Security taxes, or 7.65% of total income. A person who earned $150,000 paid $6,062, or 4.04% of overall salary, and a person who earned $300,000 paid $8,237, a total of 2.75% of overall salary. This disparity makes Social Security a **regressive tax**: a tax that is proportionately greater for people with low incomes than for people with higher incomes.

The accompanying tax rate schedule, in Table 8.1, lists the percentages of income paid for OASDI and Medicare in 1996. Each worker's employer

Table 8.1

Tax Rate Schedule for OASDI and Medicare

1997 tax rate percent* on employee earnings		
Total	OASDI[†]	Medicare
7.65	6.2	1.45
1997 tax rate percent on self-employed earnings		
Total	OASDI[†]	Medicare
15.3	12.4	2.9

*Employers also contribute these amounts.

[†]OASDI tax applies to first $62,700 of annual income; there is no cap for Medicare.

Source: Social Security Administration (1996).

matches that amount and pays it directly to the federal government. If a person is self-employed, he or she is responsible for paying both portions. The federal government holds the money in a special account, the **Social Security Trust Fund**. Money in the Trust Fund can be used only for the OASDI program. The money is used to pay benefits for those who become eligible upon retirement or as a result of disability. Eligibility requirements include having worked for at least forty quarters (ten years) in covered employment and reaching the retirement age of 65 (by the year 2022, the retirement age will be 67). There are some exceptions and variations to this rule, and the specifics change from year to year. In order to be absolutely certain of eligibility, each person should check with a local Social Security Administration office. The details of the program are also available in book format from the Social Security Administration (Social Security Administration, 1993a).

The Social Security Administration keeps track of the contributions made by each worker and that person's employer. This amount is used to calculate how much retirees receive per month as their benefit when they become eligible. The average monthly benefit for a retired worker in 1994 was $697 (U.S. Bureau of the Census, 1996a).

The majority of women who receive Social Security benefits do so as wives or survivors of eligible workers (Iams & Ycas, 1988). A wife or widow can choose to receive benefits based on her own work history or based on the earnings of her spouse. For most women, monthly benefits are greater if based on the earnings of their husbands. A woman still living with her husband receives 50% of his entitlement. Thus, a married couple typically receives 150% of the husband's benefits. If a woman becomes a widow, she is entitled to the full 100% of her late husband's benefits.

How Important Is Social Security?   The monthly Social Security benefit plays a vital role in keeping many elderly persons financially out of poverty. For elderly persons with incomes below the poverty line, 68% of their total income comes from OASDI benefits. More than half of all Social Security beneficiaries have less than $6,000 of annual income from sources other than Social Security (House Committee on Ways and Means, 1994). Without monthly social security benefits, millions of senior citizens would be in poverty or financially dependent on their children or other family members. This is particularly true for women and minorities. Sixty percent of older African-American women living alone are in poverty, compared to 24% of older white women and 17% of older white men (Binstock, 1990). In 1994, the poverty rate for all women over 65 years of age, living alone or with spouses and families, was 14.9%, more than twice that of men (7.2%) (Center on Budget and Policy Priorities, 1996). The inequalities of the workplace, particularly racism and sexism, are compounded with age. For many elderly persons the OASDI program is a safety net that prevents them from falling into poverty after they retire. Over the past thirty years, the poverty rate for the elderly has dropped from 35% to less than 12% (Binstock, 1990; U.S. Bureau of the Census, 1996a). This decrease in poverty among the elderly is directly related to increases in the Social Security program and serves as evidence of the program's effectiveness.

There is a common belief that Social Security is a retirement program, but in reality OASDI does not provide sufficient benefits for a comfortable retirement of leisure and travel. The average benefits from the program are less than $8,400 a year—not even enough income, by itself, to support people in retirement.

Not all older people rely heavily on Social Security, however. Receipt of Social Security benefits is not linked to economic means. Thus, for some workers it is a monthly check that is not necessarily needed. The universality of the program allows that whether people are rich or poor, as long as they paid into the program, they are eligible to receive benefits. Unlike public assistance, Social Security is regarded as a right.

People believe they have a right to receive benefits because they have paid into the system. If a person dies before reaching retirement, however, he or she will not receive anything (although the person's survivors will receive benefits). If, on the other hand, a person lives for many years past retirement, he or she may receive more money than actually was paid in. The Congressional Research Service calculated that retirees in 1980 received through monthly benefits the equivalent of all the contributions paid in over their work lives in just three years of retirement (Pearlstein, 1993). In 1995, the typical single-earner couple who retired could expect to receive two-and-one-half times the total amount they had contributed (Crenshaw, 1996). Historically, for most Social Security recipients the amount of money they have received in benefits has been more than the total they paid in over their working years.

The Future of Social Security.   Over the years, generous benefits were set by Congress based on how much money was paid into the Trust Fund each year. This form of redistribution did not take account of changing demographics. During the early years of the Social Security system there were many more people working than receiving benefits. As the population ages and people live longer, the number of people receiving benefits increases, while the number of people working and paying into the system decreases. This imbalance has led to ominous predictions that the Social Security system would soon run out of money. In 1983, policy analysts calculated that the system would be bankrupt in ten years. This never occurred because lawmakers made legislative decisions to change the program. The key changes were as follows: the retirement age limit was raised from 65 to 67 years, to be phased in over time; cost-of-living increases in benefits were delayed; the withholding tax was increased; and the taxable income ceiling was raised. These legislative changes created a surplus in funds that is supposed to accumulate to cover the increase in the number of retirees during the next century. As planned, Social Security revenues currently exceed outlays. The trust funds are growing, and there is projected to be an overall surplus in the system for the next thirty years (Aaron, 1996). Experts tend to regard the program as well entrenched and here to stay (Myers, 1997).

Social Security seems to be a permanent expectation of Americans of all income levels. To ensure the continuation of the program, some very difficult political decisions must be made. Policy-makers will have to decide how to continue to keep the system financially solvent as baby boomers expand the number of retirees and as people live longer. The policy choices to maintain Social Security include cutting benefits, limiting eligibility, raising taxes, or some combination of all three. Those choices are typically not supported by voting constituencies, and hence elected officials try to stay away from them as long as possible. With millions of older people currently receiving benefits, and most workers paying into the system, politicians are likely to find a way to maintain the primacy of the Social Security system.

Health Care

Medicare, or officially the Health Insurance program, was established by Title XVIII of the Social Security Act in 1965. It operates similarly to the OASDI program. Part of the Social Security tax all employees and employers pay goes toward funding Medicare. When a person becomes eligible to receive Social Security benefits, he or she is also eligible for Medicare coverage. (The health care components of the Medicare program are discussed more fully in chapter 6.)

As a program for the elderly, Medicare is extremely important. It provides coverage for many routine medical procedures as well as very specialized care. Because of rising medical costs and the development of new procedures over the past thirty years, however, the cost has become a major policy problem. The elderly in 1980 accounted for only 11% of the population, but accounted for 31% of all money spent on personal health care (Montgomery & Borgatta, 1987). As discussed in chapter 6, even the Medicaid program, which provides care to low-income people of all ages, is used more heavily by the elderly. In 1994, 12% of Medicaid recipients were elderly, yet they accounted for 31% of all money spent on this program (U.S. Bureau of the Census, 1996a).

How much should be paid for health care and who should pay for it are pressing social welfare policy questions. As the population ages and medical technology becomes more advanced, the expense of health care will increase. Currently, for those who are covered by the Social Security system, Medicare covers a large portion of the health care costs for the elderly, but it does not include all medical expenses.

One of the most costly health care concerns for the elderly is long-term care. **Long-term care** covers a wide array of services for elderly, chronically ill, and persons with disabilities that are necessary for day-to-day living and personal care. While Medicare covers some of the expenses of long-term care, it does not cover them all. For example, Medicare covers nursing home care for a period of up to 100 days. After that period has ended, an elderly person must either use private insurance or personal finances to pay for continued nursing home care. Because of this shortfall in Medicare coverage, people often "spend down" or deplete their financial assets in order to become eligible for Medicaid, which does provide unlimited nursing home care (U.S. General Accounting Office, 1994a).

The average cost of a year in a nursing home was $34,000 in 1991. About 1.5 million older Americans live in nursing homes (U.S. General Accounting Office, 1994b). Caring for people as they age is becoming extremely costly for individuals and the government. This is a social welfare policy issue that has yet to be adequately addressed. As people age, the issue of long-term care takes on greater significance. While 9% of people aged 65 to 69 needed assistance with performing daily activities because of health problems, 45% of people 85 years of age and older did (U.S. Bureau of the Census, 1990). Reliance on Medicare and Medicaid is costly to taxpayers, but private insurance, personal savings, and family members are not able to fully support the need. Alternative solutions to long-term care are needed as our population ages. Other services such as home health care and day treatment programs for senior citizens attempt to fill the need for such care. The goal of these services is to keep senior citizens at home and out of institutions for as long as possible.

Older Americans Act of 1965

The growth of social welfare programs during the 1960s expanded services for the elderly. In 1961, the first White House Conference on Aging was held (Axinn & Levin, 1992). It highlighted the growing needs of older people, and in part led to the passage of the **Older Americans Act (OAA) of 1965** (P.L. 89–73). The OAA subsidized social services and the development of **Area Agencies on Aging (AAA)** to coordinate the provisions of the Act (Jansson, 1997).

In addition to the AAAs, the legislation also authorized a number of social services. Each local agency has a great deal of discretion in planning and implementing the services. The general services supported by funds through the OAA include transportation, senior centers, recreation, nutrition, and health-related programs such as immunizations. The overall goal of the Act was to create a governmental agent to coordinate the various existing services and create new ways to better serve older people. Some of the specific programs that are coordinated today through the provisions of the OAA include group meals, Meals on Wheels, senior centers, adult day care centers for older people with impairments, home-based care, and employment services (Gelfand, 1994).

In general, the services offered through the OAA are available to all persons 60 years of age or older, regardless of means. In practice, however, due to limited resources and low funding levels over the years, services tend to be directed to those most in need (Torres-Gil, 1992). The struggle between universality and targeted services is a result of incremental cutbacks in federal and state funds over the past ten years. As is true in so many areas of services to the elderly, the expanding population of older people will challenge the resources of the programs of the OAA and most likely demand social welfare policy changes over the next several years.

Intergenerational Relations: Conflict Versus Cooperation

As more people live longer, the emphasis on programs and services for seniors gains strength. The political power and influence of senior citizens has brought attention to what is sometimes described as the public policy divide between the young and the old (Pearlstein, 1993). Observers have pointed out that for every dollar the federal government spends on children, it spends four dollars on the elderly (Taylor, 1991). Child welfare advocates argue that several forces combine to favor spending on the elderly over spending on children. There is a sense of self-interest involved:

> While we cannot recapture our own childhoods, all of us anticipate being old someday. At some level we all perceive programs and benefits for the elderly as *mechanisms through which we transfer resources to ourselves in the future* (Hewlett, 1991, pp. 187–188).

Another way to view the evolution of senior services is to recognize that government support for people as they age has freed the younger generation from responsibility (Torres-Gil, 1992). The benefits and services provided over the past thirty years have helped to reduce the proportion of poor elderly, to extend life expectancy, and to enhance the political power of older Americans. These social welfare policies have given the elderly more autonomy and allowed their children to be more mobile and not have to worry as much about day-to-day responsibilities nor cost of care for their aging parents.

Hewlett (1991), while arguing for more support for children, views the investment in children and their future productivity as providing the prosperity needed to support older generations. She advocates that social welfare policy should emphasize support of all children to the same extent that support for all seniors is accomplished. From a social welfare policy perspective, she is suggesting taking a more institutional and preventive approach.

Without taking a preventive approach, we run the risk of polarizing social welfare services. There is a tremendous danger in viewing social welfare policy in divisive terms. To pit the old against the young is to fall into the perpetual cycle of residual social welfare policy. Programs such as social insurance and Medicare demonstrate that people can receive social welfare benefits by virtue of age, regardless of their economic means. The challenge is to develop social welfare policies and programs that do the same for children, families, and younger adults. The major intergenerational divide is that children are predominantly served under means-tested public assistance programs, and the elderly are served under social insurance institutional programs. This is the division that needs resolution.

More social welfare programs should be patterned after Social Security. The idea of investing in a social insurance system that helps ensure the health and well-being of a future generation of taxpayers could be incorporated into programs that serve children. By creating similar program structures for seniors and children, the intergenerational divide should disappear.

Final Thoughts on Social Welfare Policy for Older Americans

As the population of elderly persons continues to grow, the political power of senior citizens will also increase. Policy-makers will need to be more attentive to the wishes of the aged. Advocacy groups such as the American Association of Retired Persons (AARP) with over 30 million members, represent very powerful special-interests. As such, they will dominate social welfare policy discussions of issues related to aging. Thus, social welfare policies relevant to aging in America will remain a critical part of our social welfare system.

Key Concepts

Old-Age, Survivors, and Disability
    Insurance (OASDI)
Social Security Trust Fund
Medicaid
Older Americans Act of 1965

Social Security
regressive tax
Medicare
long-term care
Area Agencies on Aging

Exercises

1. Contact your local Social Security Administration Office. Ask for an application for a "Request for Earnings and Benefits Estimate Statement." Send it in to find out your history of earnings and contributions under Social Security. Within six weeks you will receive a free statement that lists your contributions and estimates what your monthly retirement benefits will be.

2. Contact a relative, neighbor, or friend who is 65 years of ago or older. Ask if he or she would be willing to discuss with you the senior services and benefits he or she receives. Are they adequate? What would he or she like to see increased or changed?

3. Visit a senior center in your community. What services are available? Who is eligible to participate in the center's activities? How is the senior center funded? Who administers the programs? Are social workers involved? If so, how?

References

Aaron, H.J. (1996). The myths of the social security "crisis." *The Washington Post National Weekly Edition, 13* (40), 21–22.

Axinn, J., & Levin, H. (1992). *Social Welfare: A history of the American response to need* (3rd ed.). New York: Longman.

Binstock, R.H. (1990). The politics and economics of aging and diversity. In Bass, S.A., Kutza, E.A., & Torres-Gil, F.M. (eds.), *Diversity in aging* (pp. 73–99). Glenview, IL: Scott, Foresman.

Center on Budget and Policy Priorities. (1996). *Poverty and income trends: 1994.* Washington, DC: Author.

Crenshaw, A.B. (1996). A stock answer to social security worries. *The Washington Post National Weekly Edition, 13* (32), 22.

Derthick, M. (1979). *Policymaking for Social Security.* Washington, DC: Brookings Institution.

Gelfand, D.E. (1994). *Aging and ethnicity: Knowledge and services.* New York: Springer.

Hewlett, S.A. (1991). *When the bough breaks: The cost of neglecting our children.* New York: HarperCollins.

House Committee on Ways and Means. (1994). *Overview of entitlement programs: 1994 Green book.* Washington, DC: U.S. Government Printing Office.

Iams, H.M., & Ycas, M.A. (1988). Women, marriage, and social security benefits. *Social Security Bulletin, 51* (5), 3–9.

Jansson, B.S. (1997). *The reluctant welfare state* (3rd ed.). Pacific Grove, CA: Brooks/Cole.

Meyers, R.J. (1997) Will Social Security be there for me? In Kingson, E.R., & Schulz, J.H., (eds.), *Social Security in the 21st century* (pp. 208–216). New York: Oxford University Press.

Montgomery, R.J.V., & Borgatta, E.F. (1987). Values, costs, and health care policy. In Borgatta, E.F., & Montgomery, R.J.V. (eds.), *Critical issues in aging policy* (pp. 236–252). Newbury Park, CA: Sage Publications.

Pearlstein, S. (1993). Battling for a slice of the pie: The young challenge their elders. *The Washington Post National Weekly Edition, 10* (17), 22.

Richardson, V.E. (1993). *Retirement counseling.* New York: Springer.

Social Security Administration. (1993a). *Social Security handbook 1993* (11th ed.) SSA No. 65–008. Washington, DC: U.S. Department of Health and Human Services.

Social Security Administration. (1993b). *Social security programs in the United States.* SSA No. 13–11758. Washington, DC: U.S. Department of Health and Human Services.

Social Security Administration. (1996). *Social Security bulletin: Annual Statistical Supplement.* Washington, DC: U.S. Department of Health and Human Services.

Taylor, P. (1991). Like taking money from a baby. *The Washington Post National Weekly Edition, 8* (18), 31.

Torres-Gil, F.M. (1992). *The new aging: Politics and change in America.* New York: Auburn House.

Trattner, W.I. (1994). *From poor law to welfare state* (5th ed.). New York: The Free Press.

U.S. Bureau of the Census. (1990). *Persons needing assistance with everyday activities.* SB-12–90. Washington, DC: U.S. Government Printing Office.

U.S. Bureau of the Census. (1993). *Voting and registration in the election of November 1992.* P20–466. Washington, DC: U.S. Government Printing Office.

U.S. Bureau of the Census. (1996a). *Statistical abstract of the United States, 1996* (116th ed.). Washington, DC: U.S. Government Printing Office.

U.S. Bureau of the Census. (1996b). *65+ in the United States*. Current Population Reports (pp. 23–190). Washington, DC: U.S. Government Printing Office.

U.S. General Accounting Office. (1994a). *Long-term care: Other countries tighten budgets while seeking better access*. GAO/HEHS–94–154. Washington, DC: U.S. Government Printing Office.

U.S. General Accounting Office. (1994b). *Long-term care: Support for elder care could benefit the government workplace and the elderly*. GAO/HEHS–94–64. Washington, DC: U.S. Government Printing Office.

Mark Richards/PhotoEdit

Chapter 9

Civil Rights

The issue of *rights*—what people deserve and are entitled to—versus *social welfare services*—what government or groups in power are willing to provide—dates back to the earliest history of this country. Questions regarding the government's role in ensuring and protecting rights, what is or is not a right, and what rights exist for whom, dominate social welfare policy debates today. Affirmative action, abortion rights, gay rights, and immigration policies are all examples of social issues that bring to question what are civil rights and what are social welfare services. **Civil rights** describes the rights to which people are entitled because they are members of society. Rights are often ensured and protected through laws, resources, and services; but social welfare services, on the other hand, are provided only when deemed necessary by a majority of voters. Civil rights are protected and guaranteed by law, while social welfare services are created and dispensed in accord with the decisions of policy-makers. Therefore, social welfare services are more easily changed and rescinded.

While the legal and political rights of citizens have been a public concern throughout American history, civil rights protections have been, and continue to be, slow in coming for some members of society. For example, early citizenship rights such as eligibility to vote were restricted to white men, generally those who owned property. Women were not protected by government laws to the same extent as men for most of American history. For hundreds of years, African-Americans and American Indians were not allowed the same rights as whites because of racial discrimination. In spite of the limited nature of early civil rights in this country, however, periods of social upheaval, political organizing, and public outcry have brought about major civil rights changes. These efforts still continue today.

Discussions of people's civil rights raise the issue of inequality. When one group has rights and protections that others do not, it creates a sense of relative inequality. When only men had the right to vote, for example, there was an inequality for women. When only whites could sit in the front of public buses, African-Americans were being treated in an unequal way. For those people or groups who perceive that their rights or access to services and resources are blocked, there is an imbalance. That imbalance is inequality.

In this text, we posit that there are certain tenets—such as citizenship, freedom of expression, and protection from discrimination—that are or should be a right of *all* people, regardless of age, income, sex, race, ability, ethnicity, or sexual orientation. In order for those rights to be guaranteed, they must be supported by the power of public law and government. When laws are created and enforced to uphold civil rights, people are protected in every facet of their lives from discrimination. In this chapter we will trace the history of civil rights in America, discuss those rights, and evaluate the implications for social welfare policy.

The Constitution: Cornerstone of Civil Rights

The foundation in law for protection of people's rights rests with the Constitution. Following the Revolutionary War, the newly established leaders of the nation turned their attention to developing a system of government that was more democratic than the previous system of rule by the British monarchy. The Constitution, as it was originally passed and later amended, serves as the basis for civil rights and protections in America. It provides the framework for our system of government, our electoral process, the rights related to personal expression and behavior, and protection of the nation's and citizen's well-being.

The United States Constitution, consisting of seven articles, was agreed to in 1789. Article I outlines the legislative branch, while Articles II and III establish the executive and judicial branches, respectively. The separation of powers was deemed necessary to provide a system of "checks and balances" with the design of "separate institutions sharing functions" (Oleszek, 1989, p. 3).

Furthermore, the Constitution settled the question of whether the government should be representative of the national citizenry or a federation representing states (Jacobson, 1987). A national government would be based on representation according to population, while a federal system would be based on representation of the states. For large states with great numbers of people, representation according to population was advantageous. For small states, equal representation for each state was much more appealing. The system that prevailed was a compromise between these two positions.

The form of government established was based on a bicameral, or two-chamber, system. The House of Representatives was elected by the people according to population, and the Senate consisted of two representatives from each state, regardless of the state's size. Senators were originally chosen by state legislatures, but in 1913 the Constitution was amended to allow for direct election of senators by citizens. This system remains in effect today.

Although the question of representation was settled through development of democratic process, participation in the process of selection was limited. The right to vote was initially addressed by the Constitution in a general way, with the specifics left to states. Over time, the Constitution was amended to more clearly delineate the parameters of the right to vote. Voting as a specific right took decades to resolve, and is discussed in further detail in the next section.

The **Bill of Rights** identifies the central tenets of civil rights in America. It consists of the first ten amendments to the Constitution, which were ratified in 1791, two years after the first Constitutional Convention and the original passage of the Constitution. The First Amendment protects freedom of religion, speech, and the press; the right of people to assemble peaceably; and the right of people to petition government:

> Congress shall make no law respecting an establishment of religion, or prohibiting the free exercise thereof; or abridging the freedom of speech, or of the press; or the right of the people peaceably to assemble, and to petition the Government for a redress of grievances.

These protections create a foundation of civil rights in this country. Other amendments were added as the struggle for civil rights expanded the meaning of these liberties. Today the Constitution and all its amendments serve as the basis for legal decisions in this country.

The History of Voting Rights in the United States

The right to vote was actually not clearly spelled out by the Constitution. The specifics of who was eligible to vote were left to the states to decide. Consequently, after ratification of the Constitution and prior to the Civil War, voting was predominantly a right of white men who owned property.

This meant that many other Americans were denied the right to vote. Because voting entitles one to a voice in government and political decisions, and voting was restricted to white men, most public policies ignored or did not protect the rights of all people. Women, slaves, and those who did not own land were not envisioned as full citizens. For almost one hundred years, these omissions in civil rights were ignored by those in power. Not until after the Civil War did the government begin to make concessions to protect the rights of more citizens.

Rights of African-American Men

The Civil War began the movement that was to expand the rights of African-Americans. Until the Civil War, black slaves brought over from Africa lacked any civil rights or personal protections. In fact, they were considered the property of their owners. One of the political outcomes of the Civil War was that the federal government intervened and passed the Fourteenth Amendment in 1868 and the Fifteenth Amendment in 1870.

The original intent of the Fourteenth Amendment was to establish the full rights of citizenship and equality for all, including African-Americans:

> All persons born or naturalized in the United States, and subject to the jurisdiction thereof, are citizens of the United States and of the State wherein they reside. No State shall make or enforce any law which shall abridge the privileges or immunities of citizens of the United States; nor shall any State deprive any person of life, liberty, or property, without due process of law; nor deny to any person within its jurisdiction the equal protection of the laws.

The words "persons" and "citizens" in the Constitution referred to men. Consequently, the rights of citizenship were extended to all men but not to women. Two years later, in 1870, the issue of voting rights was clearly spelled out in the Fifteenth Amendment, which gave the right to vote to any male, regardless of race or color:

> The right of citizens of the United States to vote shall not be denied or abridged by the United States or by any State on account of race, color, or previous condition of servitude.

Although the intent of the Fourteenth Amendment was to give freedom and civil rights to former slaves, interpretation in the courts limited its impact. The Supreme Court's interpretation through the *Plessy v. Ferguson* decision in 1896 mandated that equal protection did not preclude segregation. The decision justified separate but equal public facilities. However, the government will to enforce the decision was minimal, and the historical result was that segregation and "separate and unequal" dominated public policy and practice (Dye, 1992).

Theoretically, these constitutional amendments gave African-American men the right to vote. In practical terms, particularly in the South, local rules and regulations made it impossible for most former slaves to actually vote. Rampant throughout the South were rules such as poll taxes and literacy tests that were used to bar people from registering to vote. Without paying a tax and passing a literacy test, a man could not register to vote. Without first registering, a man could not cast a vote in any election.

After the Civil War, in spite of emancipation, former slaves who stayed in the South were poor and had very little access to education. Southern state and local governments maintained local rules that kept African-Americans marginalized by making it impossible for them to obtain adequate educational and financial resources. These local rules and regulations, together with rampant racial discrimination, prevented former slaves from owning land, running businesses, or holding well-paying jobs. Moreover, poll taxes and literacy tests were not the only barriers that kept African-Americans from voting. Voter registration was conducted by local officials. When African-Americans would attempt to register, intimidation and fear tactics were used to discourage them (Polenberg, 1980). Thus, local laws and practices effectively nullified the impact of the Fourteenth and Fifteenth Amendments.

The impact of these blocking tactics lasted for almost one hundred years. This example illustrates how the power of local control and policy-setting can be more powerful and effective than federal government rule. In addition, the poll tax and literacy tests are classic examples of **institutional racism** in which public laws and regulations are used to differentiate and discriminate according to race.

For African-Americans in the South, voting did not become a reality until passage of the Twenty-Fourth Amendment in 1964 and the Voting Rights Act of 1965. The Twenty-Fourth Amendment, which barred the use of poll taxes, was reinforced by the congressional passage of the Voting Rights Act. The 1965 Voting Rights Act put an end to literacy tests and assigned federal registrars to enroll voters. The impact of these laws was immediate. For example, in Selma, Alabama, one of the cities where civil rights were most strongly contested, on the day of enactment 381 African-Americans were registered to vote. That was more than the total number who had registered in the previous sixty-five years (Polenberg, 1980).

Women's Suffrage

For women, the legal right to vote was slow in coming. Woman activists began their struggle as early as the 1840s to achieve **suffrage**, the right to vote. Frustration over the denial of women's roles in making public policy decisions prompted women to organize to gain the right to vote. In 1848, Elizabeth Cady Stanton and other early reformers organized the first women's rights conference, the Seneca Falls Convention (Boulding, 1992). This meeting marked the official beginning of the women's suffrage movement in America.

The Civil War shifted reform activities to the abolition of slavery. Women's groups tried unsuccessfully to include sex in the protections of the Fourteenth and Fifteenth Amendments. Abolitionists were concerned that adding provisions for women's rights would complicate their efforts (V. Klein, 1984). Thus, women's rights groups, primarily the National Woman Suffrage Association formed by Susan B. Anthony and Elizabeth Cady Stanton, continued to organize and press for the right to vote without the support of other rights movements. The Nineteenth Amendment took decades to pass. It was first introduced in 1878, and reintroduced into every congressional session until 1920 (V. Klein, 1984). Like all women's rights issues, it sparked tremendous controversy and met with extreme resistance.

As we discussed in chapter 2, the Progressive Era came about in response to the social changes wrought by industrialization and urbanization at the turn of the century. Women were deeply affected by these changes. More women were in the labor force and were part of other social reform movements. It was the impact of World War I, however, that finally influenced the political acceptance of women's suffrage (Axinn & Levin, 1992). The role of women during the war effort made it clear that women were active participants in the nation's economic and political realms. Thus, in 1920 the Nineteenth Amendment to the Constitution was ratified: "The rights of citizens of the United States to vote shall not be denied or abridged by the United States or by any state on account of sex." This marked the culmination of a seventy-year struggle. Women's rights organizations, having fought for the right to vote for so long, lost momentum and for the most part remained relatively dormant for the next forty years.

Protection from Discrimination

The Civil War was the first time that the federal government intervened to protect people from discrimination based on race. While the Civil War may have helped to officially end slavery, however, it did not accomplish much in the way of protecting African-Americans from discrimination, harassment, and exclusion based on the color of their skin.

After the Civil War and until the 1960s, race relations were tainted by a sense of racial superiority on the part of whites (Polenberg, 1980). Discrimination on the basis of race covered both social and economic spheres. In the South, discrimination through segregation in all facets of life served to keep African-Americans and whites separate. The Jim Crow laws, state rules and regulations that enforced segregation, dominated in Southern states. "Jim Crow" was a minstrel-show character who portrayed blacks as childlike, irresponsible, and lazy; this was the image Southern whites wanted to perpetuate (Davis, 1991). They did so through many restrictions, including laws that barred African-Americans from many public facilities used by whites, prohibited African-Americans from sitting in the front seats of buses, and forced them to use restricted entrances to buildings. Public law was used to deny African-Americans the privileges that whites enjoyed. The Jim Crow system held, and federal intervention and protection from discrimination did not occur until almost one hundred years after the Civil War.

In the North, racial discrimination was less overt. African-Americans could register to vote, and public facilities were not segregated. There were two areas in which racial discrimination played a significant role, however: housing and employment (Polenberg, 1980). In Northern cities with sizable populations of African-Americans, neighborhoods were segregated by race and very few areas of employment were open to African-Americans. Decades after the Civil War, the living conditions of African-Americans in the United States were significantly lower than those of white Americans. Even the progressive reforms of the New Deal ignored issues of racial inequality. In America during the 1940s, groups considered racially different "worked at the hardest jobs, earned the least money, lived in the most wretched homes, and died most frequently of preventable diseases" (Polenberg, 1980, p. 30).

Following World War II, after African-Americans had actively participated in defending this country and worked at home in defense plants, awareness of the need for civil rights protections grew. Powerful black leaders such as the Reverends Martin Luther King, Jr., and Ralph Abernathy began their educational training during the postwar years at seminaries, and took advantage of rare opportunities to study in the North for their advanced degrees. The life and work of Dr. Martin Luther King, Jr., epitomizes the gradual and painful shift in race relations in this country. Taylor Branch (1988), in his book *Parting the Waters*, thoroughly documents the civil rights struggle through the experiences and work of Dr. Martin Luther King, Jr. Branch provides a history of the civil rights movement interwoven with events from the life of the man most notably involved in the movement, stating that "King's life is the best and most important metaphor for American history in the watershed postwar years" (Branch, 1980, p. xii).

Through civil disobedience and nonviolent efforts such as the Montgomery bus boycott and sit-ins at lunch counters, public awareness of the racial segregation of the South intensified. Public support for civil rights legislation grew as a result of the efforts of charismatic and visionary leaders such as Dr. King, growing political activism within the black community, increased media coverage, and backing from church groups. What further propelled the movement was a shift in the support of the courts. The Supreme Court, with changes in membership, began to broaden "the constitutional rights of citizens and, at the same time, to sanction governmental efforts to remove barriers to social equality" (Polenberg, 1980, p. 177). Through court decisions, public universities were integrated and military forces were used to ensure the right of African-American students to attend. The mood in the country had shifted. Propelled in part by the public's growing sense of civil fairness and in part by their fear of what might happen if civil rights protections were not extended, legislators enacted public policy to protect the civil rights of all citizens regardless of race.

In 1964, legislation drafted by the Kennedy administration and passed under Johnson's presidency guaranteed federal protection for the civil rights of African-Americans. The Civil Rights Act of 1964 (P.L. 88–352) prohibited racial, sexual, or ethnic discrimination in employment (Axinn & Levin, 1992). The law required desegregation of public facilities and prohibited institutions that received federal funds from discriminating in the hiring of employees. This legislation also created the Equal Employment Opportunity Commission (EEOC), charged with implementation and enforcement of the act (Jansson, 1997).

Changes took place gradually as the new policies were enforced. Resistance was great, as this represented a major social shift in American culture. What was important for members of different racial groups was that finally there were public laws on record protecting them from discrimination.

Affirmative Action

One effect of the civil rights movement was the development of policies supporting affirmative action. **Affirmative action** involves efforts to correct historical imbalances in opportunities due to race and sex. These policies have recently been drawing a tremendous amount of public attention and serious reconsideration.

The provisions of the Civil Rights Act prohibited discrimination in hiring based on race, gender, national origin, or religion, and also stated that hiring should not involve preferential treatment to equalize prior existing imbalances. As a public policy, affirmative action grew out of federal regulations, presidential executive orders, and the courts, not directly from the Civil Rights Act of 1964. Thus, over the next fifteen years, affirmative action primarily evolved out of federal regulations attached to federal contracts.

Affirmative action regulations called for efforts to equalize race and sex imbalances through hiring practices. For example, in 1968, the Labor Department required affirmative action plans as a condition of receiving a federal contract. The Supreme Court indirectly supported this practice in 1971 by prohibiting labor practices that maintained the status quo of racial imbalances. By 1972, federal regulations required colleges and universities to institute affirmative action plans (Polenberg, 1980). Affirmative action plans require proof of efforts to ensure that qualified people of color and women are "included in any pool of applicants and are represented fairly in the work force, in schools, and in the awarding of government contracts" (National Organization for Women, 1996).

The questions of whether affirmative action policies work and whether they are fair gained public attention during the mid-1990s. In many areas of employment, affirmative action policies seem to have made a difference. From 1970 to 1990, the number of African-American police officers increased almost threefold, while African-American representation in fire departments rose from 2.5% to 11.5% (Taylor, 1995). In many other areas of employment, however, gains have been minimal.

Preferential treatment and quotas have drawn unfavorable public attention to affirmative action. As designed, affirmative action policies are not to set quotas, but rather are meant to require institutions

> to develop plans enabling them to go beyond business as usual and search for qualified people in places where they did not ordinarily conduct their searches or their business.... The idea of affirmative action is *not* to force people into positions for which they are unqualified but to encourage institutions to develop realistic criteria for the enterprise at hand and then to find a reasonably diverse mix of people qualified to be engaged in it (Wilkins, 1995, p. 3).

Although this definition seems clear, the interpretation of affirmative action has varied greatly, While federal regulations developed during the 1970s expanded the use of affirmative action, conflicts arose during the next decade. Many employers argued that qualified female and minority candidates did not exist.

For example, Harvard Law School made this argument in 1990. In response to demands that the law school practice diversity and hire an African-American woman, the official response was that in order to do so the school would have to, in the words of the associate dean, "lower its standards" (Williams, 1991). It seems very difficult to believe that a school such as Harvard University did not have the resources, contacts, or know-how to find and recruit one qualified African-American woman to teach in its law school. The assertion that there were absolutely no African-American women qualified to take such a role illustrates precisely the attitude that makes affirmative action policies necessary.

While the Supreme Court upheld affirmative action policies into the 1980s, by 1989 that position had changed. With a more conservative court, a number of decisions ruled against the use of affirmative action to remedy past racial imbalances and discrimination (Axinn & Levin, 1992). In response to these restrictions, Congress passed the Civil Rights Act of 1991. The Act reaffirmed the right of employees to bring suits alleging discrimination against employers (Jansson, 1997).

Public sentiment of the 1990s reflects criticism of affirmative action. States have passed laws to minimize the impact of affirmative action. For example, in 1996 the state of California passed legislation that no longer requires affirmative action in state government programs. Immediately following the election, affirmative action supporters filed suit in federal court and won a temporary restraining order so that the law could not take effect. It remains to be seen what will be the impact of such reversals in public policies, how the courts will respond, and whether other states and the federal government will follow. While there have been implementation problems with affirmative action, the principles of protecting civil rights and recognizing past imbalances due to race and sex remain important issues that will require continued attention by policy-makers and social reformers.

Women's Rights

As we discussed earlier in the chapter, the major accomplishment toward expansion of rights for women was passage of the right to vote in 1920. Since that time, there have been numerous other policy debates regarding the civil rights of women.

The Equal Rights Amendment.   The most frequently mentioned struggle for women's rights was the fight to pass the Equal Rights Amendment (ERA). This constitutional amendment was written to extend civil rights protections for women and to prohibit discrimination based on sex.

Extending the civil rights coverage of the Constitution is not a new issue. Suffragists as far back as the mid-1800s had proposed an equal rights amendment. As already discussed, efforts to include women's rights as part of the Fourteenth Amendment met with failure. Even securing the right to vote did not provide enough public policy momentum to secure an equal rights amendment. Four decades later, however, the reform atmosphere of the 1960s and women's growing involvement in political movements ignited another wave of interest in an equal rights amendment. In 1972, after forty-nine years of attempts, Congress passed the ERA by an overwhelming margin (E. Klein, 1984). Before an amendment to the Constitution can become law, however, it must be ratified by a majority of state legislators in three-fourths of all the states. During the first year, ratification was secured in twenty-two states. Through legislative extension, the ERA had a ten-year limit on securing those ratifications. The obstacle in passing the ERA was in getting state legislators in the remaining states to agree to support the amendment.

Unfortunately, time, resources, and negative publicity efforts prevailed. While to supporters the ERA simply represented an extension to women of the rights that all men and racial groups already possessed, it represented to opponents a radical change in the social structure of America. In the end, although a majority of Americans supported the ERA, there were not enough state legislators willing to vote for it (Freeman, 1984). In 1982, at the end of the deadline, the ERA was still three states short of the thirty-eight needed for ratification (E. Klein, 1984).

The defeat of the ERA may have been caused in part by a shift in political sentiment. The mood of the nation with regard to civil rights and public responsibility had shifted from the 1970s to the 1980s, leading to reduced legislative support for the ERA. The amendment was also a victim of the rise in political organization of anti-ERA groups, mobilization of Christian fundamentalist groups, and differing priorities among women's groups (Mansbridge, 1990).

Animosity toward the ERA and women's rights groups continues. In his campaign for the election of a Republican president in 1992, Pat Robertson, a leader of the Christian Coalition, warned that the ERA was part of a "feminist agenda" that represented "a socialist, anti-family political movement that encourages women to leave their husbands, kill their children, practice witchcraft, destroy capitalism, and become lesbians" (Wicker, 1992, p. E3). Although the defeat of the ERA took a tremendous toll on the women's movement and continues to incite strong responses such as Robertson's, numerous women's groups gained valuable political experience that has helped them continue to advocate for public policies promoting the civil rights of women.

Equality in Education: Title IX.   Enactment of the right to vote and protection from discrimination in employment through the Civil Rights Act of 1964 were significant gains for women. Nevertheless, the American political system has provided limited legislative support for the enactment of policies designed to ensure *equality* based on gender. Although related, there is a difference between **nondiscrimination** and **equality**. People can be protected from discrimination but still lack equality. For example, if a school system guarantees nondiscrimination, it can guarantee schools for all children by creating separate schools for boys and girls. The schools may not be similar or equivalent. On the other hand, equality requires that those schools provide equivalent services and resources. Thus, equal rights goes further than protection from discrimination.

A significant piece of legislation that did support gender equity was Title IX of the Education Amendment to the Civil Rights Act, passed in 1972. The legislation stated that:

> No person in the United States shall, on the basis of sex, be excluded from participation in, be denied the benefits of, or be subjected to discrimination under any educational program or activity receiving federal financial assistance.

The implementation and enforcement of Title IX has been fraught with problems since passage. The greatest resistance to implementation of the policy has centered around the provisions related to academic institutions and athletics. Those provisions:

> which sought equalization of sport opportunity and rewards...engendered the most extreme, organized, and concerted lobbying pro and con, generated the most impassioned pleas, and garnered the most extraordinary claims about the benefits or pending disasters that will befall society if the legislative mandates are implemented (Boutilier & SanGiovanni, 1983, p. 171).

Interpretation of the legislation meant that sports programs at elementary and secondary schools and universities, which had traditionally committed the vast majority of resources to sports programs for male students, would now be required to equally support programs for female students. Supporters fought for even greater commitment, and detractors complained that such equality would be impossible to achieve and that attempting to do so would ultimately dilute the athletic accomplishments and reputations already made by institutions.

Title IX has had a significant impact on the lives of girls and women. Between 1972 and 1988, the number of high school girls who participated in athletics increased from 300,000 to 1.8 million. According to the National Association of Girls and Women in Sports, prior to passage of Title IX only 2% of college athletic budgets were committed to women's sports. By 1988, 16% of college athletic budgets were earmarked for women's sports. Finally, athletic scholarships for women increased from nonexistent in 1972 to more than over 10,000 by 1988 (Hogan, 1988). In 1984, however, the scope of the legislation was significantly narrowed through the Supreme Court ruling in favor of Grove City College (*Grove City College v. Bell*). The court decision stated that Title IX covers only specific programs in institutions of education. This meant that if a specific program did not directly receive federal funds, it was not covered by Title IX protections (Terpstra, 1984). Institutions were able to demonstrate that not all programs, such as athletics, benefited directly from federal funds. Thus, these programs were not under Title IX. This court decision had ramifications for other civil rights laws as well.

In 1988, the tide turned. Congress overrode President Reagan's veto and passed the Civil Rights Restoration Act. The Act restored the original intent of Title IX and protected other civil rights laws from dilution (Congressional Quarterly, 1988). The 1988 legislation defined "program" or "activity" to include an entire institution that received federal funds and thus brought back the original intent of Title IX. The rocky history of Title IX demonstrates the difficulty in protecting and expanding rights that promote gender equality. It also demonstrates the difficulty of protecting the positive impact of such civil rights legislation. For example, the 1996 Summer Olympics showcased numerous American women who were the first generation to have grown up under Title IX. For these women, equal rights to compete athletically seem normal (Kuttner, 1996).

The Abortion Controversy.   Another right which has sparked tremendous public debate is the issue of abortion and who has the right to control the use of it by women. The controversy surrounding the right of a pregnant woman to choose whether or not to have an abortion is still unresolved. The controversy is complex. For those who are "pro-choice" (who believe a woman should be allowed to make her own decision) access to legal abortions is a civil right that should be protected by law. For those who are opposed to legal abortion, it is viewed as a moral issue of preserving life by protecting the fetus from abortion. Susan Faludi (1991) in her comprehensive analysis of the state of women's issues in America, challenged these differences. She argued that at issue was not the rate of abortions, which in fact had decreased during the 1980s, nor was it "protection of the unborn." Rather, for the antiabortion movement, whose leaders were predominantly young men:

> The real change was women's new ability to regulate their fertility without danger or fear—a new freedom that in turn had contributed to dramatic changes not in the abortion rate but in female sexual behavior and attitudes.... Women also became far more independent in their decisions about when to have chil-

dren, under what marital circumstances, and when to stop…to many men in the antiabortion movement, the speed with which women embraced sexual and reproductive freedom could be frightening…this revolution in female behavior had invaded their most intimate domain (pp. 403–404).

The social upheaval implied by the right of women to choose whether or not to have an abortion is a major component of the conflict. For many people, legal abortion represents a threat to the traditional family. It is believed to lead to pre-marital sex, divorce, and use of contraceptives, and it touches on a deep social anxiety of what might be the consequences if women are free to control when and if they choose biological motherhood (Gelb & Palley, 1987). These social concerns make the issue of legalized abortions a very heated and controversial political and social welfare issue.

Abortions were legal in America and did not take on illegal status until the mid-1800s. As women's rights groups emerged and gained recognition, so too did the battle over the right to an abortion (Faludi, 1991). For almost one hundred years, abortions were illegal and difficult to obtain, but in 1973, the Supreme Court decision in *Roe v. Wade* stated that a woman's right to privacy permitted her to make the choice whether or not to have an abortion, that states could only intervene during the second trimester to ensure the mother's health, and that abortions could only be prohibited after the sixth month of pregnancy (Biskupic, 1993).

As was true during the previous century, antiabortion movements arose in response to the growth in women's rights organizations. While Congress has been hesitant to vote directly on the legality of abortion, it has restricted it through legislation that limits the use of federal dollars to pay for abortions. The Supreme Court, which has become more conservative since *Roe v. Wade*, has also put limitations on access and availability. In spite of restrictions that vary from state to state, however, abortions are still legal in this country.

Today, the anger surrounding the right to a legal abortion has escalated to dangerous levels. Hundreds of bombings and attacks on clinics have been occurring at alarming rates. In 1990, 100 violent incidents were reported, and in 1992 that number had jumped to 667 (Boodman, 1993). In Florida, in 1993, a member of an antiabortion group shot and killed a clinic doctor, and in 1994 clinic workers were killed by a protester in Boston. According to National Abortion Federation statistics, in 1994 incidents of disruption and violence against abortion providers totaled 1,802, including 4 murders, 8 attempted murders, 3 bombings, 42 incidents of vandalism, and 59 bomb threats (National Abortion Federation, 1995). These escalations and murders prompted passage of the Freedom of Access to Clinic Entrances Act (FACE) in 1994, which limits the extent of protesting antiabortionists can engage in at abortion clinics. Recent data reveal that the FACE Act has been a very effective piece of federal social welfare policy. In 1996, the number of violent incidents against clinics had dropped to less than 400 compared to more than 1,800 during the preceding year (Pear, 1996).

The issue of a woman's right to have an abortion is far from settled. Voters have mixed feelings, and politicians are reluctant to deal with the issue directly. Opponents of abortion have been working for more than twenty years to reverse *Roe v. Wade*. Major women's rights organizations have been supporting legal abortion for more than a century. It is likely that this dispute will continue for years to come.

The area of women's rights seems to be one of the most controversial of civil rights issues. It seems to cut across race, class, and religious boundaries, perhaps because it touches on values and beliefs that are integral to so many parts of our lives. The rights of women affect our families, homes, workplaces, and every sphere of our personal lives. Because of the highly personal nature of sex roles and gender identities, it would seem that issues that have been highly politicized and unresolved for 150 years, such as abortion and equal rights, will continue to be major public policy concerns.

The Rights of People with Disabilities

How society defines disability and how many people fit that definition are subject to great debate. Estimates of how many people live with disabilities in this country range from 25 million to 120 million, depending on the source. The reason the estimates are so varied is because there is a lack of consensus among researchers, advocates, and people with disabilities, about what exactly is a disability (LaPlante, 1991). Without an agreed-upon definition and understanding of what it means to have a disability, it becomes difficult to protect the civil rights of people with disabilities. In spite of this difficulty, the need for protection of rights is very important.

Persons with disabilities face numerous social and economic barriers to full participation in our society. While 25% of all American households earn less than $15,000 per year, twice as many households of people with disabilities earn less than $15,000 per year (West, 1991). Furthermore, while participation in the labor force among the general population increased by 10% from 1970 to 1990, it decreased by 4% among people with disabilities (Yellin, 1991).

As many as 66% of all working-age Americans with disabilities are unemployed (Kirkpatrick, 1994). The major reasons for this exclusion are employers' attitudes, inaccessible workplaces, and inadequate levels of education. Public policy to address these inequities in employment and access for people with disabilities took a long time in coming.

The Americans with Disabilities Act of 1990 (ADA) (P.L. 101–336) was the first significant piece of legislation providing civil rights protection for people with disabilities. The Act prohibits discrimination against people with disabilities in the areas of employment, public accommodations, transportation, and public services. The law includes the mandate that work places and public facilities provide "reasonable accommodation" for people with disabilities. In addition, all new buildings that provide public services must be wheelchair accessible (Perritt, 1990).

The impact of the ADA is significant. For example, reasonable accommodation in the workplace may mean changing existing facilities to be readily accessible and usable by people with disabilities; restructuring of jobs; modifying people's work schedules; modifying equipment; altering training techniques and materials; and/or providing interpreters or other support personnel (Orlin, 1995). The provisions of the ADA can remove long-standing barriers to many occupations for people with disabilities. A policy analysis of the ADA is outlined in Figure 9.1.

Gay and Lesbian Rights

Civil rights protections by the federal government cover race, gender, ethnicity, religion, and ability, yet one group that has actively campaigned for civil rights legislation without success is the gay and lesbian community. Sexual orientation—whether people define themselves as homosexual, heterosexual, or bisexual—is far from accepted as a right to be protected. In large part this results from disagreement over whether homosexuality is a legitimate part of a person's identity. For many people, homosexuality cannot be accepted due to personal values. While this belief is a personal right, is it sufficient reason to deny gays and lesbians federal protection from discrimination?

For the vast majority of gays and lesbians in America, discrimination is a significant part of their daily lives. Fear of revealing one's sexual orientation is based on the life experiences of most gays and lesbians. In a national study covering eight U.S. cities, 94% of the gay men and lesbians surveyed reported having experienced some type of victimization related to their sexual orientation. In addition, almost two-thirds said they feared for their safety (Berrill, 1990).

Lack of civil rights protections means that if an employer discovers that an employee is gay, the employer can fire the worker and the employee has no legal recourse. If a landlord refuses to rent an apartment to a gay person, or a bank refuses to give a mortgage to buy a house, again the person is not protected. On April 25, 1993, in spite of intimidation and lack of protection from job loss or refusal for housing, hundreds of thousands of gay men, lesbians, and civil rights supporters marched on Washington, D.C., for gay civil rights. The march provided a sense of public legitimacy and gave a face to gay America (Berke, 1993). While it was not the first of such marches, it was the largest, and galvanized a political push for Congress and the president to respond.

Efforts in 1993 centered on passing legislation that would prohibit the military from asking about a person's sexual orientation. While this was a far cry from full civil rights, it was regarded as an entry point from which to gain momentum and push for full civil rights. The legislative effort failed, and advocates focused on presidential intervention. While President Clinton promised to change the regulations as part of an Executive Order, the Congress prevailed and blocked the change.

Figure 9.1

Social Welfare Policy Analysis Model: Americans with Disabilities Act of 1990

Social Issue

- Lack of access and opportunities for people with disabilities
- Employment discrimination against people with disabilities

Goal

- Eliminate discrimination against people with disabilities
- Ensure equality of opportunity and access
- Increase employment opportunities for people with disabilities

Policy or Legislation

- Americans with Disabilities Act of 1990 (P.L. 101–336)

Implementation

- Federal mandate to eliminate discrimination in places of lodging; facilities for general public gathering; public transportation; service and social services establishments
- Federal mandate to eliminate discrimination in the workplace through reasonable accommodation
- Enforcement through federal agencies
- Penalties for lack of compliance

Affected Populations

- People with disabilities
- Public and private establishments where people gather
- Employers

Actual Impact

- Greater access to public resources and establishments
- Accessibility planning by developers of new facilities
- Costs for redesigning existing facilities
- Decreased employment discrimination

Intended Impact

- Ensure equality of opportunity and access
- Prevent workplace discrimination and create access to employment opportunities

Gay rights advocates shifted their strategy and moved to push for civil rights protections in the area of employment. In 1994, the Employment Non-Discrimination Act was introduced in Congress. It was reintroduced during the next Congressional Session and voted on by the Senate in the closing months of 1996. The bill would prohibit employers, employment agencies, and labor unions from using an individual's sexual orientation as the basis for employment decisions, including hiring, firing, promotion, or compensation, and it would also protect people from discrimination based on sexual orientation (Human Rights Campaign Fund, 1994). The bill was defeated by a narrow margin in the 1996 Senate vote, but advocates planned to reintroduce the policy in the next session.

With a Republican majority in the Congress after the 1994 election, passage of gay civil rights legislation of any form seemed unlikely. For example, as a response to possible state legislation that might legalize gay marriages in Hawaii, the Congress passed the Defense of Marriage Act of 1996. This law does not actually ban gay marriages; rather, it permits states to not recognize as legal such action by another state (Schmitt, 1996). There are questions about whether this legislation is constitutional, and in the meantime the Hawaii courts have upheld the right of gay couples to marry (Goldberg, 1996). The two congressional votes in 1996 and the judicial struggles in Hawaii demonstrate the power of social values in shaping public policies.

Gay rights advocates, finding the federal government unresponsive, have been broadening their focus and using grassroots organizing, local changes, and court cases to further their fight for civil rights protections. For example, in 1996 the Supreme Court in *Romer v. Evans* upheld the rights of gays and lesbians to the "equal protection under the law" provisions of the Fourteenth Amendment. The state of Colorado had passed legislation that would have prohibited cities and localities from passing anti-discrimination protection laws for gays and lesbians. The Supreme Court ruled that this prohibition was unconstitutional. Some states and local governments have passed anti-discrimination policies that outlaw discrimination based on sexual orientation, and many large corporations have followed suit in the workplace. These actions represent progress toward ending discrimination based on sexual orientation, but there is still more to be done to ensure equality.

American Indians and Civil Rights

Recognition of the rights of American Indians was slow in coming to this country. The earliest European settlers were insensitive at best, and hostile at worst, to the rights and needs of the peoples who were already living in North America. The history of protected rights for American Indians is replete with promises that were never kept and treaties that were deliberately broken. It is a history that spans more than 500 years.

Traditionally, the American Indian populations lived under different cultural rules and had very different ways of life compared to the white settlers. These ways of life were deemed inferior by white, European settlers. Race played a significant role in this viewpoint, because the superiority of white culture was already assumed based on relationships with other populations, particularly African slaves. The key to understanding the poor treatment of American Indians by whites is knowledge of the cultural differences.

American Indian tribes lived communally and regarded the land as belonging to all, people and animals alike. The idea of private ownership of land was foreign. White settlers, ignoring or misunderstanding these beliefs, assumed the superiority of their own system of land ownership and disdained the communality of tribal life. These differences, coupled with driving colonial forces demanding that early settlers stake out land on behalf of their home country, created irreconcilable differences between whites and American Indians. The colonists had come to America to stay, and they "had little use for Indians. The Indians were 'savages' (being hunters) and 'devil-worshippers' (not being Christians); they were nuisances who blocked the growth of this new English-speaking colonial world" (Nabokov, 1992, p. 20). Ethnocentric and racist attitudes dominated relations between settlers and American Indians, and the consequences of these feelings remain today.

Prior to the widespread development of farms and ranches in the West, large-scale public policies concerning American Indians did not exist. Early settlers drove tribes westward, and local treaties were used to contain tribes. Most public policies were handled through the Bureau of Indian Affairs, which dates back to 1824. The Bureau was, and still is, under the Department of the Interior and was created to provide a link between the federal government and American Indian tribes. The early role of the Bureau was to assist in containment and control of tribes.

Accelerated westward expansion made it necessary for white settlers to gain lands occupied by American Indians. These lands had already been promised to American Indian tribes in exchange for lands in the East. During the 1870s, the courts and an organized movement arose to contain American Indian tribes and control tribal ownership of land. In 1886, the Supreme Court ruled that American Indian tribes were "wards of the nation" dependent upon the United States (Nabokov, 1992). This clearly denied American Indians sovereign rights and citizenship. In 1887, Congress enacted the Dawes Act, which limited to 160 acres the amount of land each head of an Indian family could receive and pushed Indians to live in smaller and smaller regions (Jansson, 1997). These two pieces of public policy effectively contained and controlled all aspects of American Indian life.

Civil rights protection for American Indians was largely ignored by makers of public policy. Outside of granting citizenship in 1924 as a result of American Indians' military service in World War I, the periods of social reform such as the Progressive Era and the New Deal achieved little in the way of guaranteeing rights for American Indians. The Dawes Act had legalized ways for whites to acquire Indian land, and from 1887 to 1934, two-thirds of American Indian land was taken away (Nabokov, 1992).

Although American Indians fought in World War II, in many states they still could not vote. Their rights to own property were curtailed, and the Bureau of Indian Affairs handled all their economic, social, and educational affairs. The spirit of self-determination and rights for American Indians blossomed with the social reforms of the 1960s. Demonstrations including land takeovers, road blocks, and armed defense brought to light the anger and resentment of the majority of American Indians. The most publicized of such events was the 1973 armed takeover of the town of Wounded Knee, South Dakota, by the American Indian Movement (AIM) (Nabokov, 1992). Using the media coverage and events that followed to publicize the historical treatment of American Indians, the movement was able to tap into the social reform mood of the country.

The current status of American Indian rights is twofold. While all American Indians are United States citizens who can vote and own land, economic and social rights are still lacking. Poverty statistics on American Indians are not regularly published by the Bureau of the Census, but local censuses done on reservations often find the majority of residents below the poverty line. Tribal governments struggle to maintain sovereignty, while also trying to find ways of integrating into the dominant American economic culture. One of the most controversial issues today is gambling enterprises on Indian reservations. Sovereign rule allows tribal governments to open their land to gambling, but many worry that the social costs ultimately will be enormous. Perhaps the difficulty in these decisions rests with the fact that the American Indian control of social and economic decisions today was attained only after the abundant land and natural resources that were once available to American Indians had been taken away.

Attitudes Toward Immigration

Another civil rights issue that has gained public attention is the rights of immigrants. Immigration has a long history in this country, with the vast majority of Americans tracing their roots to earlier generations of immigrants. At times in our history, we have glorified the idea of immigrants coming to this country with nothing and prospering. At other times in history we have regarded immigrants as taking jobs away from legal citizens and draining public social welfare services. Recent debate has centered around the latter perception, but research suggests a different picture:

> In contrast to public perception, immigrants do not increase unemployment by taking jobs held by Americans, nor do they drain increasingly scarce public revenues through [social] welfare programs. Quite the contrary—the evidence demonstrates that immigrants create more jobs than they take, and they contribute more in taxes than they consume in social program benefits (Stoesz, 1996, p. 161).

During the 1990s, in states with significant numbers of recent immigrants, particularly poor immigrants, negative public attitudes have come to the forefront. The focus of that negative attention has been on the legal status of immigrants. Poor economic conditions in Mexico and military hostilities in Central America during the 1980s and 1990s brought thousands of legal and illegal immigrants to this country. Large numbers of these immigrants settled in border states such as California and Texas. Anti-immigrant sentiments have grown in these regions, and states have reacted through the policy arena. In an effort to discourage immigrants from coming to this country, particularly illegal immigrants from Mexico and Central America, California voters in 1995 passed Proposition 187, which terminated public social services to illegal immigrants living in California. The services terminated included schooling for children, food assistance, and medical care. The legislation was immediately challenged through the court system. While the issue is being debated through the courts, the governor of California signed an executive order to cut off state services to illegal immigrants (Golden, 1996).

A federal law was also passed that limits public social welfare services for legal and illegal immigrants. The Personal Responsibility and Work Opportunity Reconciliation Act of 1996 bans legal immigrants from receiving food stamps and Supplemental Security Income (SSI), and states have the option of withholding Medicaid and Temporary Assistance for Needy Families (TANF) until they receive citizenship. Illegal immigrants are completely banned from these programs.

Conflicting public attitudes toward immigrants reflect the contradictions between nativist tradition, which emphasizes "pure" Americans, and the reality that this is a country of people whose families came here from elsewhere. Thus, issues involving immigration are likely to receive ongoing attention in social welfare policy debates.

Final Thoughts on Civil Rights

Until the 1960s, federal involvement was minimal in securing the rights of different population groups. State and local control dominated the political, social, and legal arenas. Local actions such as poll taxes were able to override the impact of federal efforts to provide voting rights for people, but political shifts that occurred during the 1960s changed the structure of government.

Two significant trends emerged during the 1960s (Melnick, 1994): (1) expansion of federal responsibilities for public well-being, and (2) increasing fragmentation of power at the national level. During the 1960s and 1970s, federal involvement in protection of people's civil and economic rights expanded greatly. The federal government took the leading role in securing civil rights for African-Americans, began the War on Poverty, created new social welfare programs such as Medicare and Medicaid, expanded social insurance coverage and benefits, and took leadership roles in promoting gender equality and civil rights for people with disabilities.

At the same time that the federal role expanded, the power of federal agencies became more fragmented. The strength of political parties lessened, interest groups proliferated, presidents became less powerful, and Congress became more divided. To achieve the lofty goals of so many programs and policies aimed at opening opportunities for people, more and more federal agencies had to be created and developed.

The expansion of the federal role and the fragmentation of federal control were accompanied by an increase in federal spending for social welfare services. The increased spending by the federal government allowed for greater federal control. Control was developed through the creation of federal regulations and stipulations that accompanied the receipt and use of federal moneys. One of the outgrowths of this increased control was federal influence in the expansion of civil rights and public opportunities.

Affirmative action is an example of how federal government funding of state and local programs can influence the course of social welfare policy and civil rights. In order for any public or private organization to receive federal funds, each agency must have in place a policy of nondiscrimination and make concerted efforts at giving access to opportunities for groups who have historically been disadvantaged. Making efforts to open opportunities to groups who have historically been outside is the intent of affirmative action. Because the federal government provides funds contingent upon these efforts, organizations are forced to either follow the provisions or forfeit federal funding.

While the expansion of federal legislation and enforcement has had the greatest impact on advancing civil rights in America, changes in the federal role could prove to diminish those protections. The goals of the 104th Congress during 1995 and 1996 were to remove federal government regulation from state and private concerns. Efforts to give states more control and fewer federal restrictions could have the effect of lessening the protection of civil rights. If each state is free to decide whether or not to protect people's rights, we could see a return to the conditions that originally brought the federal government into the role of enforcer of civil rights. Historically, when left to their own devices, states have not acted as champions of civil rights. Voting rights, protection from discrimination and racism, access to legal abortions, affirmative action, and other personal rights were attained only through federal intervention. If there really is a turning back to state rule, it may include a turning back of civil rights.

Key Concepts

civil rights

institutional racism

affirmative action

equality

Bill of Rights

suffrage

nondiscrimination

Exercises

1. Divide into small groups, with each group selecting a national civil rights organization, such as the NAACP, NOW, the Anti-Defamation League, or Human Rights Campaign. Find out if the group has a local chapter. Visit the local office and ask for materials describing the group's mission and current efforts. Share the information in class. If there are no local offices of civil rights groups, consult the Internet for information.

2. Identify one social movement and find a book in which the author describes events from a first-hand perspective. Examples include *Parting the Waters* by Taylor Branch, which focuses on the civil rights movement of the 1960s; *Stonewall* by Martin Duberman, which explores the gay rights movement; and *No Pity* by Joseph Shapiro, which discusses the fight for rights for people with disabilities. What can we learn from reading an experiential account of fighting for civil rights? What did you learn?

References

Axinn, J., & Levin, H. (1992). *Social welfare: A history of the American response to need.* (2nd ed.). New York: Longman.

Berke, R.L. (1993, April 26). Crossroad for gay rights. *New York Times*, pp. A1, B8.

Berrill, K.T. (1990). Anti-gay violence and victimization in the United States. *Journal of Interpersonal Violence, 5* (3), 274–294.

Biskupic, J. (1993). Argument without end. *The Washington Post National Weekly Edition, 10* (14), 10–11.

Boodman, S.G. (1993). Bringing abortion home. *The Washington Post National Weekly Edition, 10* (25), 6–7.

Boulding, E. (1992). *The underside of history* (Vol. 2). Newbury Park, CA: Sage Publications.

Boutilier, M., & SanGiovanni, L. (1983). *The sporting woman.* Champaign, IL: Human Kinetics Publishers.

Branch, T. (1988). *Parting the waters: America in the King years, 1954–63.* New York: Simon & Schuster.

Congressional Quarterly. (1988). Grove City bill enacted over Reagan's veto. *CQ Almanac, 44,* 63–68. Washington, DC: Author.

Davis, F.J. (1991). *How Is Black?* University Park, PA: Pennsylvania State University Press.

Dye, T.R. (1992). *Understanding public policy* (7th ed.). Englewood Cliffs, NJ: Prentice Hall.

Faludi, S. (1991). *Backlash: The undeclared war against American women.* New York: Crown Publishers.

Freeman, J. (1984). The women's liberation movement: Its origins, structure, activities, and ideas. In Freeman, J. (ed.), *Women: A feminist perspective* (3rd ed.) (pp. 543–556). Palo Alto, CA: Mayfield.

Gelb, J., & Palley, M.L. (1987). *Women and public policies.* Princeton, NJ: Princeton University Press.

Goldberg, C. (1996, December 4). Judge in Hawaii says the state cannot prohibit gay marriage. *The New York Times*, pp. A1, A19.

Golden, T. (1996, August 28). California governor acts to end state aid for illegal immigrants. *The New York Times*, p. A1.

Hogan, C.L. (1988, February 14). The eroding of Title IX. *Chicago Tribune*, section 6, p. 4.

Human Rights Campaign Fund. (1994, summer). Employment Non-Discrimination Act of 1994 introduced in house and Senate. *Momentum*, p. 1.

Jacobson, G.C. (1987). *The politics of congressional elections* (2nd ed.). Boston: Little, Brown.

Jansson, B.S. (1997). *The reluctant welfare state* (3rd ed.). Pacific Grove, CA: Brooks/Cole.

Kirkpatrick, P. (1994). Triple jeopardy: Disability, race and poverty in America. *Poverty & Race*, 3 (3), 1–3.

Klein, E. (1984). *Gender politics*. Cambridge, MA: Harvard University Press.

Klein, V. (1984). The historical background. In Freeman, J. (ed.), *Women: A feminist perspective* (3rd ed.) (pp. 519–532). Palo Alto, CA: Mayfield.

Kuttner, R. (1996). Fair play for female athletes. *The Washington Post National Weekly Edition*, 13 (14), 5.

LaPlante, M.P. (1991). The demographics of disability. In West, J. (ed.), *The Americans with Disabilities Act* (pp. 55–77). New York: Milbank Memorial Fund.

Mansbridge, J.J. (1990). Organizing for the ERA: Cracks in the facade of unity. In Tilly, L.A., & Gurin, P. (eds.), *Women, politics, and change*. New York: Russell Sage Foundation.

Melnick, R. S. (1994). *Between the lines: Interpreting welfare rights*. Washington, DC: Brookings Institution.

Nabokov, P. (ed.). (1992). *Native American testimony: A chronicle of Indian-white relations from prophecy to the present, 1492–1992*. New York: Penguin Books.

National Abortion Federation. (1995). *Incidents of disruption and violence against abortion providers fact sheet*. Washington, DC: Author.

National Organization for Women. (1996). *The NOW fact sheet on affirmative action*. Washington, DC: Author.

Oleszek, W.J. (1989). *Congressional procedures and the policy process* (3rd ed.). Washington, DC: Congressional Quarterly, Inc.

Orlin, M. (1995). The Americans with Disabilities Act: Implications for social services. *Social Work*, 40 (2), 233–239.

Pear, R. (1996, September 24). Violent protests at abortion clinics have declined, and new federal law is credited. *The New York Times*, p. A13.

Perritt, H.H. (1990). *Americans with Disabilities Act handbook*. New York: Wiley.

Polenberg, R. (1980). *One nation divisible: Class, race, and ethnicity in the United States since 1938*. New York: Penguin.

Schmitt, E. (1996, September 11). Senators reject gay marriage bill and job-bias ban. *The New York Times*, pp. A1, A11.

Stoesz, D. (1996). *Small change: Domestic policy under the Clinton presidency*. White Plains, NY: Longman.

Taylor, W.L. (1995). Affirmative action: The questions to be asked. *Poverty & Race*, 4 (3), 2–3.

Terpstra, J. (1984). Grove City: Dead end or detour? *Title IX Line*, 4 (3), 2–4.

West, J. (1991). The social and policy context of the act. In West, J. (ed.), *The Americans with Disabilities Act* (pp. 3–24). New York: Milbank Memorial Fund.

Wicker, T. (1992, August 30). The Democrats as the devil's disciples. *The New York Times*, p. E3.

Wilkins, R. (1995). Racism has its privileges. *Poverty & Race, 4* (3), 3–5.

Williams, A.J. (1991). *The alchemy of race and rights*. Cambridge, MA: Harvard University Press.

Yellin, E.H. (1991). The recent history and immediate future of employment among persons with disabilities. In West, J. (ed.), *The Americans with Disabilities Act* (pp. 129–149). New York: Milbank Memorial Fund.

J. Marshall/The Image Works

Chapter 10

Economics and Social Welfare Policy

Current social welfare policies and programs have been shaped both by social factors and by economic conditions. Social forces are central to the development of social welfare policy, but changes in the economic system have played a crucial role in influencing this country's public policy response. The history outlined in chapter 2 demonstrates numerous instances when economic change precipitated policy change. The most significant example was the impact of the Great Depression on the social welfare system of this nation: the Social Security Act was passed in response to the most significant economic downturn in our history. This legislation permanently altered the role of government in relation to individual economic well-being.

Although economic trends play a critical role in the development of social welfare policies, however, the link is often overlooked by those who provide direct human services. Social work and economics are often viewed as unrelated disciplines. Social workers tend to be unfamiliar with the subject of economics. The realm of economics seems to be technical and rigid to the social service provider who is trained in human behavior.

Economics can be described as "the science that deals with the production, distribution, and consumption of commodities" (*American Heritage Dictionary,* 1976). Economics is viewed as a science, while social work is more often considered an art:

> A rigorous intellectual approach associated with scientific thinking is resisted.... It [rigorous intellectual assessment] is perceived on the one hand as a threat to the uniqueness of the individual. On the other hand, since it seems cold and impersonal, it is perceived as a threat to the skill of the social worker, to the sensitivity and the artistic element that are regarded as so important in social work (Bartlett, 1970, p. 38).

The separation between social work and economics appears to be the difference between an art and a technical science, but this is not the only distinction. There are significant ideological differences between the two disciplines.

Ideological Differences Between Social Work and Economics

There are three fundamental ideological differences between social work and economics. The first is the emphasis placed on competition for resources. The foundation of economics is the competitive marketplace where those who have the most to offer can outbid all others. Social welfare services are designed to minimize the extreme effects of competitive distribution. The second difference is economists' emphasis on cost/benefit analysis. Economics is concerned with finding the least expensive way to produce the greatest results. The best ways to help people cope or adapt, and methods of producing environmental change, often are not the least expensive social welfare policy alternatives. The third difference rests upon economists' use of mathematical calculations and concrete criteria to explain social and human behaviors, while social workers more often use case studies and practice experience to guide analyses of behavior. These differences can lead to conflict between the ideologies of economics and social work.

Competitive Marketplace

Social workers tend to believe that economists are predominantly interested in finding the most efficient system of transfer for the marketplace (Page, 1977). Efficient transfer of resources minimizes social welfare outlays and stresses a competitive economic model. Those who possess sufficient means are able to acquire what they need, and conversely, those with minimal resources are left with very little. The byproducts of such competition are the economically deprived groups who lack the means to actively participate in the marketplace.

An unrestricted competitive marketplace may function economically from a theoretical standpoint, but in reality there are social repercussions. If all variables related to employment were relatively equal, such as educational opportunity and access to jobs, and if impediments such as racism, sexism, and other forms of discrimination were eliminated, then open competition would create a stable economy. Unfortunately, this is not the case.

> Structural unemployment, beyond the reach of macroeconomic demand policies, afflicts disproportionately certain vulnerable demographic groups, teenagers, young adults, minorities. Labor markets are very imperfectly competitive. The interests of unemployed outsiders are insufficiently represented... (Tobin, 1986, p. 30).

Cost/Benefit Analysis

An outgrowth of the competitive nature of the marketplace is the emphasis on comparing the cost of something with the benefits generated by the outcome. Marketplace success is achieved when what is produced is profitable over what was required to run the production process. This ideology can be contrary to social welfare services, where the outcome is often intangible or immeasurable. While we can count the dollars spent for a given program, what is the quantifiable dollar benefit of a nutrition program for infants, mental health services for a suicidal client, or literacy tutoring for an unemployed adult?

Furthermore, emphasizing cost versus benefit ignores social responsibility and conscience. Social work ideology stresses empowerment, self-determination, and advocacy, regardless of the potential for profitable return. Cost/benefit concerns can be blind to human needs. Weighing cost versus benefits is an aggregate measure that does not recognize the uniqueness of each person.

Charles Murray (1984) used the analysis of cost versus benefit in his argument against social welfare spending. Murray's point was that if the amount spent on anti-poverty measures over the past thirty years had been effective, then poverty would no longer exist today. Because poverty continues to exist, he concluded there is no reason to continue spending on social welfare services. While there are numerous fallacies to Murray's logic (as well as erroneous calculations), the issue here is that Murray looked at poverty as simply a matter of cost versus benefit. There is no acknowledgment of inequality of opportunity, discrimination, or the human experience of poverty anywhere in Murray's book. Murray also ignores the possibility that without spending on anti-poverty measures, poverty in this country might be worse.

Mathematical Calculations

Many aspects of economics are based on mathematical concepts and computations. The use of mathematics often seems intimidating and alien to human service providers. Furthermore, mathematical calculations cannot measure or quantify the uniqueness of each individual. Human variability is a key element for social work professionals and clients. In order to capture the uniqueness of individuals, social workers examine clients on a case-by-case basis. Details of a person's individual history and current social and emotional conditions are used to assess what is an appropriate intervention. This emphasis on the qualitative aspects of people's lives seems to conflict with the quantitative mathematical assessment techniques used by economists.

Regardless of the difficulties in quantifying social concerns, elected officials and policy analysts tend to regard such calculations as a stronger basis for making policy decisions. Consequently, social workers often find themselves arguing from the perspective of first-hand experience against large-scale data.

Key Economic Concepts

In spite of the ideological differences between economics and social work, economics are extremely important to the public policy debate. "Economic policy is the primary determinant of social policy and social policy outcomes" (Bellin & Miller, 1983). Because social welfare policy is interwoven with the economic structure of our society, social workers should have a working knowledge and understanding of economic phenomena. "Unless the relationship between economics and social work is strengthened, the ability of social work to influence social policy will tend to decrease" (Page, 1977, p. 49). The course of social welfare policy during the 1980s and 1990s seems to confirm this view. Before we can influence social welfare policy, we must understand economic policy. In the rest of this chapter, we will examine the key economic issues relevant to social welfare policy and discuss the relationship of economics to social well-being.

Role of the Marketplace

One of the key concepts of the economic marketplace is the balance between **supply and demand**. Products and services offered are supply, and the desire and ability to buy is demand. When there is a high demand, then the price of goods goes up. If the price goes up too high, then consumers have less means with which to buy and demand decreases. The supply stocks up, and prices are cut to encourage buying, and demand comes back. The reality of supply and demand is not as smooth as the theory. Time lags, fluctuating interest in the item or service, and competition between suppliers combine to create cycles of expansion and inflation alternating with recession and deflation (Burch, 1990).

For example, suppose automobile manufacturers develop a new vehicle, such as a minivan. People like the vehicle and want to buy it, but few are available. Because the demand is greater than the supply, there is a shortage. People are still interested in buying the vans, so the price goes up and creates inflation. Because the price is driven up by demand, not by an increase in the manufacturing expenses, profit increases. Other automobile companies see the interest and the profits, and they decide to also make minivans. Now the supply increases rapidly. The market expands while supply grows. Eventually, however, the number of people interested in buying minivans does not increase as greatly as the supply. In order to encourage customers to buy their minivans, manufacturers reduce prices and offer special incentives. This has the effect of deflation, lowering prices. The amount of profit falls. If manufacturers experience too much loss due to overproduction, some companies will lay off workers or shut down production. This can result in a recession. After a period of low production, there is a decrease in supply. Some people will still have the interest and means to buy, so demand will grow. With growth in demand, the cycle begins again.

This simplified example illustrates the cyclical nature of the marketplace. The existence of prolonged economic downturns, however, suggests that the cyclical, self-correcting nature of the economy is not adequate. The potential for negative outcomes was addressed by economist John Maynard Keynes during the 1920s. In order to control for these lapses in the cycle, Keynes advanced the idea that supply and demand could be influenced through government policies. "The crux of Keynes's message was that government spending might be an essential economic policy for a depressed capitalism trying to recover its vitality" (Heilbroner & Thurow, 1982, p. 31). The acceptance of Keynes's ideas following the Great Depression led to the direct involvement of government in the supply and demand economy.

One of the key ways for government to take a Keynesian approach is to provide money for those without employment to still purchase necessities. Thus, the Food Stamp Program, which allows people in poverty to continue to purchase food at local grocery stores, is not just an anti-poverty program but a stimulus to production. In fact, during arguments about cutting back food stamps under the 1995 policy plans of the Republican Contract with America, farmers and agricultural businesses argued against cutting back the Food Stamp Program. They pointed out that the billions of federal government dollars spent on food stamps indirectly helped agriculture by guaranteeing food purchases no matter how poor people were.

The debate as to the optimal extent of government involvement in the economy is at the center of much of today's social welfare policy debate. The two sides of the argument can be summarized as follows (Moroney, 1991): The first holds that the market system is not perfect, and therefore government must intervene to alleviate the harmful effects of economic policies. The second position reflects the belief that the market should be

left alone because government intervention can inhibit the incentive for individual work and economic growth. Most political disagreements about
the extent and form of social welfare services reflect the struggle between
these two positions.

Employment and Unemployment

One of the most strongly held economic beliefs in our society is that if a
person works hard, she or he will be rewarded. This ideology stems from our
earliest history, when Americans embraced concepts such as "pulling yourself up by your own bootstraps" and eagerly read the Horatio Alger stories
of a young man who rose from rags to riches. Implicit in this belief is the assumption that there are enough jobs available for everyone who wants to
work, and all a person needs to do is find a job and stay with it. While this
belief permeates our social consciousness, it is not entirely true. The job
market frequently fluctuates, and the existence of a job does not necessarily mean it is available to anyone who is looking. Not only do education and
ability play a part, but location and unwillingness of employers to consider
a wide range of applicants can block access to employment. Thus, even
when there are jobs available, they may not be available to all who are looking for work. The result is that there are varying numbers of people who are
unemployed and looking for work.

The Bureau of Labor statistics provide an official count for the rate of
unemployment and announce the monthly rate on the first Friday of each
month. The official definition for **unemployment** is as follows:

> Unemployed persons comprise all civilians who had no employment during
> the reference week [the week in which the data were gathered that month],
> who made specific efforts to find a job within the previous four weeks (such as
> applying directly to an employer, or to a public employment service, or check-
> ing with friends), and who were available for work during that week, except for
> temporary illness. Persons on layoff from a job and expecting recall are also
> classified as unemployed (U.S. Bureau of the Census, 1996, p. 390).

People who have given up looking for a job, who would like a job but do not
apply for one because they cannot find support such as child care or transportation which are necessary for their employment, and those who are un-
deremployed (working in jobs that are inadequate to their skills or needed
hours), are not officially counted among the unemployed. Thus, the unemployment rate does not reflect all people who are out of work. The true rate
of unemployment may be significantly higher than the official numbers represent.

In spite of the limitations in counting the number of people who are
unemployed, the data provide a valuable indication of employment trends
over the years. Table 10.1 lists the average unemployment rates since 1960.
The data reveal a strong demographic trend that reflects the disparity in
employment in this country. The averages in Table 10.2 reveal the difference

Table 10.1

Annual Unemployment Rates*, in Percents

Year	Total Males	Total Females	White Males	White Females	African-American Males	African-American Females
1960	4.7	5.1	4.2	4.6	9.6	8.3
1961	5.7	6.3	5.1	5.7	11.7	10.6
1962	4.6	5.4	4.0	4.7	10.0	9.6
1963	4.5	5.4	3.9	4.8	9.2	9.4
1964	3.9	5.2	3.4	4.6	7.7	9.0
1965	3.2	4.5	2.9	4.0	6.0	7.5
1966	2.5	3.8	2.2	3.3	4.9	6.6
1967	2.3	4.2	2.1	3.8	4.3	7.1
1968	2.2	3.8	2.0	3.4	3.9	6.3
1969	2.1	3.7	1.9	3.4	3.7	5.8
1970	3.5	4.8	3.2	4.4	5.6	6.9
1971	4.4	5.7	4.0	5.3	7.3	8.7
1972	4.0	5.4	3.6	4.9	7.0	9.0
1973	3.3	4.9	3.0	4.3	6.0	8.6
1974	3.8	5.5	3.5	5.1	7.4	8.8
1975	6.8	8.0	6.2	7.5	12.5	12.2
1976	5.9	7.4	5.4	6.8	11.4	11.7
1977	5.2	7.0	4.7	6.2	10.7	12.3
1978	4.3	6.0	3.7	5.2	9.3	11.2
1979	4.2	5.7	3.6	5.0	9.3	10.9
1980	5.9	6.4	5.3	5.6	12.4	11.9
1981	6.3	6.8	5.6	5.9	13.5	13.4
1982	8.8	8.3	7.8	7.3	17.8	15.4
1983	8.9	8.1	7.9	6.9	18.1	16.5
1984	6.6	6.8	5.7	5.8	14.3	13.5
1985	6.2	6.6	5.4	5.7	13.2	13.1
1986	6.1	6.2	5.3	5.4	12.9	12.4
1987	5.4	5.4	4.8	4.6	11.1	11.6
1988	4.8	4.9	4.1	4.1	10.1	10.4
1989	4.5	4.7	3.9	4.0	10.0	9.8
1990	4.9	4.8	4.3	4.1	10.4	9.6
1991	6.3	5.7	5.7	4.9	11.5	10.5
1992	7.0	6.3	6.3	5.4	13.4	11.7
1993	6.4	5.9	5.6	5.1	12.1	10.6
1994	5.4	5.4	4.8	4.6	10.3	9.8

*Rates apply to persons 20 years of age and older.

Sources: Economic Report of the President (1995); House Committee on Ways and Means (1994).

Table 10.2

Average Unemployment Rates by Decade, in Percents

Decade	Total		White		African-American	
	Males	Females	Males	Females	Males	Females
1960s	3.57	4.57	3.17	4.23	7.10	8.02
	(1.28)°	(.87)	(1.12)	(.78)	(2.91)	(1.60)
1970s	4.54	6.04	4.09	5.47	8.65	10.03
	(1.11)	(1.07)	(1.03)	(1.04)	(2.35)	(1.85)
1980s	6.35	6.42	5.58	5.53	13.34	12.80
	(1.48)	(1.20)	(1.34)	(1.08)	(2.81)	(2.07)

°Standard deviations are given in parentheses.

Source: Calculations based on data from *Economic Report of the President* (1995).

in unemployment by gender and race. Until recent years, the rate of unemployment for women tended to be higher than for men. Racial differences are most pronounced. African-American men and women experience rates of unemployment that are twice as high as those for white men and women.

Types of Unemployment.   Not all unemployment is the same. There are several different types of unemployment (Schiller, 1989). **Structural unemployment** reflects the structure of our economic system. Some people, in spite of wanting to work, find themselves unable to gain access to the necessary training or education required for the jobs available. For example, there may be numerous jobs open for word processing, but if a person does not attend a school with computers, or cannot afford to go on for post-high-school training, then a word processing job is out of reach. The unavailability of suitable employment is also true for the **dislocated worker**, the person who was trained and employed in an occupation no longer needed. Many manufacturing jobs have been phased out of existence with the development of computerized assembly systems.

   Seasonal unemployment reflects changes in employment over different times of the year. Retailers sell much of their goods during the winter holiday season, so they hire more workers at that time. Construction jobs tend to be available in the spring and summer when the weather permits large building projects to be undertaken. Farm workers, particularly migrant workers, find employment during the harvest but cannot find work during the rest of the year. The time of year and season have an impact on the employment needs of employers.

Unemployment that is limited to a specific region or a specific type of work is referred to as **geographic or industry unemployment**. When steel mills closed during the 1980s, for example, many workers lost their jobs. Typically, this work was concentrated in specific geographic areas, such as the Northeast. While other regions of the country were growing, communities that relied on specific industries were hurt economically.

To what extent is unemployment an ever-present reality of our nation? The policy goal of full employment has been vigorously debated since the Great Depression, and it raises a number of important points. **Full employment** means there are very few workers available for jobs paying typical wages, and those looking for jobs can find them. The economic upheaval of the Great Depression demonstrated that the goal of full employment was difficult to achieve and that economic cycles could be severe. The Great Depression convinced people that government intervention might be a suitable means of maintaining economic stability. Supporters of government intervention wanted legislation that promoted full employment. Such legislation would have placed the federal government as employer of those in need of jobs, typically through public works programs and civil service employment. Major business and agricultural groups fought full employment legislation on the grounds it would interfere with the free market, and instead of full employment, policy-makers supported the Employment Act of 1946 (Weir, 1987). The Employment Act set the goal of maximum employment through government actions such as spending and taxing to stabilize the economy (Axinn & Levin, 1992). While not adopting a commitment to full employment, the legislation did place some responsibility for the economy and employment in the control of the federal government.

Effects of Unemployment.   To social workers, it would seem that unemployment is not a desirable or healthy condition. In fact, analysis of research on the impact of unemployment suggests that having a job is crucial to self-esteem and self-definition (Aldous & Tuttle, 1988). In spite of the psychological benefits of working, public policies for full employment have never been enacted. In fact, there is an economic incentive for continually maintaining a pool of unemployed workers (Schiller, 1989). Some analysts argue that there is a trade-off between unemployment and inflation. When the rate of employment increases, more people are working and therefore have more to spend. When consumers have more money to spend, manufacturers often seek to make a greater profit by raising prices on goods and services. As prices rise, inflation can follow. If prices rise too quickly, inflation occurs faster than growth in wages. Workers begin to spend less, and supply outpaces demand. The result is a slowdown in productivity. Fewer workers are needed, and unemployment rises as inflation goes down. This trend is exacerbated by the benefit of unemployment to employers. If there are numerous people looking for work, employers can offer lower wages and quickly fill open positions. If unemployment is low, then there are fewer people willing to accept less desirable employment.

Table 10.3

Average Periods of Unemployment, in Weeks

	Mean	Standard Deviation
1950s	11.31	2.18
1960s	11.75	2.79
1970s	11.87	2.28
1980s	14.99	2.57
1990–1993	15.48	3.00

Source: Calculations based on data from *Economic Report of the President* (1995).

The social welfare policy conflict rests on the short-term advantages to unemployment. Businesses tend to prefer a pool of workers who are not in a position to make strong demands for high wages or working conditions that may seem costly to the employer. In reality, however, this short-term gain seems to be more than offset by the long-term liabilities. Low wages make for low consumption, and thus the economy as a whole suffers. Also, poor working conditions lead to dissatisfied workers. Those who are unhappy in their work tend to be less productive, less loyal, and more likely to leave. Worker turnover can become very costly over time.

As is typical of so many of our social welfare policies, our national approach to employment is residual in nature. Instead of actively promoting full employment, policy-makers have allowed unemployment to creep upward, as illustrated by the data in Table 10.2. Not only have the rates of unemployment steadily increased over the past thirty years, but the duration of unemployment has also grown (see Table 10.3). Our country's experience over the past thirty years demonstrates that when left to its own, the employment market does not provide jobs for all those who are looking, particularly for women and people of color.

Employment and Job Creation

If the employment arena does not provide enough jobs, then one solution is to have the federal government intervene and help people become employed. The employment programs of the New Deal, such as the Works Progress Administration and the Civilian Conservation Corps (discussed in chapter 2), represented the largest government effort at creating jobs by employing millions of workers. Since the New Deal, the major government employment efforts for economically disadvantaged persons centered on the Comprehensive Employment and Training Act of 1973 (CETA) (P.L. 93–203) and the Job Training Partnership Act of 1982 (JTPA) (P.L. 97–300).

These programs represented two very different approaches to government-sponsored employment.

The goal of CETA was to create public-service jobs. The CETA program was a federal, state, and local effort that enrolled as many as 750,000 participants during the peak year of 1978 (Levitan & Gallo, 1992). Unfortunately, however, CETA developed a negative reputation due to poor administration and political pressures. Public service employment jobs were doled out as political patronage rewards by local politicians, cities used CETA workers to serve in basic services so that they did not have to use their own funds, some work sites were poorly supervised, and positions never materialized into real jobs (Levin & Ferman, 1985).

In response to the negative publicity of the CETA program, the Reagan administration vowed to change the approach to employment services from public job creation to job placement in the private sector. In 1982, JTPA was passed to replace CETA. JTPA placed the responsibility for program administration with state governments and the private sector. The goal was to link those looking for jobs with existing employment. Each community was to develop a council with representatives from private employers who would direct the employment services. Compared to CETA, JTPA received less funding, did not create new jobs, and provided less social service support for participants (Levitan & Shapiro, 1987).

The effectiveness of JTPA has been minimal. While JTPA includes over 600 local programs providing services, most services are contracted out to private groups such as community colleges and trade schools. As one would expect, these organizations have had difficulty creating jobs for those with employment deficits (Blumenthal, 1987). Investigation of JTPA programs revealed improper spending without adequate federal and state government oversight (U.S. General Accounting Office, 1991). Recent research concluded that while there may be some short-term benefits from JTPA training, there was no significant improvement in earnings or employment five years after JTPA services (U.S. General Accounting Office, 1996).

As part of JTPA and other programs, the federal government has been involved in employment training in many other areas. Recent count identified 154 programs administered through 14 different federal departments and agencies. A sample of these programs is listed in Figure 10.1. These programs include numerous separate services for disadvantaged youth, disadvantaged adults, older individuals, summer employment, and dislocated workers (U.S. General Accounting Office, 1994a). Unfortunately, the effectiveness of these programs is questionable. Information on the outcomes or effectiveness of the programs is not collected by agencies, and there is no evidence that participants who do find jobs were helped by the programs or would not have achieved the same results on their own (U.S. General Accounting Office, 1994b).

As can be seen by examining the rates of unemployment over three decades (see Table 10.2), efforts to increase employment through social welfare services have not been extremely effective. The average rate of unemployment for adult workers increased in each decade from 1960 to 1990.

Figure 10.1

Partial List of Employment and Training Programs

Department of Education

School Dropout Demonstration
Migrant Education
Adult Education for the Homeless
Vocational Education
English Literacy Program
Student Literacy Corps

Department of Health and Human Services

Job Opportunities and Basic Skills Program (JOBS)
Community Services Block Grant
Refugee and Entrant Assistance
Health Career Opportunity Program

Department of Labor

JTPA Training Services for Disadvantaged Adults
JTPA Training Program for Older Individuals
JTPA Disadvantaged Youth
JTPA Dislocated Workers
JTPA Defense Diversification
JTPA Job Corps
Apprenticeship Training
Veterans Employment Program
Targeted Jobs Tax Credit
Homeless Veterans Reintegration Project

Source: U.S. General Accounting Office (1994b).

If employment and training efforts are not highly effective, then there is greater need for supportive services for those who are unemployed.

Taxes

Paying taxes ranks high among people's dislikes, but taxes play a critical role in providing social welfare services and programs. **Taxes** are compulsory payments we make to the government. They are the payments we make to ensure we have a government that will maintain law and order, protect property rights, and uphold civil rights. Without the power and strength of government, there would be no control over our social system, nor would there be protections. Therefore, taxes are the price we pay to feel safe and secure.

Progressive taxes take an increasing percentage as income rises, while **regressive taxes** are proportionately higher on low incomes. Federal income taxes are designed to be progressive taxes. The example of OASDI payroll taxes in chapter 8 demonstrates regressivity: people with lower incomes pay a greater proportion of their income to social security taxes. The issue of who should shoulder the burden of taxes is controversial. Today, most people feel they pay too much in taxes. Actually, however, the percent of people's incomes that go to cover federal, state, and local taxes has remained steady over the past twenty-five years. In 1969, the average tax rate was 29.1%, and in 1995 it was 29.6% (Center on Budget and Policy Priorities, 1996b).

Major Social Welfare Programs Tied to Economic Conditions

Economic policies are not always viewed as part of our social welfare system, and some social welfare programs are regarded as outside the domain of economics. The following programs, which are directly based on individual and social economic conditions, are integral parts of our social welfare system.

Unemployment Insurance

In order to protect workers from economic hardship during periods of unemployment, the federal government developed the **Unemployment Insurance** program. The program was enacted as part of the 1935 Social Security Act. Unemployment Insurance was created as a joint program administered by both the federal and state governments. States decide duration and amount of benefits, set eligibility requirements, and directly administer the program. The federal government provides grants for administration of the program and is responsible for maintaining the Unemployment Insurance Trust Fund.

The Unemployment Insurance Trust Fund consists of state-collected payroll tax dollars from employers. Employers pay unemployment insurance tax according to the number of workers they employ. For each dollar paid, they receive a 90-cent credit against their federal tax (Social Security Administration, 1993). Because of this tax inducement, all states willingly comply with the program. Although every state participates in the Unemployment Insurance program, the specifics of the programs vary widely from state to state.

Generally, eligibility is based on the extent of recent employment, willingness and ability to accept new employment, and involuntary termination from prior employment. Benefits are provided as a right and do not require a means test. Unemployment coverage provides a percentage of previous earnings for up to 26 weeks in most states. In 1994, the average weekly benefit was $182 for an average of 15.5 weeks (U.S. Bureau of the Census, 1996).

The Unemployment Insurance program is one of the few social welfare programs that tends to be more universal in structure. As long as a person has been dismissed from a covered job, he or she is entitled to unemployment benefits, regardless of personal wealth, income, or age. Unfortunately, however, many people need to leave jobs for reasons that are not covered, such as illness of a family member or problems obtaining child care. Also, many people work in part-time jobs and thus do not quality for unemployment benefits. In 1993, only 48% of people who were unemployed received unemployment insurance benefits (House Committee on Ways and Means, 1994). The percentage has been dropping, and in 1994 only 36% of unemployed people received benefits through the Unemployment Insurance program (Center on Budget and Policy Priorities, 1995). For many unemployed workers, benefits run out before they have found new employment. This is particularly true during times of greatest need. For example, in 1991, at the peak of economic recession, 3.5 million recipients of unemployment insurance exhausted their benefits before finding new employment (Shapiro & Nichols, 1992). Although the program provides a necessary safety net for people who lose jobs, it is not comprehensive nor does it provide for all who are unemployed.

Minimum Wage

Another public policy that is related to employment and provides wage security for workers is the minimum wage. The concept of a **minimum wage** is that the government intervenes to guarantee a base hourly wage. The instability of the market and the imbalance in power between employers and employees serve as the rationale for government intervention in wages.

The aftermath of the Great Depression spurred lawmakers to investigate labor practices. Industry support of strike breaking, labor spies, and violent attacks on workers prompted the passage of the Fair Labor Standards Act of 1938 (Axinn & Levin, 1992). In addition to standardizing work hours and controlling child labor, the legislation set a minimum wage below which employers could not legally pay workers. The hourly rate in 1938 was set at $.25 an hour, and it had risen to $4.25 by 1991 (Social Security Administration, 1994). During the 1996 congressional session, President Clinton and Congress agreed to new legislation, the Small Business Protection Act (P.L. 104–188), which raised the minimum wage to $4.75 per hour as of October 1, 1996, and to $5.15 per hour as of September 1, 1997.

Critics argue that the minimum wage is inadequate and has not kept pace with the cost of living. As shown in Figure 10.2, the value of the minimum wage has shrunk over the years. The 1997 rate of $5.15 per hour is 15% below the purchasing power of the minimum wage during the 1970s (after adjusting for inflation). To keep even with the 1970s, it would have to

Figure 10.2

Value of the Minimum Wage in 1995 Dollars

1960s	$5.65
1970s	$5.74
1980s	$4.93
1995	$4.25

Source: Shapiro (1995).

Figure 10.3

Minimum Wage Earnings in Comparison to Poverty Line*

1995

$4.25 × 40 hours per week × 52 weeks per year = $8,840 per year.
After Social Security taxes = $8,164 annual full-time income.
Poverty line for family of three in 1995 = $12,183.
Difference between full-time earnings at minimum wage and poverty threshold for family of three = –$4,019.

1997

$5.15 × 40 hours per week × 52 weeks per year = $10,712 per year.
After Social Security taxes = $9,893 annual full-time income.
Estimated poverty line for family of three in 1997 = $12,925.
Difference between full-time earnings at minimum wage and poverty threshold for family of three = –$3,032.

Source: Author calculations.

be more than $6.00 an hour (Center on Budget and Policy Priorities, 1996a).

The differences between working full-time at minimum wage and the poverty line are outlined in Figure 10.3. The disparity between the minimum wage income and living in poverty in 1997 was more than t$3,000 for a family of three. The minimum wage would have to be raised to $7.80 an hour to lift a family of four above the poverty line (Meredith, 1996). Without public assistance or benefits through the Earned-Income Tax Credit, full-time work at minimum wage still leaves a family below the poverty line. This difference highlights one of the many policy contradictions in our social welfare system. While people are categorized as living in poverty with incomes below officially recognized levels, legislation does not mandate employers to pay wages that lift workers or their families out of poverty. In 1990, more than 14 million people, or 18% of all full-time workers, earned less than the poverty line. This represented a 50% increase since 1974 (U.S. Bureau of the Census, 1992).

Opponents of the minimum wage argue that government interference in setting pay levels destroys free enterprise and causes economic imbalances. They feel that if employers are forced to pay higher wages, there will be fewer jobs available. Recent research findings suggest this is not true. In a study done in New Jersey, labor economists found that when the minimum wage was increased, even during a state economic recession, the number of jobs actually increased (Epstein, 1995). The researchers theorized that higher wages attract and keep people in jobs, thereby favoring long-term employment rather than frequent turnover.

While the concept of a minimum wage is usually relegated to economic discussions, it has important implications for social work. Most low-paid workers lack economic security during recessions or changes in the employment market. Many are not covered by unemployment insurance, and are consequently the most likely candidates for public assistance. If the minimum wages of available employment were adequate to support a family, it is likely that fewer people would be dependent on public assistance.

Earned-Income Tax Credit

Recent public policy efforts to make employment worthwhile centered on the Earned-Income Tax Credit program (EITC), which was introduced in chapter 5. Enacted in 1975, the legislation allows for a decrease in taxes paid by low-income workers. The program is administered through the filing of a tax return and therefore does not involve additional federal agencies or administrators (Social Security Administration, 1993). The average credit per family was about $945 in 1993, with 14 million families participating (House Committee on Ways and Means, 1994). The provisions of the EITC are complicated and vary according to income level and size of household. Generally, the lower the income, the higher the tax credit. In cases where the income is extremely low, families may qualify to receive a direct grant.

The program has received support from both political parties. It is supported because it rewards people for working, and it is efficient because it is handled through the existing Internal Revenue Service (Hutchinson, Lav, & Greenstein, 1992). Critics charge, however, that although the EITC helps low-income individuals, it also keeps wages low. Why should employers raise wages when the government subsidizes poor workers to accept the low wages? In effect, the EITC uses tax dollars to supplement poorly paid workers instead of placing the responsibility on the employers themselves (McDermott, 1994). This brings us back to the question of who should be responsible for determining wages: the government or the marketplace. Should wage levels be left entirely to the ebb and flow of economic conditions, or should the federal government intervene? If the government intervenes, what should that action be? Should employers be regulated, or should workers be supplemented? Those questions continually surface in the ongoing debates regarding economic policy and social well-being.

Impact of the Federal Budget on Social Welfare Policy and Practice

How do the workings of the federal budget affect social workers and their practice? The federal budget may seem far removed from the day-to-day activities of social service providers. As demonstrated throughout this book, however, the impact of government policies flows through all levels of our social welfare system and ultimately affects our direct practice. The federal budget is the main source of revenue for national social welfare programs and services. Federal money is used to fund services for children, families, health care, unemployment, retirement, education, and other areas of our social welfare. Budget cuts necessitate reductions in social welfare programs and services.

What Is a Budget Deficit?

A tremendous amount of public debate has covered the issue of the budget deficit. In spite of public attention, many people do not fully understand the potential impact or consequences of the federal budget deficit. Simply put, each year the federal government legislates a plan for what and how much should be spent on the business of government. (In chapter 11, we will outline the federal budget process and timeline.) Part of the plan includes estimates for how much money will be taken in for taxes and how much the economy will grow.

When the government overspends, it incurs a budget deficit. In order to continue financing its operations, the government must borrow to make up the shortfall. The largest amount of borrowed money is financed through the government selling treasuries to the public. This borrowed amount is referred to as the public debt. The rest of the debt is covered through money borrowed by federal agencies. The cumulative total of annual budget deficits, which includes public debt and agencies' debt, makes up the gross federal debt.

Since 1962, the federal government has run an annual deficit in every year except 1969. Until the 1980s, however, the overall debt climbed slowly. Table 10.4 lists the deficit and total debt for the past twenty years. The gross federal debt grew by $1 trillion between 1975 and 1984, but during the

Table 10.4

Annual Deficits and Overall Debt, 1975–1996
(in billions of dollars)

	Deficit	Public Debt	Total Federal Debt°
1975	$ 53	$ 395	$ 542
1976	74	477	629
1977	54	549	706
1978	59	607	777
1979	40	640	829
1980	74	709	909
1981	79	785	994
1982	128	919	1,137
1983	208	1,131	1,371
1984	185	1,300	1,564
1985	212	1,499	1,817
1986	221	1,736	2,120
1987	150	1,888	2,346
1988	155	2,050	2,601
1989	153	2,189	2,868
1990	221	2,410	3,206
1991	270	2,688	3,598
1992	290	2,999	4,002
1993	255	3,247	4,351
1994	203	3,432	4,644
1995	164	3,640	4,921
1996[†]	146	3,857	5,300

°Includes the annual deficit, accrued public debt, and other federal government obligations.
[†]Estimates.

Sources: U.S. Bureau of the Census (1996); *Budget of the United States Government, fiscal year 1997* (1996), p. 223; *Economic Report of the President* (1995), p. 365; Berry (1996).

next ten years it increased by almost $3 trillion to stand at its current level of $4.7 trillion.

While such a large debt seems disturbing, if we compare the debt to the overall national income (the gross domestic product), there is some precedent in previous years. In 1992, the gross federal debt represented 59% of the gross domestic product. From 1955 to 1959, the ratio ran from 60% to as high as 72% (House Committee on Ways and Means, 1994). It has steadily declined since the 1960s, dropping as low as 34% in 1981. Since then it has risen, and neared 69% by 1994 (House Committee on Ways and Means, 1994).

Consequences of the Deficit

The consequences of running the federal government with such a high deficit are unclear. Some policy-makers view this as dangerous to long-tern economic health, while others consider it a fact of large government. When the federal budget is decreased, resources for government programs are also decreased. As long as people will still invest in the government by purchasing securities, however, there is a cycle of transferring money from the public to the government and back again. Because there has never been a time in history when the dollar amount of the federal debt was so large, there is no precedent for interpreting the long-term impact of such a large deficit. It remains to be seen if the cycle is stable or if economic distress will be the outcome of such an imbalance.

Contentious political debate surrounds deficit reduction. While the president and Congress agree that the budget must be balanced and the debt reduced, there is little consensus on how to accomplish this goal. The political showdown in November 1995, when the government was officially closed for a week, demonstrated the extent of the disagreement. Although short-term consensus was reached to reopen government, the long-term problem of the deficit and debt remains unresolved.

Changes in the Work Force

The concern for social welfare policy in relation to employment and economics rests with current and future service needs of workers and people without work. We have discussed the shortcomings of the system and some of the major current policies designed to address those social needs, but these policies reflect the state of the work force in the past. Examination of demographic shifts suggests that new public policies will be needed in the future.

Over the past forty-five years, the composition of the labor force has changed greatly. In 1950, 33% of all women were actively engaged in the labor force, compared to 86% of all men. By 1990, almost 60% of all women participated in the labor force, while 76% of all men did so (U.S. General Accounting Office, 1992). With more women in the work force, there are more two-parent families in which both parents are employed and more single-parent families headed by working mothers. In 1960, 32% of men who worked were married to women who were also in the labor force. By 1990, the percentage had increased to almost 70% (U.S. General Accounting Office, 1992).

Other changes have affected the work force (May, 1995). From a high in 1986, the median annual income of men working full-time throughout the year dropped by 7% after inflation while for women during the same period it increased by about 1%. Median weekly earnings dropped 2% from

1986 to 1993. These changes reflect the overall decline in income as well as the gradual closing of the earning gap between men and women. The result of an overall decrease in wages means that families are struggling to maintain their standard of living. Demographic and income changes will increase the need for social welfare policies that address the social and economic needs of all people.

Final Thoughts on Economics in Relation to Social Welfare Policy

When examining the provision of social welfare services and the market economy, two questions must be asked. First, can the market economy adequately provide for the social welfare needs of all its citizens? Second, should the marketplace and rules of the market economy dictate the provision and delivery of social welfare services? For example, are medical care, nutrition, or housing best left to the cycles of supply and demand, or should there be government intervention? Are the levels of wages and unemployment protections the responsibility of industry and employers, or should the government intervene to compensate for the ups and downs of the economic system? These questions must be asked by anyone analyzing economic ideologies and social welfare policy. Social workers must be familiar with economic terms and concepts in order to effectively advocate for the social welfare needs of all members of our society.

Key Concepts

economics	supply and demand
unemployment	structural unemployment
dislocated worker	seasonal unemployment
geographic unemployment	industry unemployment
full employment	progressive taxes
regressive taxes	Unemployment Insurance
minimum wage	Earned-Income Tax Credit

Exercises

1. Examine one of your pay stubs from previous or current employment. How much did you pay in taxes? What percent of your income did you pay? How much did you pay under FICA? Does it equal the required 7.65%?

2. Research the unemployment benefits in your community and state. How many weeks are people eligible to receive benefits? What conditions or requirements must be met by recipients of benefits? What is the process to apply, and how long does it take to become eligible?

3. What kinds of jobs pay minimum wage in your community? Are there employers who offer more than minimum wage for entry-level, unskilled jobs? Where are those jobs? Why do you think the employers are offering more than minimum wage?

References

Aldous, J., & Tuttle, R.C. (1988). Unemployment and the family. In Chilman, C.S., Cox, F.M., & Nunnally, E.W. (eds.). *Employment and economic problems* (pp. 17–41). Newbury Park, CA: Sage Publications.

American Heritage Dictionary. (1976). Boston: Houghton Mifflin.

Axinn, J., & Levin, H. (1992). *Social welfare: A history of the American response to need* (3rd ed.). New York: Longman.

Bartlett, H. (1970). *The common base of social work practice*. Washington, DC: National Association of Social Workers.

Bellin, S.S., & Miller, S.M. (1983). Economic policy is the dominant social policy. *American Behavioral Scientist, 26* (6), 725–737.

Berry, J.M. (1996). The quietly shrinking deficit. *The Washington Post National Weekly Edition, 13* (22), 22.

Blumenthal, K. (1987, February 9). Job training effort, critics say, fails many who need help most. *Wall Street Journal*, p. 1.

Budget of the United States government, fiscal year 1997. (1996). Washington, DC: U.S. Government Printing Office.

Burch, H.A. (1990). *The why's of social policy: Perspective on policy preferences*. New York: Praeger.

Center on Budget and Policy Priorities. (1995). *Unemployment Insurance protection in 1994*. Washington, DC: Author.

Center on Budget and Policy Priorities. (1996a). *Assessing a $5.15-an-hour minimum wage*. Washington, DC: Author.

Center on Budget and Policy Priorities. (1996b). *Twisted tales: Overstating the taxes the typical household pays*. Washington, DC: Author.

Economic Report of the President. (1995). Washington, DC: U.S. Government Printing Office.

Epstein, G. (1995, January 23). A boost in the minimum wage doesn't always produce the expected result. *Barron's, LXXV* (4), 42.

Heilbroner, R., & Thurow, L. (1982). *Economics explained*. New York: Simon & Schuster.

House Committee on Ways and Means. (1994). *Overview of entitlement programs: 1994 Green book*. WMCP: 103-27. Washington, DC: U.S. Government Printing Office.

Hutchinson, F.C., Lav, I.J., & Greenstein, R. (1992). *A hand up: How state earned income credits help working families escape poverty*. Washington, DC: Center on Budget and Policy Priorities.

Levin, M.A., & Ferman, B. (1985). *The political hand: Policy implementation and youth employment programs*. New York: Pergamon Press.

Levitan, S.A., & Gallow, F. (1992). *Spending to save: Expanding employment opportunities*. Washington, DC: Center on Social Policy Studies, George Washington University.

Levitan, S.A., & Shapiro, I. (1987). *Working but poor*. Baltimore, MD: Johns Hopkins University Press.

May, R. (1995). *1993 poverty and income trends*. Washington, DC: Center on Budget and Policy Priorities.

McDermott, J. (1994, November 14). And the poor get poorer. *The Nation, 259* (16), 576–580.

Meredith, R. (1996, October 1). Minimum wage, minimum effect. *New York Times*, pp. C1, C6.

Moroney, R. M. (1991). *Social policy and social work*. New York: Aldine de Gruyter.

Murray, C. (1984). *Losing ground: American social policy 1950–1980*. New York: Basic Books.

Page, A.N. (1977). Economics and social work: A neglected relationship. *Social Work, 22* (1), 48–53.

Schiller, B.R. (1989). *The economics of poverty and discrimination* (5th ed.). Englewood Cliffs, NJ: Prentice Hall.

Shapiro, I. (1995). *Four years and still falling: The decline in the value of the minimum wage*. Washington, DC: Center on Budget and Policy Priorities.

Shapiro, I., & Nichols, M. (1992). *Far from fixed: An analysis of the unemployment insurance system*. Washington, DC: Center on Budget and Policy Priorities.

Social Security Administration. (1993). *Social security programs in the United States.* SSA Publication No. 13-11758. Washington, DC: U.S. Department of Health and Human Services.

Social Security Administration. (1994). *Social security bulletin annual statistical supplement*. Washington, DC: U.S. Department of Health and Human Services.

Tobin, J. (1986). The economic experience. In Obey, D.R., & Sarbanes, P. (eds.). *The changing American economy: Papers from the fortieth anniversary symposium of the Joint Economic Committee* (Senate Hearing 99-637). New York: Basil Blackwell.

U.S. Bureau of the Census. (1992). *Workers with low earnings: 1964 to 1990*. Current population reports, P-60, No. 178. Washington, DC: U.S. Government Printing Office.

U.S. Bureau of the Census. (1996). *Statistical abstract of the United States, 1996* (116th ed.). Washington, DC: U.S. Government Printing Office.

U.S. General Accounting Office. (1991). *Job Training Partnership Act: Inadequate oversight leaves program vulnerable to waste, abuse, and mismanagement*. GAO/HRD–91–97. Washington, DC: U.S. Government Printing Office.

U.S. General Accounting Office. (1992). *The changing workforce: Demographic issues facing the federal government*. GAO/GGD-92-38. Washington, DC: U.S. Government Printing Office.

U.S. General Accounting Office. (1994a). *Multiple employment training programs: Conflicting requirements underscore need for change*. GAO/T–HEHS–94–120. Washington, DC: U.S. Government Printing Office.

U.S. General Accounting Office. (1994b). *Multiple employment training programs: Most federal agencies do not know if their programs are working effectively*. GAO/HEHS–94–88. Washington, DC: U.S. Government Printing Office.

U.S. General Accounting Office. (1996). *Job Training Partnership Act: Long-term earnings and employment outcomes*. GAO/HEHS–96–40. Washington, DC: U.S. Government Printing Office.

Weir, M. (1987). Full employment as a political issue in the United States. *Social Research, 54* (2), 377–402.

Part Three

Social Welfare Policy Practice

In part three we will explore the social welfare policy-making process and discuss ways to influence social welfare policy. Social workers have an important role to play in the creation and implementation of social welfare policies. The information in these chapters will help you to become a policy practitioner who can influence the policy-making arena and assist clients to do the same.

Our focus in chapter 11 will be how policies get made on the federal, state, and local levels. In chapter 12, we provide the resources needed to analyze policy and to influence the policy-making process. In chapter 13, we describe how to conduct policy practice and influence the policy-making process. Finally, in chapter 14, we discuss the role of social work in the social welfare policy arena, identifying the important contributions social workers can make to the policy-making process.

Chapter 11

Social Welfare Policy and Governmental Policy-Making

The making of social welfare policy occurs on many different levels. Most social welfare programs are a result of governmental choices and decisions. To understand the implications and effects of social welfare policies, and to influence the development of those decisions, social workers must be familiar with the policy-making process. You may have taken a civics or government course in high school or college, but we have found that typically most social work students need to review this information. In this chapter, we present all the information needed to understand how laws are made and to identify the key legislative bodies involved in the policy-making process.

There are three key avenues through which social welfare policies are made: federal and state legislative processes, judicial decision-making, and government agency regulations. In this chapter we describe and explain where these decisions are made and the processes involved. In chapter 13, we will build on this knowledge by presenting ways that social service providers can influence the policy-making process.

The Three Branches of the United States Government

The United States Constitution outlines the basic composition and roles of the three branches of the federal government: **legislative**, **executive**, and **judicial**. These three parts are related, but each operates more or less independently of the others (see Figure 11.1). Often the relationship between the three is referred to as a system of **checks and balances**. This refers to the idea that while each branch plays a significant part in the creation of public laws and regulations, each also has the responsibility and power to offset or check the power of the other two branches.

Each branch is organized independently of the others but is also linked with them through the overall legislative process. For example, appointments to the Supreme Court are initiated by the president and approved by the Senate. After appointment, the Supreme Court justices are independent of the organization of the other branches and are therefore free to make independent policy decisions. As long as due process is followed, the other branches can challenge Supreme Court decisions. This relationship is true for all three branches of government. In the next three sections, we will explore the details of the organizational structure and policy-making role of each branch.[1]

The Legislative Branch: Congress

The major body of the legislative branch is the Congress. Congress consists of two chambers, the Senate and the House of Representatives, each with its own set of rules for operation and leadership. Although the Senate and House are independent of each other in day-to-day operations, no legislation can be passed without agreement between both chambers. This arrangement represents another set of checks and balances.

Differences Between the House and the Senate

The House of Representatives consists of 435 members, each elected from a congressional district. District boundaries, which reflect population, were

---

[1]Many sources detail the composition of our government and the legislative process through which laws and policies are made. The information in this chapter was obtained from the following sources: U.S. House of Representatives (1986); *U.S. Congress Handbook* (1995); *Guide to Congress* (1991); Congressional Research Service (1986); Congressional Research Service (1987); and Oleszek (1989).

Figure 11.1

Branches of the United States Government

Legislative Branch

CONGRESS

House   Senate

Executive Branch

PRESIDENT
Vice President

Cabinet Departments:

Agriculture	Interior
Commerce	Justice
Defense	Labor
Education	State
Energy	Transportation
Health and Human Services	Treasury
Housing and Urban Development	Veterans' Affairs

Judicial Branch

SUPREME COURT
U.S. Court of Appeals
U.S. District Courts

---

originally set by the Constitution and have been changed over the years by Congress (Jacobson, 1987). Each district includes about 575,000 people. Therefore, states with large populations have many representatives in the House, while less populous states may have only one or two. For example, in 1997 California had fifty-two representatives and Vermont had one. Each representative is elected to serve a two-year term. Thus, each member of the House of Representatives must run for re-election every other year if he or she wants to remain a member of the House. National elections are held on the first Tuesday of November during even-numbered years, at which time every seat in the House of Representatives is up for a vote.

The Senate is much smaller, with one hundred members. Each state, regardless of its size, has two senators. Each senator is elected for a six-year term. Terms are staggered so one-third of the senators run for office in each federal election. The two senate positions in each state are scheduled for re-election in different years.

The differences in representation and election between the House and the Senate provide important balances within the Congress. The general philosophy behind the differences is that representatives reflect current opinion, while senators are free to be more concerned with long-range policy. House members typically represent fewer people and are tied to smaller geographic regions. They are open to voter opinion more frequently through elections every other year and therefore are more likely to be concerned with issues of a more immediate nature. Senators, on the other hand, have more time to participate in the legislative process because they are in office for at least six years. They tend to represent a much larger constituency: an entire state. Their role tends to be more global and nationwide, rather than being focused on a specific community. With the size of congressional districts increasing as the population grows, however, members of the House are expected to represent increasingly diverse interests. If the government were to create smaller districts by population, then it would have to increase the number of House members. At this time, that outcome seems very unlikely.

Decision-making differs from the House to the Senate. The Senate, with only one hundred members, tends to be more deliberative. Compared to the workload of the 435 members of the House, the legislative work in the Senate is shared by fewer members. This means that each senator is involved more deeply in a greater number of issues. Furthermore, the length of term again plays a part. Because of their six-year term, senators do not feel a great sense of urgency to make legislation.

In the House, with the possibility of not getting re-elected looming every other year, there is more of a sense that legislation must be passed as soon as possible. In addition, the large number of members makes it impossible for everyone to be an integral part of each legislative decision. That means that representatives tend to specialize more than senators, focusing on a set of issues important to them or to their constituents.

Day-to-Day Operations of Congress

Following each national election, the newly elected members convene in January for a two-year congressional session. For example, after the 1996 elections, the 105th Congress opened in January 1997 for its first session. The second session of the 105th Congress opened in January 1998. All legislative action to be taken may be introduced at any time during a congressional session but must be completed before final adjournment of the second session.

The Congress writes federal laws, investigates matters of concern to the public, and oversees federal agencies and programs. Much of the work of Congress is done by committees. The committees of the 104th Congress are listed in Figure 11.2. Although there was discussion of reducing the committee structure after Republicans took control of Congress in 1995, little changed:

> Senior House Republicans, taking over committees for the first time in their lives [after the 1994 election] balked at wholesale changes. While Republicans made some modest changes in committee jurisdiction and eliminated three minor committees, they left most committees as they were (Cloud, 1995, p. 10).

Almost all committees are subdivided into smaller subcommittees that meet to analyze proposed legislation and policy matters, then make recommendations to the larger committee or directly to the House or Senate. Each committee has a chairperson. The chairperson represents the majority party. During the first session of the 105th Congress, the Republicans had a majority in both the House and Senate. Therefore, all committees were chaired by a member of the Republican majority. Members of Congress

Figure 11.2
Congressional Committees

Senate Committees	House Committees
Agriculture, Nutrition, and Forestry	Agriculture
Appropriations	Appropriations
Armed Services	Banking and Financial Services
Banking, Housing, and Urban Affairs	Budget
Budget	Commerce
Commerce, Science, and Transportation	Economic and Educational Opportunities
Energy and Natural Resources	Government Reform and Oversight
Environment and Public Works	House Oversight
Finance	International Relations
Foreign Relations	Judiciary
Governmental Affairs	National Security
Indian Affairs	Resources
Judiciary	Rules
Labor and Human Resources	Science
Rules and Administration	Small Business
Small Business	Standards of Official Conduct
Veterans' Affairs	Transportation and Infrastructure
Special Committee on Aging	Veterans' Affairs
Select Committee on Ethics	Ways and Means
Select Committee on Intelligence	Select Committee on Intelligence

request service on committees through the leadership of each chamber. Once appointed, they can stay on the committees from one Congress to the next. Usually, the committee chairperson is the member who served the longest on the committee.

Leadership within each chamber is decided through election by the majority. This means that the party with the majority of members controls the administration of the chamber. The highest-ranking leader of the House of Representatives is the Speaker of the House, and the highest elected leader of the Senate is the majority leader. Technically, the highest-ranking official of the Senate is the vice president, but the vice president may vote only in the event of ties. Therefore, the vice president usually does not actively participate as the leader of the Senate. The minority party in each chamber also elects minority leaders, one in the Senate and one in the House.

Members of Congress are simultaneously involved in making policy for the nation and responding to the needs of their constituents. Members of Congress hire staff members who fulfill one of two general roles, working on the development and monitoring of legislation or tending to the concerns of constituents back home. Congressional staff members are therefore very important to all the operations of a member of Congress. The typical congressional office in Washington is headed by an administrative assistant who is in charge of all operations and staff. There is also a legislative director who oversees the legislative concerns and reports directly to the administrative assistant and the elected official. The legislative staff includes aides who specialize in key areas and respond to constituents' concerns regarding legislative issues. In addition, each member of Congress has staff in his or her home district or state. These staff members focus on state or district concerns and respond to constituents locally.

For the 105th Congress, the annual salary of a senator or representative was $133,600. Salaries are higher for majority and minority leaders and the Speaker of the House. Members of Congress receive free office space and furnishings for their Washington offices, as well as funds to hire staff and pay for office expenses. While the annual salary is well above the average family income, most members of Congress must maintain two residences, one in Washington and one in their home state.

The Composition of Congress

Historically, until voting rights were extended to all Americans, almost all members of Congress were white men. Today, while women and minorities are represented in both the House and the Senate, the proportions are small (Congressional Quarterly, 1993; Congressional Quarterly, 1994). Until 1992, women with voting status never constituted more than 6% of Congress. After the 1992 election, the proportion rose to 10%, with fifty-four women serving in the Congress. In 1994, fifty-six women were elected as voting members. In 1996, sixty women were elected, the largest number of women ever serving in one Congress. Although women comprise half the population and have made political gains over the past several years, of the 535 members of Congress in 1997, only 11.2% were women. Nine women served as senators, and fifty-one women served in the House.

For minorities, 1992 was also a year of significant change. Sixty-three members of Congress were African-American, Hispanic, Asian-American, or Native American, for a total of 11.8% of Congress. That was a 50% increase from the previous election. By 1997, however, minority representation had dropped to sixty-two voting members, or 11.6%. Minority representation in Congress lags behind the minority proportion of the overall population.

How Laws Are Made

The technical flow of Congressional legislation is outlined in Figure 11.3. While the formal legislative process is very clear, however, the real process

Figure 11.3
The Flow of Federal Legislation:
How a Bill Becomes a Law

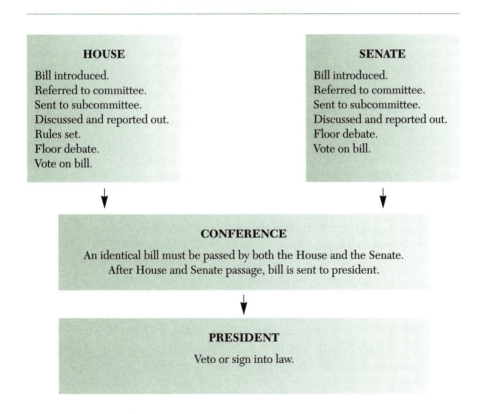

HOUSE

Bill introduced.
Referred to committee.
Sent to subcommittee.
Discussed and reported out.
Rules set.
Floor debate.
Vote on bill.

SENATE

Bill introduced.
Referred to committee.
Sent to subcommittee.
Discussed and reported out.
Floor debate.
Vote on bill.

CONFERENCE

An identical bill must be passed by both the House and the Senate.
After House and Senate passage, bill is sent to president.

PRESIDENT

Veto or sign into law.

Source: Congressional Quarterly Almanac (1989).

is laden with political maneuvering and partisan biases. It is helpful to become familiar with both the formal and informal legislative processes.

Submission of Bills.   Ideas for legislation are drafted into technical language and submitted to either the House or the Senate. A bill must be sponsored by a congressional member. Sponsorship does not necessarily mean complete support or understanding by the member of Congress. Interest groups or citizens can request that a congressional member submit a bill on their behalf.

Each bill submitted is numbered in the order of its submission during each two-year Congress. In the House, each number is preceded by H.R., with the very first bill numbered H.R. 1. In the Senate, each bill is preceded by an S., and thus the first bill is identified as S. 1.

Assignment to Committee.   Once a bill is submitted, it is referred to a committee. The office of the Speaker of the House is responsible for assignment of bills to committees and can decide ultimately which committee will be charged with reviewing the bill. Typically, the bill is assigned to the most appropriate committee based on its content, but the criteria for assignment also can be political. For example, a congressional member may request that a bill with relevance to his or her constituents be discussed in his or her committee. This allows the member to be personally involved in an issue that has local importance and may affect his or her chances for re-election.

Because committees tend to be large, they are divided into subcommittees that focus on more specialized areas. Pending bills are usually discussed and analyzed at the subcommittee level. Public hearings may be held, at which experts or people with relevant experience are asked to testify. The proceedings of public hearings are transcribed and available directly from the committees. Major hearings are published in bound form and available through the U.S. Government Printing Office.

After review and hearings, the subcommittee votes on the bill and sends it back to the full committee. The full committee reviews the bill and the subcommittee's recommendations. If the committee decides to take further action, the bill is voted on and sent to the chamber. In the House, before the bill goes to the floor for debate, it passes through the Rules Committee. This step is not done in the Senate. The size of the House and the limited terms seemed to require guidelines for discussion of pending measures. The Rules Committee sets the guidelines or rules under which a specific piece of proposed legislation can be discussed. This process can also be very political because the Rules Committee is controlled by the majority party. In the Senate, any limitations on debate of a bill are decided in the full chamber with the participation of all senators.

Passage or Defeat.   Not all bills are brought to debate on the floor of the House or Senate. Committees can choose not to discuss a bill or they can discuss it but not vote it out of committee. Thus, the committee forum becomes very important for the life of a bill. If a bill cannot garner enough support once it is assigned to a committee, it will never be debated. Also, while each chamber operates independently of the other, similar bills or even the very same bill may be discussed simultaneously in each chamber. This simultaneous attention can expedite the progress of a bill. Once a bill is referred to the full chamber, it is slated for congressional action. The Speaker of the House and the Senate majority leader decide when to schedule debate on a bill. Once a bill is on the floor, open debate allows for discussion and the possibility of amendments. If a vote is taken, there must be a majority consensus to pass the bill.

A bill passed in one chamber of Congress must also be passed in the other if it is to be sent to the president to become law. When there are differences between the two chambers, a conference committee with representatives from both the House and the Senate is convened to iron out the differences. Once that is done, and both chambers have officially voted and passed the bill, it is sent to the president for signature. The president may either sign a bill or veto it. If signed, the bill becomes law. If vetoed, it goes back to both the House and the Senate, where it may still become law if a two-thirds majority in each chamber passes it. Once a bill becomes a public law (P.L.), it receives a number, beginning with the Congress number. For example, a public law numbered P.L. 104–100 was the one-hundredth bill signed into law during the 104th Congress.

Thousands of bills are introduced during each congressional session. For example, more than 10,000 bills were introduced during both the 101st and 102nd Congresses. While many initiatives are submitted, very few actually become law. Only 4% of the bills submitted during the 101st Congress were enacted into law, and less than 6% were enacted during the 102nd Congress (Stanley & Niemi, 1994). There were 9,824 bills introduced during the 103rd Congress, and 465, or 4.7%, became laws (Langdon, 1994).

The introduction of a bill and its subsequent success or defeat are politically determined and can be affected by many outside sources. Public opinion or national events can promote a particular need for legislation. For example, the bombing of the Federal Building in Oklahoma in April of 1995 prompted development, discussion, and floor debate on an antiterrorism bill. Although pieces of the proposed legislation had been promoted previously, the occurrence of a major national event propelled the issue into a bill that gained the immediate attention of all lawmakers. On the other hand, bills can be introduced repeatedly from one Congress to the next without any consideration. In each Congress since the 1970s, the Equal Rights Amendment has been submitted to Congress for deliberation, and over the past fifteen years it has not received committee attention. As we will emphasize in chapter 13, because congressional committees are crucial to the successful passage of legislation, policymakers and those interested in influencing policy need to pay close attention to the work of congressional committees.

The Budgetary Process

The passage of the annual budget is part of our national legislative process. The bill for the proposed budget is developed by the president through the Office of Management and Budget. The proposed budget is submitted to Congress on the first Monday in February each year. It is a proposal for the upcoming fiscal year, which starts in October. After the president submits the budget proposal, Congress debates it and makes amended changes. The typical process takes place as follows:

First Monday in February—President submits proposed budget.

April 15—Congress completes action.

May 15—Appropriations bills considered.

June 30—Congress completes actions on appropriations.

August and September—Revisions based on economic forecasts.

October 1—Start of new fiscal year (Cranford, 1990).

While the flow of the calendar is clear, the process is not this smooth. Congress rarely passes a complete budget in the summer, but instead tends to debate the budget close to or right up to the beginning of the new fiscal year. Furthermore, the legislative budget process involves two different actions, authorization and appropriation. The **authorization** process, which occurs also at other times of the year, simply sets a ceiling on how much Congress might be willing to spend on a given program. The **appropriation** process sets the actual amount permitted to be spent. Often the two are not the same. This is particularly true for many social welfare programs. What is initially authorized does not actually get appropriated. Even after a specific amount is appropriated, that may not be the actual amount spent by the end of the year. The *actual amount spent* is typically referred to as the **outlay**. Table 11.1 lists the actual dollars spent, or outlays, on the major categories and social welfare programs during the 1992, 1994, and 1995 fiscal years.

Congressional decision-making about the budget actually rests on only part of the budget. The majority of the budget is already earmarked every year for mandatory spending such as Social Security, Medicare, and interest on the federal debt. Often the first two categories are referred to as **entitlements** because as long as a person meets the eligibility requirements or qualifications, he or she is entitled to receive benefits (Pianin, 1992). The part of the budget that is open to debate and congressional decision-making is considered discretionary spending. In recent years, discretionary spending has accounted for less than half of the federal budget, which represents a complete reversal of the budget over the past thirty years (Hager, 1993).

The largest outlays of the federal budget are for the entitlement programs of OASDI and Medicare. Almost 33% of the outlays in 1995 went toward these two programs. In addition, another 15% was earmarked for interest payments on the outstanding federal debt. The amount spent on national defense accounted for 18% of the budget. The anti-poverty programs

Table 11.1

Actual Federal Budget Dollars Spent (outlays in billions)

	1992	1994	1995
Total Budget	$1,381	$1,461	$1,519
Receipts	1,091	1,258	1,355
(Deficit)	(290)	(203)	(164)
Expenses (partial list)			
National Defense	$ 282	$ 282	$ 272
OASDI	290	320	336
Medicare	134	145	160
Interest on the debt	200	203	232
AFDC	15	16	17
Medicaid	68	81	89
Food Stamps	22	26	26
SSI	19	26	27
Veterans	34	38	38
Education	26	25	31
Head Start	2	3	4
WIC	3	3	3
Housing Assistance	14	9	21
International Affairs	21	17	16
Science, Space & Technology	17	16	17
Energy	6	5	5
Agriculture	22	15	10
Transportation	37	38	39

Sources: *Budget of the United States government, fiscal year 1996* (1995); *Budget of the United States government, fiscal year 1997* (1996).

of AFDC, Medicaid, Food Stamps, and SSI totaled 10% of the budget. Although OASDI and Medicare combined represent the largest category of the overall federal budget, in reality these programs are separate from the rest of the budget. OASDI and Medicare are funded from the Social Security Trust Fund. This fund is financed through the FICA payroll taxes. The money *cannot*, by law, be used for any other government program or purpose. Thus, while the Trust Fund is included on paper as part of the total budget, it is actually separate. Some government authorizations are not made to programs for individuals, but to states based on population. For example, the Title XX Social Services block grant is given to states according to their populations (Hager, 1993).

What is important to remember about entitlements is that they are mandatory, as long as eligibility criteria are met. Also, entitlements do not always represent money spent to assist people with low incomes. In fact, 80% of entitlements go to people regardless of their income (Hager, 1993). For example, most government entitlement dollars are spent for social insurance, Medicare, agricultural subsidies, and federal civil and military retirement pensions.

The handful of mandatory items discussed above, together with national defense, accounted for almost three-fourths of the entire 1995 federal budget. Unless major changes are made in these programs, balancing the budget will be very difficult and will have to focus on numerous small programs. It will also have to include areas that receive strong public or corporate support, such as agriculture, transportation, education, and international affairs.

If changing the amount of spending becomes too difficult, then the only other alternative is to increase the amount of money received. As shown in Table 11.2, the majority of tax receipts come from individuals, either through income taxes, or Social Security taxes. The corporate sector contributes less than 12% of the total dollars collected in taxes. The government borrows what it needs to balance the budget (as explained in chapter 10), and in 1995 12% of the actual federal spending required borrowed funds.

The federal budget is both a piece of legislation and an important part of social welfare policy. It presents the priorities of lawmakers. Examination of federal spending and the budget provides another tool for conducting social welfare policy analysis and assessing policy priorities. When a social issue gains recognition as a problem or need, it is then supported through funding. For example, the public health implications of AIDS were recognized by medical personnel and epidemiologists as early as the mid-1980s, but federal funding for research and treatment through legislation specifically earmarked for HIV/AIDS concerns did not appear as a budget item until 1990.

Table 11.2

Federal Budget—Receipts (in billions of dollars)

	1992	1994	1995
Individual income taxes	$ 476	$ 543	$ 590
Corporate taxes	100	140	157
Social insurance	414	462	484
Excise taxes	46	55	57
Other	54	58	66
Total	$1,091	$1,258	$1,354
Federal deficit	(290)	(203)	(164)
Gross federal debt	3,973	4,644	4,921

Sources: Budget of the United States government, fiscal year 1996 (1995); *Budget of the United States government, fiscal year 1997* (1996).

On the other hand, if a social program loses its importance, it is likely to lose some or all of its funding. For example, under three different presidents, the EITC was expanded, but the new congressional majority of 1995 proposed cutting the program by as much as $21 billion over seven years (Center on Budget and Policy Priorities, 1995). This shift represented a change in legislative priorities.

The State Legislative Process

Every state has control over its legislative process and is therefore free to develop its own legislature, but most state governments tend to operate very similarly to the federal government and consequently to each other. The major difference between state governments is their size. Larger states have full-time representatives that meet throughout the year. States with small populations often have part-time legislators who meet for only part of the year. Some good ways to find out about a state's government are to visit the capitol, call or write for information, or use published guides such as *The Book of the States*, published by the Council of State Governments (1995).

Each state is headed by a governor elected directly by the people. All states have a deliberative legislative body, often called the General Assembly. Usually this body is divided into two chambers, the House and the Senate. Therefore, each of us lives in a community that is represented by a state representative and a state senator, as well as a federal representative and federal senators.

Most state chambers operate using the same process as the federal government. All laws must be passed by both chambers of the General Assembly and signed into law by the highest-ranking state official, the governor. Like the president, the governor can sign a bill into law, or veto it. The General Assembly can override the veto, but this typically requires a greater than majority vote. For example, in Ohio and Illinois, a three-fifths vote is required to override the governor's veto, while in New York a two-thirds majority is required. Control of each chamber is through election; thus, the majority party controls the leadership and administration of the state lawmaking process.

In general, the role of state governments is to enact laws, authorize and appropriate funds for state and local governments, develop revenue (typically through taxation), and oversee and regulate the state judicial system. While state governments are most concerned with their own state, they are also involved in federal policy-making. Governors, state legislators, and state administrators often take active roles in suggesting policy initiatives through various means. State advisory councils, state congressional delegations, and state associations located in Washington are some of the formal organizations used to influence policy (Krane, 1993). Governors exert a significant amount of influence on federal policy-making. Governors can pledge political support to a president, presidential hopeful, senator, or representative with the expectation that the individual, once elected, will return the support. That support could take the form of financial or administrative resources directed to the state.

Another way that states influence federal policy is through state initiatives and demonstration programs. Many federal initiatives that are passed into law are based on programs or laws first passed by states. In this way, states serve as testing grounds to see if certain policy efforts will work. If they are successful, then the federal government is more likely to adopt the efforts for the entire nation. The federal government encourages this experimentation on the state level by offering funding through grants for demonstration programs.

The link between states and the federal government rests primarily on the financial support states receive. Typically, states choose to provide federal social welfare programs because of the financial incentive. Programs such as Medicaid are funded through matching grant programs. If states agree to follow federal guidelines, they are entitled to receive money from the federal government. During the 1990s, however, governors and state representatives began to voice frustration with the requirements attached to federal funds. The result following the 1994 election was a move toward lumping funds together into a block grant and letting states have more control over how they use the money. Developing the 1996 TANF block grants as a replacement for the AFDC matching grants is an example of this shift from federal to state control. One contingency of this freedom is a limit on the amount of money the federal government will give to states. These proposals follow an already diminishing amount of federal funds available to states. Between 1980 and 1989, federal money to states decreased by more than $50 billion a year (Uchitelle, 1990).

While states want more autonomy from federal rules and regulation, they are dependent on federal financial support. As federal spending decreases, state governments will be faced with difficult choices. They will have to decide whether to cut services or to raise the needed revenue themselves through state and local taxes. Social welfare services will be particularly vulnerable, as these programs tend to depend most heavily on the federal-state partnership.

The Executive Branch

The executive branch of the federal government, led by the president, provides a balance to the actions of the Congress. While Congress is responsible for all legislative powers, the Constitution requires the president to provide information on the state of the union and recommend legislative measures that are deemed necessary (Oleszek, 1989). Without the president's signature, most bills would not become public law. While Congress can override a presidential veto, the required two-thirds vote is very difficult to obtain. It is easier to get a simple majority to agree. The threat of a presidential veto can be very powerful in convincing lawmakers to make changes that will make a bill acceptable to the president.

The executive branch includes the vice president and the Cabinet. As of 1997, the Cabinet consisted of the directors of fourteen departments (listed in Figure 11.1). The president appoints the members of the Cabinet with confirmation by the Senate. A president may appoint others to serve in the Cabinet. The role of the Cabinet member is to advise the president and direct the affairs of the federal agencies under their respective departments.

The executive branch also includes other offices that serve the president. Most notable is the Office of Management and Budget. This office is responsible for tracking the appropriations and outlays of each federal agency and for preparing the annual budget document submitted to Congress each February. Other executive branch offices that have been developed over the years include the National Security Council, the Environmental Protection Agency, the National Drug Control Policy, and the Central Intelligence Agency (*U.S. Congress Handbook*, 1995).

The Judicial System

The last of the three policy-making bodies is the judicial branch. While the legislative branch creates laws, and the executive branch proposes budgets and concurs in law-making, the judicial branch interprets laws. The role of the courts is to "interpret legislation, clarify or define legal intent, and protect against violations of the Constitution" (Pierce, 1984, p. 143).

The highest court in the country is the Supreme Court. It consists of nine judges who are appointed by the president and confirmed by the Senate. Supreme Court justices are appointed for life. There are also hundreds of federal judges who are also appointed for life. This freedom from election or reappointment is thought to free the judges from any political influence. Nevertheless, the timing of judicial appointments and the party affiliation of the appointing president can make the initial appointing process very political. For example, in 1992 after Bill Clinton was elected president, there were more than 100 vacancies among the 846 federal judge positions (High court run on gold watches, 1992). The ability to appoint so many judges can allow a president to leave a lasting mark on the judiciary.

Cases are brought to the Supreme Court after they have been tried and appealed through the lower federal courts. A decision to actually hear a case is based on the discretion of the justices. If four or more justices agree to hear a case, it is placed on the calendar to be reviewed. In 1991, 6,770 cases were filed with the Supreme Court, with about 200 actually argued (Stanley & Niemi, 1994). In 1994, 8,100 cases were filed, and only 136 were actually argued (U.S. Bureau of the Census, 1996).

The impact of the courts on social welfare policy can be significant. For example, as a result of the *Roe v. Wade* court decision in 1972, abortion became a legal procedure. Members of Congress, although often speaking in favor of legislation outlawing all abortions, have refrained from actually taking a full-floor vote on the legality of abortion. In part this is due to their own vulnerability to the potential political consequences of such a vote, while judges are immune to political fallout.

Federal and State Government Regulatory Agencies

In addition to elected and appointed government positions, there are millions of paid employees who are directly involved in the social welfare policy system. While legislators develop public policy, **federal agencies** are primarily responsible for implementing those policies. Most government laws are passed in the form of general outlines with overall goals. The specifics are yet to be developed. For example, a bill that is passed to change eligibility for AFDC/TANF benefits will outline the general intent. The specific rules and regulations will need to be developed by the federal agency responsible for administering the program. In the case of AFDC/TANF, that would likely be the Office of Family Assistance within the Administration for Children and Families, which is part of the Department of Health and Human Services. The chart in Figure 11.4 outlines the flow of regulation for the AFDC/TANF program.

Figure 11.4
Administrative Flow for AFDC/TANF Program

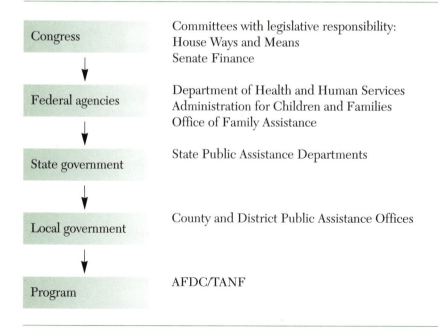

Congress	Committees with legislative responsibility: House Ways and Means Senate Finance
Federal agencies	Department of Health and Human Services Administration for Children and Families Office of Family Assistance
State government	State Public Assistance Departments
Local government	County and District Public Assistance Offices
Program	AFDC/TANF

Source: Adapted from U.S. General Accounting Office (1987).

Each Cabinet-level department is subdivided into numerous offices and agencies responsible for operations and management of federal government programs and services. Listed in Figure 11.5 are the administrative agencies of the Department of Health and Human Services. The breadth and depth of each department is extensive. Some other familiar federal agencies are the Agency for International Development (AID); the Bureau of Alcohol, Tobacco and Firearms; Bureau of Indian Affairs; Central Intelligence Agency (CIA); the Drug Enforcement Administration (DEA); the Federal Bureau of Investigation (FBI); the Internal Revenue Services (IRS); and the United States Postal Service. While department secretaries and many agency directors are presidential appointments, agency personnel tend to be hired employees who may or may not be politically aligned with the president. Many federal agency employees serve for many years under

Figure 11.5
Offices Within the Department of Health and Human Services

Office of the Secretary

The Administration on Aging

Public Health Service

Substance Abuse and Mental Health Service Administration

Agency for Toxic Substances and Disease Registry

Centers for Disease Control and Prevention

Agency for Health Care Policy and Research

Food and Drug Administration

Health Resources and Services Administration

Office of the Assistant Secretary for Health

Indian Health Services

National Institutes of Health

The Administration for Children and Families
    The Administration for Children, Youth, and Families
    The Administration on Developmental Disabilities
    The Administration for Native Americans
    The Office of Child Support Enforcement
    The Office of Community Services
    The Office of Family Assistance
    The Office of Refugee Resettlement

Health Care Financing Administration

Social Security Administration

Source: Office of Management and Budget (1994).

different presidents, Congresses, and political parties. All federal agencies are involved in writing the rules and regulations for programs under their jurisdictions. Local social welfare service agencies are typically bound by those rules and regulations. Thus, federal agency decisions have tremendous impact on the development and delivery of social welfare services in our local communities.

Final Thoughts on Governmental Policy-Making and Social Welfare Policy

The federal and state governments, the executive branch, the judicial system, and regulatory agencies together create, implement, and oversee our social welfare policies. Each takes a different role, but none can operate by itself. A great deal of public hostility toward government, particularly the federal government, surfaced during the mid-1990s. While there are reasons to be frustrated with public policy, government in America is not removed from the people. National elections are held every two years, and as we will see in chapter 13, elections provide a major opportunity for citizens to participate in the policy-making process. State and local governments hold frequent elections as well. Furthermore, government employees represent a wide spectrum of citizens. In 1993, there were 18.8 million federal, state, and local government employees. These employees accounted for almost 16% of the adult employed labor force (U.S. Bureau of the Census, 1996). The reality is that in large part, the government *is* the people. To what extent individuals choose to participate and exercise their right to be an active part of government is a personal decision. In the next chapter, we will look at ways to participate in government and to actively influence the policy-making process.

Key Concepts

legislative branch	executive branch
judicial branch	checks and balances
authorization	federal agencies
appropriation	outlay
entitlements	

Exercises

1. Try to arrange a visit to your state capitol while the General Assembly is in session. Sit in on a committee hearing. What procedures were fol-

lowed? Who were the key participants? What issue was discussed, and what positions were taken?

2. Choose a public law related to a social welfare policy issue. Using resources from a Federal Depository Library (identified in chapter 12), trace the bill's legislative history. When was the issue introduced to Congress? Who introduced it? What committee handled the bill? Were there key players involved in the bill? How long did it take for the bill to go from introduction to passage? Was the bill changed throughout the legislative process? If so, how?

References

Budget of the United States government, fiscal year 1996. (1995). Washington, DC: U.S. Government Printing Office.

Budget of the United States government, fiscal year 1997. (1996). Washington, DC: U.S. Government Printing Office.

Center on Budget and Policy Priorities. (1995). *An unraveling consensus? An analysis of the new Congressional agenda on the working poor.* Washington, DC: Author.

Cloud, D.S. (1995). Shake-up time. *Congressional Quarterly, 53* (Supplement to No. 12), pp. 9–10.

Congressional Quarterly. (1993). *The new Congress, 51* (Supplement to No. 3). Washington, DC: Author.

Congressional Quarterly. (1994). *The freshmen-elect, 52* (Supplemental to No. 44). Washington, DC: Author.

Congressional Quarterly Almanac. (1989). How a bill becomes law. Washington, DC: Congressional Quarterly, Inc.

Congressional Research Service. (1986). *An introduction to the legislative process on the House floor.* Washington, DC: Library of Congress.

Congressional Research Service. (1987). *An introduction to the legislative process on the Senate floor.* Washington, DC: Library of Congress.

Council of State Governments. (1995). *The book of the states, 1994–1995* (Vol. 30). Lexington, KY: Author.

Cranford, J. R. (1990). New budget process for Congress. *Congressional Quarterly Weekly Report, 48,* 3712.

Guide to Congress (4th ed.). (1991). Washington, DC: Congressional Quarterly, Inc.

Hager, G. (1993). Entitlements: The untouchable may become unavoidable. *Congressional Quarterly Weekly Report, 51* (1), 22–30.

High court run on gold watches. (1992, Nov. 16–22). *The Washington Post Weekly, 10,* (3), 31.

Jacobson, G. C. (1987). *The politics of congressional elections* (2nd ed.). Boston: Little, Brown.

Krane, D. (1993). State efforts to influence federal policy. In Jennings, Jr., E.T., & Zank, N.S. (eds.), *Welfare system reform: Coordinating federal, state, and local public assistance programs.* Westport, CT: Greenwood Press.

Langdon, S. (1994). Clinton's high victory rate conceals disappointments. *Congressional Quarterly Weekly Report, 52* (50), 3619–3623.

Office of Management and Budget. (1994). *Catalogue of federal domestic assistance* (28th ed.). Washington, DC: U.S. Government Printing Office.

Oleszek, W.J. (1989). *Congressional procedures and the policy process* (3rd ed.). Washington, DC: Congressional Quarterly, Inc.

Pianin, E. (1992). A budget out of control. *The Washington Post National Weekly Edition, 9* (41), 9.

Pierce, D. (1984). *Policy for the social work practitioner.* New York: Longman.

Stanley, H.W., & Niemi, R.G. (1994). *Vital statistics on American politics* (4th ed.). Washington, DC: CQ Press.

Uchitelle, L. (1990, March 25). Will all this tax talk lead to new taxes? *The New York Times,* (pp. E1, E4).

U.S. Bureau of the Census. (1996). *Statistical Abstract of the United States 1996* (116th ed.). Washington, DC: U.S. Government Printing Office.

U.S. Congress Handbook. (1995). McLean, VA: Dale Pullen.

U.S. General Accounting Office. (1987). *Welfare: Issues to consider in assessing proposals for reform.* Washington, DC: U.S. Government Printing Office.

U.S. House of Representatives. (1986). *How our laws are made.* No. 99–158. Washington, DC: U.S. Government Printing Office.

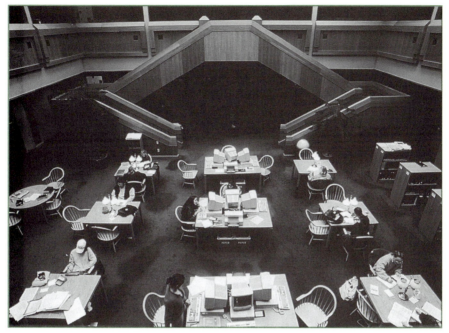

Chapter 12

Sources of Information for Social Welfare Policy Analysis and Practice

The challenge in conducting research in the public policy arena is knowing where to look for information that specifically addresses the creation, development, and implementation of social welfare policies. Numerous sources are available to anyone interested in tracking social welfare policy, but finding and using these sources may seem difficult at first. Libraries are certainly excellent places to start, but there are specific collections, types of libraries, and unique resources that are most useful. In this chapter we will outline key resources for social welfare policy analysis, explain where to find those sources, and describe how to use them.

Familiarity with public policy sources is important as you begin to analyze social welfare policy. Moreover, much of the information in this chapter is critical for understanding the mechanisms of the policy process discussed in chapter 11, and for participating in the policy arena as described in chapter 13. Therefore, the sources described in this chapter are presented to familiarize you with the array of information available to help you analyze social welfare policy, understand the policy process, and influence policy-making.

Most major libraries, and many smaller ones, have reference sections with government-related sources. Many major libraries are designated federal depositories. These libraries are classified as official receptors of government documents available to the public. Most major university libraries and state libraries are federal depositories. These are excellent places to conduct social welfare policy research because the collections are extremely detailed. Other libraries are selective depositories and receive a portion of the available government documents. (Most of the sources listed here, unless otherwise noted, can be found at libraries that serve as federal depositories.)

Gaining Familiarity with Issues and the Legislative Environment

The easiest way to begin to familiarize yourself with social welfare policy issues is to read daily newspapers. Major newspapers such as *The New York Times* and *Washington Post* are indexed, and the indices can be found in book form and on computer databases in major libraries. The newspaper indices can be used to look for subjects that are relevant to the particular public policy or social issue to be researched. For issues of national interest, the *Washington Post* and *The New York Times* are excellent sources. The *Washington Post* offers in-depth coverage of events related to the federal government. For news related to business and economic events, the *Wall Street Journal* provides detailed reports.

In 1979, the House of Representatives passed legislation permitting televised coverage of House proceedings. This vote opened the procedures of Congress to the viewing public. The Cable-Satellite Public Affairs Network (C-SPAN), a private non-profit network, has been televising the proceedings of the House since 1979 and of the Senate since 1986. Programming includes live coverage of each legislative chamber while it is in session. C-SPAN gives the public a chance to view the day-to-day workings of Congress. In addition to House and Senate floor proceedings, C-SPAN includes television coverage of committee hearings, congressional testimonies, presidential speeches, and related public policy events. C-SPAN coverage centers on the events themselves, and little commentary is usually provided. Our discussion in chapter 11 clarified the political process and the procedures followed in Congress. Using that chapter as a guide, watching C-SPAN provides a live demonstration of the federal policy-making process.

Use of daily newspapers and C-SPAN can provide a framework for beginning to understand policy issues. For more detail, the *Congressional*

Quarterly Weekly Report is invaluable. It tracks all major congressional legislation and provides related news reports and analyses. It also covers political events, Supreme Court proceedings, and elections, giving every recorded vote on major legislation. It is published weekly, and every year a compilation of the reports is published as the *Congressional Quarterly Almanac.* The *Almanac,* which is organized by year and congressional session, should be used to investigate the legislative history of an issue. Both the *Almanac* and the *Weekly Report* are indexed by topics so legislation and congressional action can easily be tracked. Even libraries that are not federal depositories may subscribe to the *Congressional Quarterly.*

In addition, the publishers of the *Congressional Quarterly* offer a number of support documents. Most of these are costly, and thus they are usually found in organizations with legislative services, in congressional offices, and in legislative libraries. These documents include the *Congressional Monitor*, issued daily, and *Congress in Print*, which comes out weekly. The *Monitor* lists all committee and subcommittee action and provides a daily calendar of congressional events. *Congress in Print* comes out weekly and lists all available committee and congressional publications.

Another news source for tracking public policy is the *National Journal*. This weekly news magazine covers congressional action and the work of government agencies. The magazine includes features and background information on government policies and politics. The editors of the journal also publish *The Almanac of American Politics*. This annual provides information on all members of Congress as well as descriptions of congressional districts in each state.

Other sources concerning the federal legislative environment include the *American Congressional Dictionary* and the *Guide to Congress*, both published by Congressional Quarterly. These sources provide definitions and explanations for terms related to Congress and to the legislative process. Information on the judicial branch is also included.

Reviewing these sources can help you gain familiarity with the public policy environment and a general sense of what issues are currently being debated. The indices of these sources should also be consulted after you have identified a specific topic for analysis. Armed with general information, you can begin to focus more narrowly on your chosen topic.

Background Research on a Social Issue or Problem

Background information on specific social concerns is available from a variety of sources. Policy analysis resources can be obtained from government agencies, congressional offices, professional associations, and policy research groups. Many of these publications must be secured directly from their issuers and are not available in libraries.

Congressional support services are provided through the research efforts of several agencies. While the agencies' mandates are to serve Congress, most of their publications are available free to the public. The General Accounting Office (GAO) studies issues relevant to government operations and prepares written reports analyzing these issues for Congress. The topics of GAO reports come from requests placed by members of Congress. The reports cover a wide variety of issues, many of which are related to social services.

The Office of Technology Assessment (OTA) prepares scientific and technological analyses at the request of congressional committees. The OTA research includes analyses of health issues. The Congressional Budget Office (CBO) conducts economic forecasts and budget analyses. Reports from both offices are available to the public.

Many federal departments and agencies compile data and develop analyses of social welfare policy and program concerns. For example, the Office of Family Assistance, an agency under the Department of Health and Human Services, keeps statistics on the AFDC program and publishes annual compilations that are available upon request. The Centers for Disease Control and Prevention, an agency under the National Institutes of Health, publishes quarterly statistics on health and morbidity that are available free through subscription. A complete listing of all federal agencies can be found in the *Catalogue of Federal Domestic Assistance*. This catalog, which lists federal programs, projects, and services, can be found in all federal depository libraries.

In addition to government sources, a great deal of policy information can be acquired from professional associations and policy research groups. Many professions have national offices in Washington, D.C., that are responsible for tracking legislation relevant to their membership. For example, the National Association of Social Workers (NASW) is one of many professional organizations with a legislative affairs office. The NASW's legislative staff monitors legislation relevant to the concerns of social workers and publicizes those issues to the national membership. Other professional organizations such as the American Medical Association and the American Psychological Association also have legislative affairs offices.

Other organizations that monitor federal legislation and the impact of policies include groups concerned with civil rights and social welfare policy involving particular population groups. Organizations such as the National Association for the Advancement of Colored People (NAACP), the National Organization for Women (NOW), and the National Gay and Lesbian Task Force (NGLTF) can provide current information on policies affecting their constituent groups. In addition, many other non-profit organizations produce extensive social welfare policy materials regarding special populations. For example, the Children's Defense Fund publishes numerous books and reports assessing the social needs of children in poverty, and these materials are used by many public policy analysts.

Policy research groups tend to be non-profit organizations that provide analyses of national policy issues. Many organizations dedicated to policy analysis track the impact of public policies on populations typically served by social workers. Examples of such groups include the Center on Budget and Policy Priorities, which analyzes issues involving the welfare of low-income persons, and the National Women's Political Caucus, which covers legislative concerns relevant to women. The Center for Law and Social Policy is a public-interest law firm specializing in policy research, education, and advocacy on behalf of low-income families.

These policy research groups, and most others, publish newsletters, reports, and other publications that are available directly from the organizations. These sources, which tend to be specialized according to their area of interest, are excellent sources for up-to-date information. When you have identified organizations that focus on your area of interest, you can get on their mailing lists to stay informed of recent developments.

Often, fully understanding the dimensions of a social issue requires knowledge of the extent of a social problem. National statistics and incidence data on numerous social welfare issues are published in the annual *Statistical Abstract of the United States*. The *Abstract* provides statistics on economic, political, and demographic categories for the entire population. Data range over the past fifteen to twenty years, although the *Historical Statistics of the United States* covers statistics dating back to the 1790s. These two sources can be found in almost any library.

The *Social Security Bulletin* is published quarterly by the Social Security Administration. It includes articles related to social insurance and public assistance as well as a variety of statistics on many social welfare programs. Each year, a compilation of data is published as the *Annual Statistical Supplement*.

The Bureau of the Census also publishes collections of statistical data. Bureau of the Census reports include studies of population data, labor trends, and economic indicators. A newsletter called the *Monthly Product Announcement* lists all data sets and reports released by the U.S. Department of Commerce and the Bureau of the Census. Materials can be ordered directly from the Bureau or through the Government Printing Office (GPO).

Documents for Analyzing Specific Social Welfare Policies

Sources such as those already discussed can provide a thorough understanding of the background of an issue. Deeper social welfare policy analysis, however, requires delving into primary source materials. These sources include documents published by the federal government in the form of reports, committee hearings, proceedings of the House or Senate, federal announcements, and actual legislation. The quantity and breadth of materials can be overwhelming, but like all new learning, it can be mastered with time and experience.

Primary Documents

The GPO is the official publisher of government documents. The main office is in Washington, D.C., but the GPO has twenty-five bookstores located throughout the country. The GPO is the source for most documents published by the federal government. It also publishes a newsletter, the *Monthly Catalog of U.S. Government Publications*, which lists everything available through the GPO. The GPO also issues *Selected U.S. Government Publications*, a list of the most popular publications. This monthly listing is available from the Superintendent of Documents.

Copies of congressional bills currently pending or public laws passed during the current Congress, called slip laws, are available directly from congressional document rooms. The House and Senate Document Rooms will send bills introduced within their respective chambers in response to requests from the public. The House Document Room will take requests over the phone or through the mail, but the Senate Document Room will respond only to mailed requests. The Document Rooms usually provide copies of bills and laws only from the current congressional session.

The process for passage and codification of laws, as explained in detail in chapter 11, can be confusing. A number of sources can, however, make it easier to track the evolution and codification of laws. Verbatim records of activity on the floors of the House and Senate are published in the *Congressional Record* each day Congress is in session. The *Congressional Record* includes all the speeches, votes, bills, and resolutions introduced during the day. It is organized by date and can be very lengthy as it records every detail of each day Congress is in session. Federal depository libraries receive the *Congressional Record*.

The *Federal Register* publishes all federal agency regulations and proposed regulations, as well as other documents from the executive branch. The *Federal Register* is a daily publication that includes proposed changes to agency regulations and announcements of grants available for programs or research. For those interested in following changes in agency rules and regulations, this is the most valuable source. The *Federal Register* includes solicitations for public input on the proposed changes to federal agency regulations. The *Federal Register* is also very lengthy, although it is indexed. Sometimes government agencies will develop their own mailing lists and send out related announcements directly. A federal agency should be contacted directly for a request to be added to their mailing list.

Once a bill is passed by Congress and signed into law, it is given a number. Initially, it is printed as a slip law and is available through the Document Rooms or at many depository libraries. Later, it is published in the annual *United States Statutes at Large*. These annual volumes contain the laws and resolutions enacted during each congressional session. The *Statutes* includes a section with legislative histories of bills that have become public law.

Eventually all laws are organized and codified into the *United States Code*. The laws are organized by subject, and the listing is updated every six years. Between revisions, the *United States Code Supplement* is published with the legislation to be included in the next collection. Both the *Code* and the *Statutes* can be found in federal depository libraries.

Another primary source is the *Weekly Compilation of Presidential Documents*. This collection publishes all the public statements and announcements of the president. It includes proclamations, executive orders, news conferences, public speeches, and messages to Congress.

Each year, the president releases the *Budget of the United States Government* in early February. This book opens with the president's report on the state of the budget and outlines proposals for the next fiscal year. This is the document that serves as the basis for congressional discussions and actions on passing the annual budget. The book includes the actual expenditures for each federal program over the last several years, as well as an index by agency and program. A number of support documents that are published at the same time can help to explain the budget. The budget and support materials are available through the GPO and in most libraries.

Support Resources for Using Primary Documents

To find your way through all the information and Congressional activity of each chamber, you can turn to a number of support sources that cover and explain Congressional activity. These collections organize and index by topics or legislation the proceedings of Congress.

The Congressional Information Service (CIS) is a commercial enterprise that publishes an index with summaries of congressional activities. The *CIS Index* lists summaries and abstracts of congressional hearings, reports, and documents, indexing them according to topic, name, and bill number. It is an excellent tool for conducting general searches by subject or for tracking a specific piece of legislation. The *CIS Annual* is a yearly compilation of the material presented in the index. Many large libraries subscribe to these sources, and they can usually be found in a government documents reference section. The CIS also publishes the *CIS Federal Register Index*, which serves as a guide to the *Federal Register*. It provides indices by subject, policy area, federal agency, and legislation.

Another company, Commerce Clearing House, also publishes an index of the activities of Congress. The *Commerce Clearing House Congressional Index* consists of looseleaf binders of weekly reports on legislation. The information is organized by subject, name of legislation, and author of the bill. Also included are biographical information on congressional members and data on how they voted on each piece of legislation. Commerce Clearing House also publishes reports on social welfare policy issues that can serve as good background material for policy analysis.

After every Congress, the Congressional Research Service (CRS), the agency that provides research assistance to members of Congress, publishes a summary of all bills enacted into law. The *Major Legislation of the Congress* divides congressional activity into numerous subject areas, such as education, taxation, social services, and transportation. The book includes a summary of the action taken and an explanation of the relevant legislation that was enacted into law. The legislative summaries include the public law number, references to other related documents, and legislative histories. Most libraries keep this source in the government documents reference section.

The Office of Management and Budget (OMB) annually publishes supporting documents and guides for the *Budget of the United States Government*. For details on the analysis of specific program areas and economics, the OMB publishes the *Analytical Perspectives*, and for historical information, the *Historical Tables, Budget of the United States Government*. These sources can usually be found at federal depository libraries. In 1995, the The OMB offered a new guide designed specifically for the general public, *A Citizen's Guide to the Federal Budget*.

Information on the government itself is available through the *United States Government Manual*. This annual publication describes the agencies of the legislative, judicial, and executive branches. The history and purpose of each agency is provided. The manual also lists the principal officials of each agency. Finally, Congressional Quarterly publishes an excellent overall source called the *Guide to Congress*. For information on individual members of Congress by district within each state, use *The Almanac of American Politics*. The *Almanac* also provides information on each state and on the characteristics of each district's population.

Other Sources of Information on Social Welfare Issues, Policies, and Programs

Government documents and published manuals are not the only sources available to assist you in analyzing and tracking social welfare policies. Many professionals and members of organizations can provide background information and insights into the development of social welfare policies and programs. State and local governments can also provide resources and information relevant to social welfare policy.

Key Informants

One way to gather policy-relevant information is to get in touch with people who are closely involved in the policy arena. Public officials, particularly elected officials in your area, tend to respond quickly to requests for information. Every congressional office is staffed with people who are responsible for addressing constituents' concerns. A request for background information or details on specific legislation can be made to the offices of members of Congress either by mail or telephone. Congressional offices in Washington include staff members who are assigned to topic areas and can be very helpful in providing policy information. When calling a congressperson's office, ask for the person, or legislative aide, responsible for the subject in which you are interested.

All members of Congress have, in addition to their Washington office, an office back in their home district. With advance notice, it is often possible to meet with members of Congress when they are home. Insight into how to maximize the impact of a meeting with an elected official is discussed in the last two chapters. Generally, it is important to be able to state what you need in a clear, direct, and concise manner.

Other individuals who can be very helpful are representatives of advocacy groups. While the larger groups often have written materials to send, some will schedule interviews and provide information first-hand. This is particularly likely for local chapters or offices that may be located in your community. Key informants can be valuable if you are doing social welfare policy research in a location where it is difficult to access state or national sources. As is true for all interviews with key informants, it is important to first conduct enough background research to allow you to be clear and specific about the information desired.

State and Local Policy Resources

A number of sources can be used to compile data related to the impact of public policy on states and localities. The Bureau of the Census publishes statistics in the *County and City Data Book* and the *State and Metropolitan Area Data Book*. The *Municipal Yearbook* publishes data on economics and demographics for cities. While not all cities are included, a section with a directory of the names of municipal officials and the telephone numbers of city halls is included. *The Book of the States* provides information on all state governments. This source is published annually by the Council of State Governments. It lists governors, state legislators, and information on each state by voting district. These sources can be found in many libraries.

State libraries usually subscribe to news reports that are relevant to residents of the state. For example, *State Policy Reports* and *State Budget and Tax News* provide in-depth coverage and analysis of public policies related to statewide concerns for all fifty states. Typically, each state compiles statistical data on the state and its local communities. Usually the information can be found through a state university or agency. The list on the next page gives examples of the statistical data available in several states.

Each year, the GPO publishes *Federal Expenditures by State*, which provides data compiled by the Bureau of the Census on federal grants and payments made to state and local governments. It lists grants made to nongovernmental recipients as well.

In addition, a number of associations provide state governments and localities with policy-related information pertinent to their communities. The National Governors' Association (NGA) and the National Conference of State Legislators (NCSL) keep state governments abreast of national public policy. In addition to these major organizations, every state has its

Examples of Statistical Data Available in States[*]

Arizona
Arizona Statistical Abstract
Arizona Economic Indicators
Arizona's Economy
University of Arizona
Dept. of Economic and
   Business Research
College of Business and Public
   Administration
McClelland Hall, #204
Tucson, AZ 85721-0001
(520) 621-2155

California
California Statistical Abstract
Department of Finance
915 L Street, 8th Floor
Sacramento, CA 95814
(916) 322-2263

California Almanac, 6th ed.
Pacific Data Resources
P.O. Box 1922
Santa Barbara, CA 93116-1922
(800) 422-2546

Maryland
Maryland Statistical Abstract
Regional Economic Studies Institute
Towson State University
Towson, MD 21204-7097
(410) 830-3765

New York
New York State Statistical Yearbook
Nelson Rockefeller Institute of
   Government
411 State Street
Albany, NY 12203-1003
(518) 443-5522

Wisconsin
1995–1996 Wisconsin Blue Book
Wisconsin Legislative Reference
   Bureau
P.O. Box 2037
Madison, WI 53701-2037
(608) 266-0341

Texas
Texas Almanac
Dallas Morning News,
   Communications Center
P.O. Box 655237
Dallas, TX 75265
(214) 977-8261

Texas Fact Book
University of Texas
Bureau of Business Research
Austin, TX 78713
(512) 471-5180

[*]For listings for each state, see U.S. Bureau of the Census (1996), *Statistical Abstract of the U.S.: 1996* (116th ed.), Appendix 1, pp. 931–934 (Washington, DC: U.S. Government Printing Office).

own office in Washington, D.C., located in a building called the Hall of States. The NGA and NCSL are also located in the Hall of States, and these organizations can forward requests for information to the appropriate state office.

The U.S. Conference of Mayors has an office that serves as a policy resource for major cities. Its reports and policy summaries are available to the public.

For information on policies specific to a state or locality, you should contact a state library or local government office. All states have libraries with both federal and state documents and references. The most comprehensive libraries usually are located in the state capitol city, but regional agency offices throughout states can have libraries with state and local social welfare policy resources. For example, a regional children's services office or public assistance center may have information on state and local policies and how federal laws are implemented locally.

Alternative Sources

Most of the resources already mentioned are published by official government units or established organizations. A number of policy groups and media track public policy from non-mainstream perspectives. Journals and magazines such as the *Nation, Mother Jones,* and the *Guardian* analyze public policy from a liberal or leftist orientation. Conservative think tanks such as the American Enterprise Institute and the Heritage Foundation also publish materials available to the public. To become familiar with all the dimensions of a policy, and to understand the opposing viewpoints, you may find it helpful to consult sources outside of the mainstream. Alternative sources can shed new light on issues and widen your understanding of the complexity of social welfare policies.

New Technologies

The development of the CD-ROM is expanding the amount of accessible information for policy analysis. Major libraries now carry indices of many sources on compact disks. The information is loaded into a computer, and users can access the information through a terminal in the library. The advantage to CD-ROM resources is that a tremendous amount of information can be stored on each disk.

Government agencies such as the Bureau of the Census are releasing data sets on CD-ROM. This advent in technology means that individuals with CD-ROM drives on their computers can purchase data sets that were formerly available in a format that only large computer systems could handle. CD-ROM capabilities are available with most new computers and as the use of them increases, so too will the data and information available on disks.

Expanded access to cable television has created ways to gain information on local public policy events. Local access stations cover school board meetings, town hall meetings, and other local government events. Public service groups also use public access cable stations to provide information on local concerns.

The Internet and the World Wide Web offer new access to materials related to social welfare policy. The list below gives Web sites for sources of

Sources of Information on the Internet / World Wide Web

Organizations

Center on Budget and Policy Priorities
http://www.cbpp.org

Urban Institute
http://www.urban.org

Center for Law and Social Policy
http://www.clasp.org

Institute for Research on Poverty
University of Wisconsin, Madison
http://www.ssc.wisc.edu/irp/

Poverty and Race Research Action Council
e-mail: prrac@aol.com

Handsnet
Welfare reform watch and analysis.
http://www.igc.apc.org/handsnet2/welfare.reform/index.html

Electronic Policy Network
Information and analysis of economic issues, welfare reform, family and health policy, and national politics.
http://epn.org/

American Public Welfare Association
http://www.apwa.org

Federal Government Information

Government Printing Office
http://www.access.gpo.gov/su_docs/

Library of Congress Site
Contains current proposals; legislation; committee reports; Congress this Week; bill text, summaries, and status; Congressional Record; historic documents; and congressional e-mail information.
http://www.thomas.loc.gov/

U.S. Department of Health and Human Services
http://www.os.dhhs.gov

FedWorld
Site links to federal agencies. Government information and documents, wide variety of reports.
http://www.fedworld.gov/

CapWeb
Guide to Congress. Information on the workings of Congress, including information about members of the House and Senate and the congressional process.
http://policy.net/capweb/congress.html

Bureau of the Census
http://www.census.gov/

Sources of Information (cont.)

State Government Information

Council on State Governments
http://www.csg.org

National Conference of State Legislatures
http://www.ncsl.org

National Governors' Association
http://www.nga.org

valuable social welfare policy information. The Internet provides immediate access to government documents and advocacy groups and can be interactive, but a word of caution is in order for users of this evolving technology. World Wide Web pages and user groups on the Internet are readily available to any organization or individual who wants to create a site. That means that material can be posted that is biased, misguided, or even completely erroneous. Unless you are confident of the source, use care in basing your knowledge on material gathered through the Internet.

Final Thoughts on Sources of Information for Social Welfare Policy Analysis and Practice

In this chapter we have provided an extensive listing of sources that can be used for social welfare policy analysis and practice. Depending on the goal of your research, some sources are more appropriate than others. Some published materials are easier to use than others. The best approach is to go to a federal depository library and become familiar with the resources available there. Start in the reference section and then explore the collection of federal documents identified in this chapter. As you become familiar with these sources, they can become extremely helpful in providing current information on the status of public policies and the background necessary to do a thorough social welfare policy analysis. It is also important to keep informed of current political events that affect social welfare policies. This can be done by using media sources, particularly daily newspapers. Once these sources become familiar, conducting a thorough policy analysis and taking action within the policy arena are manageable tasks.

Exercises

1. Go to your university library or public library. Find out if it is a federal depository. Does it have a government documents section? Browse through the reference section. Is there a state or local government section? Become familiar with the resources available. Use the items listed in this chapter as a guide.

2. Identify a social welfare policy issue in which you have an interest. See if you can identify a key informant who can provide more information on the topic. Ask your instructor, field supervisor, or classmates if they can help you identify someone. Try to make an appointment for an informational interview. Prepare your questions in advance and find out what you can about your topic.

3. Every day for two or three weeks, read a national newspaper, such as *The New York Times*. You can do this at your local library. How extensive is the paper's coverage of social welfare policy? Did you learn something new related to a social issue of interest to you?

Resource List for Sources of Information on Social Welfare Policy

Federal Government Resources

General Accounting Office
Document Handling and Information
  Services Facility
P.O. Box 6015
Gaithersburg, MD 20877
(202) 275-6241

GAO reports and summaries of reports; up to five copies are available free of charge. You can send in a written request to be added to the monthly summary distribution list.

Office of Technology Assessment
Publications Office
Washington, DC 20510
(202) 224-8996

Publication list.

Congressional Budget Office
Publications Office
House Office Building Annex #2
Second and D Streets SW
Washington, DC 20515
(202) 226-2809

Publication list.

Government Printing Office
710 N. Capitol Street NW
Washington, DC 20402
(202) 512-1808, 512-0132

Source for almost all documents published by the government.

Superintendent of Documents
U.S. Government Printing Office
Washington, DC 20402

Write to be added to distribution list.

Customer Services
Bureau of the Census
Washington, DC 20233
(301) 763-4100

Write or call for subscription to the Monthly Product Announcement *newsletter.*

Public Bills, Resolutions, and Reports

House Document Room
Room B-18
House Annex #2
Washington, DC 20515
(202) 225-3456

Senate Document Room
Room B-04
Hart Senate Office Building
Washington, DC 20510
(202) 224-7860
(202) 228-2815 (FAX)

You can order up to twelve different bills or reports. Include a return address label.

Information on Elections

Federal Election Commission
999 E Street NW
Washington, DC 20463
(800) 424-9530

Campaign financing information.

Organizations

National Organization for Women
1000 16th Street NW
Washington, DC 20036
(202) 331-0066

Center for Law and Social Policy
1616 P Street NW, Suite 150
Washington, DC 20036
(202) 328-5140

Center on Budget and Policy
   Priorities
777 North Capitol Street NE,
   Suite 705
Washington, DC 20002
(202) 408-1080

National Association for the
   Advancement of Colored People
1025 Vermont Avenue NW
Washington, DC 20005
(301) 358-8900

National Women's Political Caucus
1275 K Street NW, Suite 750
Washington, DC 20005-4051
(202) 898-1100

For information: (800) 729-6972

LEAP Asian-Pacific American Public
   Policy Institute
327 E. 2nd Street, #226
Los Angeles, CA 90012-4210
(213) 485-1422

American Indian Research and Policy
   Institute
749 Simpson Street N
St. Paul, MN 55104
(612) 644-1728

National Council of La Raza
   (Latino Issues)
1111 19th Street NW, #1000
Washington, DC 20036
(202) 785-1670

Human Rights Campaign (Gay and
   Lesbian Issues)
1101 14th Street NW, Suite 200
Washington, DC 20005
(202) 628-4160

State and Municipal Organizations

National Conference of State
  Legislatures
4444 North Capitol St. NW,
  Suite 500
Washington, DC 20001
(202) 624-5400

For information on publications: (303) 830-2054

National Governors' Association
4444 North Capitol St. NW,
  Suite 250
Washington, DC 20001
(202) 624-5300

U.S. Conference of Mayors
1620 I St. NW
Washington, DC 20006
(202) 293-7330

© Joel Gordon

Chapter 13

Policy Practice: Influencing the Course of Social Welfare Policy

Knowledge of how policies are made gives us the ability to take an active role in the process and to influence the outcome. In the field of social work, involvement in the policy-making process is very important. One role of social workers is to advocate on behalf of those who are disadvantaged and marginalized, and effective advocacy often involves the ability to influence and challenge politicians and other policy-makers.

Participating in the political system is a powerful way to bring about change. Like other forms of social work intervention, this requires direct involvement. In this sense, social workers need to become skilled **policy practitioners**. Many of the skills social work students develop in working directly with clients are well suited to use in influencing the direction and substance of social welfare policy. Therefore, social welfare policy practice is more than a theoretical construct—it is an active component of social work. In this chapter, we present tactics to use as a policy practitioner, and we outline how to conduct policy practice and directly influence the policy-making process.

Legislative Advocacy

There are a number of ways to advocate for legislation and to influence policy. The most common are through voting and lobbying. Other methods include contact with elected officials through telephone calls, letters, and personal visits, as well as more formal means such as providing public testimony or developing policy briefs and analyses. We often think of these actions as belonging to professional lobbying groups, but social work practitioners, students, and clients are well suited to do this kind of political work. In this section, we cover all of the methods listed above, and we present key tactics to enhance the effectiveness of one's efforts.

Voting and Voter Registration

Every citizen 18 years of age or older has the right to vote in all elections in this country. We often take this right for granted, but it is a fairly recent development. Women were not granted the right to vote until 1920. For African-Americans, voting did not become a publicly enforced right until passage of the Voting Rights Act in 1965. Young people became eligible to vote in 1971, when the voting age was lowered from 21 to 18. In spite of the freedom for all to vote, Americans do not tend to participate in elections. Compared to citizens of other democracies, Americans stay away from the polling place. In a comparison of voting rates during the 1980s, voter turnout in the United States was about 53%. This compares poorly with rates of 94% in Italy, 89% in Austria, 81% in West Germany, 78% in France, 76% in the United Kingdom, 74% in Japan, and 67% in Canada. The United States ranked twentieth out of a comparison of twenty-one democracies (U.S. General Accounting Office, 1990).

It is important to try to understand why people vote or do not vote. Table 13.1 displays statistics on voting demographics from 1978 to 1994 during presidential and congressional elections. While the voter turnout was low for presidential elections, it was even lower for congressional elections when there was no presidential race. From 1964 through 1992, an average of 62% of people of voting age actually voted during presidential elections. From 1966 through 1994, the percent of eligible voters who voted in congressional elections held between presidential years was less than 49%. Post-election analyses revealed that voter turnout for the 1996 presidential election may have been the lowest since 1924, between 49 and 50% (Schmitt, 1996).

The demographic breakdown of who is more likely to vote reveals some of the impetus. The least likely people to register to vote and actually vote

Table 13.1

Percent of Eligible Citizens Who Voted in Presidential and Congressional Elections, 1978–1994

	1978	1980	1982	1984	1986	1988	1990	1992	1994
Total voting-age population (in millions)	152	**157**	165	**170**	174	**178**	182	**186**	190
Percent who voted	46%	**59%**	49%	**60%**	46%	**57%**	45%	**61%**	45%
Race									
White	47%	**61%**	50%	**61%**	47%	**59%**	47%	**64%**	47%
African-American	37	**51**	43	**56**	43	**59**	39	**54**	37
Hispanic	24	**30**	25	**33**	24	**29**	21	**29**	19
Sex									
Male	47%	**59%**	49%	**59%**	46%	**56%**	45%	**60%**	45%
Female	45	**59**	48	**61**	46	**58**	45	**62**	45
Age									
18–24	24%	**40%**	25%	**41%**	22%	**36%**	20%	**43%**	20%
25–44	43	**59**	45	**58**	41	**54**	41	**58**	39
45–64	59	**69**	62	**70**	59	**68**	56	**70**	56
65+	56	**65**	60	**68**	61	**69**	60	**70**	61

[Results from presidential election years are shown in **boldface**.]

Sources: U.S. Bureau of the Census (1991); U.S. Bureau of the Census (1993); and U.S. Bureau of the Census (1996).

are young adults and members of minority groups. The most active group is older adults. Until the mid-1980s, men voted in slightly greater proportions than did women, but today women register and vote to a greater extent than men.

Politicians are well aware of the patterns in voting. Because of this knowledge, they are more likely to tailor their positions to the preferences of those most apt to vote. For this reason, some policy analysts regard voting as a weak way to influence policy. Lindblom (1980) argues that voters' ignorance and their tendency to vote for candidates and not directly for policy issues makes voting a weak instrument for influencing public policy. First, unless people actively pursue information on candidates, voters are aware of only the polished, public relations view of a candidate. Outside of presidential elections and other well-publicized contests, people often do not know the names of their elected representatives. This lack of knowledge and interest skews election results. Second, even knowledgeable voters are unlikely to find a candidate who agrees with them on all issues. Many voters either pick candidates based on superficial information or on their positions regarding a few key issues. Voting does not give people a chance to voice preferences for particular policies.

This pessimistic view of voting may describe the current state of elections, but it does not have to be this way. The fact that policy-makers are swayed by those who vote does not negate the value of the election process. Rather, the challenge is to ensure that more people vote and that voter turnout is proportionate to the population. For example, much was made of the mandate for Ronald Reagan in 1980. His election as president was regarded as a loud call for changes in public policies. While Reagan did win as president, his mandate was less than clear. Ronald Reagan received votes from 27.9% of the eligible voters, compared to Jimmy Carter's receipt of 22.6%. More than 70 million people who were eligible to vote did not do so. Ronald Reagan won a plurality of those who bothered to cast a vote. The 1960 election of John F. Kennedy against Richard Nixon was even more telling. Kennedy received votes from a mere .1% more of the population that was eligible to vote. Only 119,000 votes cast separated the two candidates (author calculations based on data from U.S. Bureau of the Census, 1996).

These examples demonstrate that even in major elections, getting more people to vote could change the outcome. Also, because not all people who are eligible to vote actually do so, efforts to target those who do vote can be extremely successful. While political candidates are well aware of this, social service providers and recipients generally are not.

For social workers and their clients, voting can be an empowering act:

> Promoting and enhancing client self-determination is a basic value of social work. Voting is one of the mechanisms that permits the citizens in a democratic nation to have a voice in determining the nation's domestic and foreign policies (Haynes & Mickelson, 1991, p. 54).

To vote, a person must first be registered. Rules for registration vary by state but typically require filing forms at least thirty days before an election and each time a person moves to a new address. As Table 13.2 demonstrates, voter registration is skewed, particularly by age and race. Also, those who are financially secure are more likely to register than are people with lower incomes. These trends can be seen in registration and voting patterns. For example, in the 1992 presidential election, 41% of people with annual incomes between $10,000 and $15,000 voted, compared to 74% of people who earned more than $50,000. In 1994, voter registration was 59% for people who earned between $10,000 and $15,000 and 83% for people who earned more than $75,000 (Merida, 1996).

Voter registration became easier in 1995 upon implementation of the National Voter Registration Act. The Act requires states to offer voter registration to all people applying for or renewing drivers' licenses, and it allows people to register in social service agencies and through mail-in applications. This legislation makes voter registration more accessible and easier. Social workers and their agencies can participate in voter registration.

Table 13.2

Percent of Eligible Citizens Registered to Vote in Presidential and Congressional Elections, 1978–1994

	1978	1980	1982	1984	1986	1988	1990	1992	1994
Total voting-age population (in millions)	152	**157**	165	**170**	174	**178**	182	**186**	190
Percent who registered	63%	**67%**	64%	**68%**	64%	**67%**	62%	**68%**	62%
Race									
White	64%	**68%**	66%	**70%**	65%	**68%**	64%	**70%**	64%
African-American	57	**60**	59	**66**	64	**65**	59	**64**	58
Hispanic	33	**36**	35	**40**	36	**36**	32	**35**	30
Sex									
Male	63%	**67%**	64%	**67%**	63%	**65%**	61%	**67%**	61%
Female	63	**67**	64	**69**	65	**68**	63	**69**	63
Age									
18–24	41%	**49%**	42%	**51%**	42%	**48%**	40%	**53%**	42%
25–44	60	**66**	62	**67**	61	**63**	58	**65**	58
45–64	74	**76**	76	**77**	75	**76**	71	**75**	71
65+	73	**75**	75	**77**	77	**78**	77	**78**	76

[Results from presidential election years are shown in **boldface**.]

Sources: U.S. Bureau of the Census (1991); U.S. Bureau of the Census (1993); and U.S. Bureau of the Census (1996).

Sometimes voter registration is mistakenly viewed by some people as a partisan political act. For an action to be partisan, however, it must promote a position or a side of an issue. Registering people to vote takes no political side; it simply allows them the opportunity to participate and thereby privately choose a side. Thus, social workers can be involved in encouraging clients and coworkers to register to vote without any conflict of interest.

Voting is a significant way to register public opinion and take a position on policy issues, but it is not the only way to do so. Some of the other ways are discussed below.

Lobbying

The term lobbying conveys some powerful images today, most of them negative. The common view of lobbyists is that of extremely highly paid political specialists who use less-than-honorable means to influence politicians. While influence is definitely related to money and access (as will be discussed later in regard to the power of political action committees, or PACs), **lobbying** is a general term for all activities used to persuade policymakers. Lobbying can encompass educating elected officials about the pros and cons of pending legislation, publicizing important issues, and providing technical information. On the negative side, lobbyists present one-sided information: they only tell and support with evidence their points of view. Thus, size of an organization and resources can affect whose position actually gets heard.

The characteristics and skills of successful lobbyists are extensive. Mahaffey (1982, p. 76) provides the following list:

- Friendly, articulate, outgoing, flexible, persuasive;
- Work independently;
- Follow organization's general directives;
- Know when to talk and when to listen;
- Know how to wait, patience;
- Knowledge of parliamentary procedure.

In addition, lobbyists must be good strategizers. They must be able to plan effective campaigns to gain political support for an issue.

Groups that do not have the resources for professional lobbyists can come together to form a coalition. Organizing around a particular issue can increase the level of influence groups can exert on policy-makers. Pooling of resources can also mean that lobbying efforts not available to each group alone can be acquired for a coalition of groups.

The key to successful lobbying is to stay focused on the issue of concern, particularly in the early stages of policy development. As described in chapter 11, the efforts of committees and subcommittees on both the federal and state levels of government are crucial to the passage of a bill. The period when a bill is being discussed in committee is the most crucial time to apply lobbying pressure. Whether done through formal or informal networks, using professionals or constituents, personal contact with legislators early in the legislative process can be most effective in achieving the desired outcome.

Meeting with Elected Officials

Organizations, agencies, and individuals need not employ a professional lobbyist to achieve results. Personal meetings can be arranged with elected officials or their staff members. These meetings can have an impact on the course of legislation.

Senators all have offices in their home states as do congressional representatives in their home districts. State representatives also have offices in their home communities. Visiting Washington may not be feasible, but it is often possible to arrange an appointment with an elected official in his or her local office. You can improve your chances for a personal visit if you include media coverage. This can be as simple as informing the staff member making the arrangements that you will have a photographer with you to take pictures for a newsletter. Elected officials are apt to participate in events that will bring them positive publicity with the people who elect them.

If the elected official is not available for a meeting, staff members usually are. Try to find out which staff person handles the issue you are interested in discussing. Speaking to a staff member can be a very effective way to influence the elected official. Members of Congress and state representatives rely on their staff members to do research and brief them on key issues. Often staff members rely on information provided by lobbyists and advocacy groups to get different perspectives on an issue. Constituents who take the time and effort to present their position can make a strong impression, influence the staff person, and thereby reach the elected official.

Whether a meeting is held with a staff member or the elected official, be sure to identify yourself as a constituent. Elected officials have limited time. They are most responsive to those who elect them or will re-elect them. Prepare for your meeting in advance by drafting a very brief presentation. You do not need to be an expert on legislative details. Rather, use your knowledge and experience of social issues to prepare your presentation. Very politely present your position and briefly support it. Use of personal experiences, clients' experiences, or anecdotal cases can be very helpful. Be sure to describe what you would like the elected official to do.

You should ask what position the official has taken thus far on the issue. Do not argue against his or her position; rather, offer to restate yours. In addition, it is very acceptable to leave information such as a prepared fact sheet with a business card. Overall, be brief, concise, and polite. After the meeting, follow up with a thank-you note. Using these approaches will help ensure the opportunity for another meeting in the future.

Mail and Telephone Contact

If it is not possible to arrange a personal meeting, you can write a letter. It may seem that a letter is not a very persuasive tool, but it can be extremely effective. Researchers asked congressional staff people to list types of communication to which members of Congress respond, and the number one answer was spontaneous constituent mail (Religious Action Center, 1989).

With the advent of computers and word processors, hand-written letters are more convincing than ever, but they must be clear and legible. The most effective letters are clearly personal, not mass-produced. The letter should be short, preferably no longer than one page. State your position, being as specific as possible. If you are writing in regard to a piece of legislation or pending government action, identify it clearly. The tone of the letter should be positive and respectful. Be sure to include your name and address on the letter and to request a response.

The typical congressional representative receives an average of 100 letters on each issue (Peck, 1991). Although the official may not read every letter, he or she will read a representative sample and get a tally of the number of favorable and unfavorable letters. For example, many offices log in each letter received and record the issue and position. Then, at the end of the week, the elected member receives a list or graph of constituent positions. The numbers often influence how a member votes.

The above guidelines apply for phone calls as well. Unless you are able to speak with a staff member about the issue, simply leave your name and address and state your position clearly. Staff members usually keep a tally of the positions taken by the phone callers. These are also reported to the elected official. The general attitude in political offices is that anyone who takes the time and effort to write a letter or make a phone call will also take the time to vote. Therefore, your efforts are taken seriously and can influence the outcome of legislation.

As a social welfare policy practitioner, you may want to organize a letter-writing effort. It is better to present individual positions than to rely on an orchestrated activity such as form letters, pre-printed postcards, or petitions. One way to accomplish this is to invite a number of people (colleagues, community members, students) to come to a letter-writing meeting. At the meeting, present background on the issue of concern to inform and educate people. Have on hand different types of envelopes and stationery as well as stamps. Have people write individual letters stating the position clearly. Collect the signed and addressed letters. Over the course of a few days or weeks, depending on the level of action on the issue, mail the letters. This will leave the legislator's office with the impression that many different individuals are concerned.

When writing to or calling federal senators and representatives, use the following addresses and salutations:

HOUSE
The Honorable _____
U.S. House of Representatives
Washington, DC 20515
"Dear Representative _____"

SENATE
The Honorable _____
U.S. Senate
Washington, DC 20510
"Dear Senator _____"

Call the Capitol switchboard at (202) 225-3121 and ask for the legislator by name. You will be connected to the office.

For letters and calls to the president, use the following:

The Honorable _____
President of the United States
The White House
1600 Pennsylvania Avenue, NW
Washington, DC 20500
"Dear President _____"

An outline to guide you in writing legislators is given in Figure 13.1 and a sample letter is provided in Figure 13.2.

Providing Legislative Testimony

A more formal way to influence the policy process is to provide **legislative testimony** before a congressional or general assembly committee or sub-committee. These meetings are called public hearings. To gather information on different sides of an issue, legislators schedule public hearings. On the federal level, hearings are scheduled frequently and are open to the public. The next time you visit Washington, you may be able to sit in on a hearing. The times and locations are printed weekly in the *Washington Post*. Schedules of public hearings can also be obtained directly from the committee staff. On the state level, hearings are also open to the public. The schedules of hearings are sometimes reported in the local newspaper or can be obtained through the office of the General Assembly clerk.

The people who testify at a federal hearing are usually selected by the staff of the committee. The presenters tend to be experts or individuals who have been directly affected by the issue being discussed. Although not many people have an opportunity to give testimony in Washington, sometimes federal committees conduct field hearings. These public hearings are held in communities throughout the country. It is easier for the average person to gain access to testify at a field hearing. The planning and scheduling of field hearings is handled by the committee staff.

Figure 13.1
Guide to Public Policy Letter Writing

1. Be concise. Try to limit yourself to one page.
2. Be aware of your audience. Remember you are writing to an elected official.
3. Be polite. You may want support on another issue in the future.
4. Be explicit. Do not assume the reader knows the issue.
5. State your purpose. Identify a specific piece of legislation if possible.
6. State your position. Cite statistics and facts if available.
7. Provide a personal point of view on the issue.
8. If you are opposing a policy, suggest alternatives.
9. Request a response. Include your full name and address.
10. Remind the legislator that you live in his or her district or state.

Source: Adapted from Michigan Program in Child Development and Social Policy (1992).

Figure 13.2
Sample Letter to Legislator

Date

Address of Elected Official

Dear _____ :

I am very concerned about the cuts in funding proposed by the Congress for homelessness and housing programs run by the Department of Housing and Urban Development. These proposed cuts come at a time when the problem of homelessness is getting worse and more people are in need of shelter and housing services.

Over the past ten years, funding for housing programs has been cut significantly. Our local program, [name of program], depends on federal support to provide [list services]. To make it possible for us to continue providing these much-needed services, I would appreciate your support for increased funding for the homelessness and housing programs of HUD. [Include specific legislation, name and number of pending bill, if possible or relevant.]

Please do everything in your power to increase the funding and resources needed to help house people who are homeless. Thank you for your consideration, I look forward to learning of your position on this important issue.

Sincerely,

[Your name and address]

State hearings tend to be more accessible than federal hearings. In many state houses, anyone interested in testifying simply attends the hearing and signs up on a list as a witness. Also, written testimony can be submitted and it will be made available at the hearing. Local community boards also have open meetings and hearings. Information on pending issues and scheduled hearings is usually available through the town or city hall. A visit to your local community government offices can provide you with information on hearings and testifying.

Testimony at a public hearing should be clear, concise, and addressed to the committee members. You should explain and defend any points that you make. Legislators will ask questions for clarification. It is helpful to learn about the committee and its members before you testify, including any special procedures, committee practices, and the voting patterns of the members (Kleinkauf, 1981). Contact the staff beforehand to clarify what is expected and most helpful.

Elected officials are responsible for passing laws but often do not have a clear understanding of every issue upon which they are expected to vote. Public hearings, in addition to staff aides and lobbyists, are important sources of information. Often, public testimony serves more to educate than to persuade. Therefore, if you plan to testify at a public hearing it is best to write out your testimony, state your position clearly, consider using exhibits such as charts and diagrams, and summarize the highlights of your testimony in a few sentences (Daly, 1980).

Social service providers frequently testify, particularly on the state level. While they have the expertise to explain an issue, the testimony of a client or community resident can be even more effective (McInnis-Dittrich, 1994). Personal experiences can be very moving and can serve to empower people by including them in the civic process through which changes are made.

Preparing Policy Briefs

Another way to voice your position on a particular issue is to present research and data in the form of a **policy brief**, a one- or two-page fact sheet that presents evidence to support a position. A policy brief can provide legislators and their staff with information upon which to base or justify a vote. Staff members themselves often prepare policy briefs or fact sheets on particular issues. The key to a useful policy brief is accuracy and brevity. Legislators are extremely busy and find themselves pulled in many different directions. They are unlikely to read anything that is long and involved. For this reason, most reports developed by lobbyists, advocates, or community groups usually include an executive summary that resembles a policy brief. The executive summary is short and highlights the most important points for the benefit of government officials and their staffs.

When developing a policy brief, be clear about the issue being presented. Define the issue in the beginning and present only necessary background information. The background information should provide the context for the issue. Build the policy brief from the general to the specific. Provide the overall framework, and then follow with the details. Use common language, but avoid slang or jargon. Because you should limit your policy brief to no more than two pages, be sure to eliminate any unnecessary words or ideas. Although you have a message to present and a goal for doing so, try to be as objective as possible. When presenting a position based on values, use data and facts to support your position. If possible, list options and possible policy alternatives. Figure 13.3 shows a sample policy brief designed to discourage state lawmakers from cutting the Ohio General Assistance program.

When a group, organization, or individual is committed to active involvement in the policy process, these methods for legislative advocacy can be very effective in influencing social welfare policy. They require time,

Figure 13.3
Sample Policy Brief

General Assistance Cuts

The Governor of Ohio proposes to eliminate the state General Assistance program. The General Assistance program provides a critical safety net for low-income persons who are ineligible for other assistance. It is a program of last resort. Dismantling the General Assistance program in Ohio will leave thousands of men and women with no other source of financial support.

- In 1993, almost one million adults received General Assistance (GA) benefits through programs in thirty-one states.

- In Ohio, 103,000 adults received an average of $98 per month for a cost of $117 million per year.

- 34% of GA recipients also receive medical assistance, the only form of medical coverage available to them.

- Almost half of all GA recipients are on the program for less than a year. The average length of time is twenty-one months.

- Most GA recipients are able to stay in private housing. Half live alone and half share with others. Without GA benefits many would not be able to maintain private housing.

- The cost of shelter is about $20 a day. If, after elimination of the program, 25% of GA recipients were forced to seek refuge in homeless shelters, the annual cost would be $183 million.

The Governor's proposal to cut the General Assistance program is dangerous to the well-being of poor citizens of Ohio. For thousands of people, it is the only source of financial assistance during times of need. Overall, cutting General Assistance is not a cost-effective policy measure.

Source: Developed from data prepared by the Coalition on Housing and Homelessness in Ohio (1994).

effort, and organization, but participating in the process is much less draining than trying to work through or live with poorly planned and executed policies. Policy practice means taking a proactive stance towards policy-making, and legislative advocacy is one mode of action.

Building Public Awareness

Legislative advocacy centers on the law-making process and the policy-makers themselves. Often, there are important social issues that do not receive legislative attention because the need is not perceived to be great enough. Sometimes, the need is ignored because the social issue affects only people who are of marginal importance to lawmakers. This is particularly true of many of the issues and populations with whom social workers are involved. In these instances, it is important to raise public awareness and gain the attention of lawmakers. There are a number of ways to accomplish these goals, such as holding public meetings, issuing press releases to the media, and distributing printed materials such as leaflets and fliers.

Public Forums

Legislators and all elected officials live in the public eye. Meeting potential voters and supporters is crucial to their continued existence as elected officials. If an event promises positive public exposure, or if their absence might be noted and perceived as evidence of a lack of concern, elected representatives will make every effort to attend.

Plan to hold a **public forum** or meeting at a time that is best for legislators. When they are in session, Mondays and Fridays are usually good days because floor activity tends to take place during the middle of the week. If you are inviting elected officials to attend a gathering in their home district, find out when the legislature is not in session so your meeting will not conflict with their scheduled time to be in the state house or Washington. Mornings are usually best, and be very specific and prompt about the starting time. When inviting local officials, find out from their staff what are the best times for them to appear at a public event.

Plan to include some form of publicity by inviting photographers, newspaper or television news reporters, or representatives from affiliated organizations. To have the greatest possible impact, try to ensure adequate attendance. If you think you will have a small turnout, plan to use a small conference room and to convene a meeting rather than a public forum. It is always better to overcrowd a room than have it appear empty. Forty people in a room for thirty makes a stronger impression than forty people scattered throughout a hall that seats two hundred.

Extend a written invitation several weeks in advance of the event, and follow up with a phone call. Working around the legislator's schedule, set the date, time, and location in advance. Be prepared for changes; in the event of a schedule change you will have less time to plan and prepare for the event. You will probably be working with a staff member, rather than the elected official. Follow up with a thank-you letter to the legislator as well as anyone else who helped with the meeting or public forum.

Getting Media Attention

To keep an issue alive and gain public support, publicity is crucial. As mentioned before, newspaper or television coverage can be strong leverage in getting the attention of elected officials. Publicity also helps to elevate a social issue to the level of legislative action.

One of the easiest methods to gain publicity is through press releases. Prepare a brief notice for an event and send it to each local television station, radio station, and newspaper before the event. Use a catchy heading to attract attention. Examples might include announcements of findings of a new study or warnings of pending social change. Have a fact sheet or summary of testimony available for the media. This saves the reporter's time and enhances the chance that the points you want to get across will be accurately reflected in the coverage.

Letters to the editor of a newspaper are another way to gain media coverage. After such a letter is printed, it can be reproduced and used as part of a publicity packet. Also, local radio or television talk shows can be an excellent medium to publicize your position, as long as you are prepared for the format of radio or television. Beforehand, speak with the host or staff to learn about the best way to present your points in the context of their show. You may want to role-play with a colleague beforehand to help you prepare.

Fliers, Handouts, and Leaflets

Part of an effective strategy for building public awareness is to have information ready for all events. As mentioned previously, fact sheets, fliers, position papers, policy briefs, and written testimonies all help to reinforce your message at public and legislative events. Each time materials are prepared, save them for possible future use. If possible, include letters and case examples from people affected by the issue. Ask their permission to use their "stories," and keep these items on file.

Fact sheets and fliers should attract and hold the reader's attention, and they must be accurate and concise. Any information should be able to stand alone so that if these items are passed on to others, all the important points are clear. Plan to share your written materials with other groups so that the information gets out to a larger audience. Include the name and telephone number of a contact person for anyone interested in more information.

Written information can also serve as a resource. For example, when we held a public forum on homelessness, in addition to a fact sheet we used two other handouts: a list of service providers and a list of agency needs. These resources accomplished several tasks. Legislators and media personnel who needed more in-depth information had an up-to-date list of services and contact people for follow-up information. Also, for community residents who wanted to do something immediately, there was a list of items and resources needed by the local agencies who served the homeless. This also helped to publicize the needs of the service providers.

Building public awareness is a very important part of the policy-making process, and the keys to successful publicity are raising awareness and keeping the issues at the forefront of public attention. Using multiple techniques elevates sensitivity to an issue. Patience and persistence are always needed to effectively sustain a public awareness campaign.

Levels of Influence

Unfortunately, not all issues receive the attention they deserve. Influence is also not evenly distributed. Regardless of the efforts and planning that go into legislative advocacy and building public awareness, some groups receive more attention than others. Financial resources play a critical role in gaining political influence.

Two groups tend to exert significant influence over the policy-making process: business interests and PACs.

Business Interests

A healthy economy is considered necessary for political stability. The business sector carries out activities that are necessary for the functioning of society—building houses, providing transportation, producing food, creating jobs. Therefore, the needs and concerns of business leaders are important to elected officials:

> Governments award to business managers a privileged position in the play of power in policy making. The privileged position goes so far as to require that government officials must often give business needs precedence over demands from citizens (Lindblom, 1980, p. 74).

Furthermore, many elected officials themselves come from the elite of business and the market economy. In 1994, 28% of U.S. Senators and 12% of members of the House of Representatives were millionaires, compared to less than .5% of the general population (Simpson, 1994).

The belief that what is good for business is good for America pervades the policy arena. Consequently, business interests play a significant role in the development of policy. Social workers and their services usually are not viewed as a direct part of the market system, but this dichotomy between the market and social welfare services is artificial. When businesses do not have trained workers or healthy employees, and when citizens cannot afford to buy the products that are made by businesses, everyone suffers. Thus, the market and the social welfare system are inextricably linked. The task for social workers as policy practitioners is to identify and publicize the link between market needs and social needs.

Political Action Committees

Another powerful interest competing for legislative attention are **political action committees** (PACs). PACs are organized to collect voluntary contributions and in turn distribute them for political purposes. Any group can form a PAC as long as it meets federal and state regulations and is independent (not part of a non-profit or for-profit group, business, organization, or advocacy group). Federal legislation passed in 1974 allowed for the

Table 13.3
Ten Largest Political Action Committees by Spending, 1991–1992

PAC	Dollars Spent
1. Democratic Republican Independent Voter Education Committee	$11,825,340
2. American Medical Association PAC	6,263,921
3. National Education Association PAC	5,817,975
4. NRA Political Victory Fund	5,700,114
5. Realtors PAC	4,939,014
6. Association of Trial Lawyers of America PAC	4,392,462
7. American Federation of State, County, and Municipal Employees	4,281,395
8. UAW Voluntary Community Action Program	4,257,165
9. National Congressional Club	3,864,389
10. National Abortion Rights Action League PAC	3,831,321

Source: Stanley & Neimi (1994), Table 6-6, p. 180.

establishment of PACs. From 1974 to 1992, the number of PACs grew from 608 to 4,195 (Stanley & Niemi, 1994). Each PAC is allowed by law to give a maximum contribution of $10,000 to a single candidate for each election cycle (Babcock & Morin, 1990). There is no limit on the number of PACs that can identify with a specific industry or position, as long as each PAC is officially independent. Table 13.3 lists the ten largest PACs by spending during the 1991–1992 election cycle.

PACs and businesses are particularly influential due to a loophole in the law. Federal rules limit how much a PAC can contribute ($10,000 per candidate per election), and individual personal contributions are limited to $1,000 per candidate per election. *Political parties*, however, can receive unlimited donations as long as the money goes into a separate account and is used for administrative costs or to help build the party (A lucrative loophole, 1992). These donations, while not directed to specific candidates, help parties to organize and also free up other money that can be directed to candidates of the party. During the 1993–94 election cycle, PACs collected $392 million, of which 48% went to candidates and the rest to finance the political parties and other expenses (U.S. Bureau of the Census, 1996).

Final Thoughts on Policy Practice

There is no denying that money can influence policy, and donations have a direct influence on politicians. Nevertheless, all elected officials must ultimately rely on votes. If groups can organize to affect the ability of politicians to garner votes, they can determine who is elected to public office. New policy-makers prioritize issues differently. With new priorities, social problems can gain the public and legislative attention they deserve. Social welfare service providers and their clients represent a tremendous source of untapped political power to effect change in voting, representation, and ultimately social welfare policy.

Policy practice is within the reach of all social workers. It can be as basic as registering to vote and voting, or as involved as running a political campaign or even running for office. The most important policy practice role is to become involved in one's community. Active participation in community affairs can open the way for involvement in local policy decision-making, which may in turn lead to a national role. When greater numbers of social workers and social service agency clients become involved in the policy-making process, social welfare policies will become more responsive to people's needs. In the final chapter, we will outline ways for social workers to become policy practitioners.

Key Concepts

policy practitioner   policy brief
lobbying   public forum
legislative testimony   political action committees (PACs)

Exercises

1. Find out your state's requirements for a person to become a deputy registrar to register people to vote. Could you qualify? How might you organize a voter registration campaign? Can you conduct one at your school? At your place of employment? At your field agency?

2. Attend an open public hearing or city government meeting. What issues were discussed? Who led the meeting? Did you observe community or citizen involvement? What did you learn by attending?

3. Develop a policy brief on an issue of concern. From your knowledge of the issue, identify an elected official who can assist with the concern. Prepare a letter and send it to the elected official. Try to set up an appointment to meet with the elected official or a staff member, and present your position.

4. As a class, choose a social welfare topic of local concern. Develop a plan for collecting information on the issue and divide the work among yourselves. Plan to hold a forum to present your findings. Invite other students, community residents, elected officials, and/or the media. Follow the guidelines for holding a public forum outlined in the chapter.

References

Babcock, C.R., & Morin, R. (1990, June 25–July 1). Following the path of self-interest. *The Washington Post Weekly Edition, 7* (34), 14.

Coalition on Housing and Homelessness in Ohio. (1994). *Fact sheet on General Assistance.* Columbus, OH: Author.

Daly, J.J. (1980). How to tell your story to a legislative body. In *The nonprofit organization handbook* (pp. 5-121 to 5-135). New York: McGraw-Hill.

Haynes, K.S., & Mickelson, J.S. (1991). *Affecting change: Social workers in the political arena* (2nd ed.). New York: Longman.

Kleinkauf, C. (1981). A guide to giving legislative testimony. *Social Work, 26* (4), 297–303.

Lindblom, C.E. (1980). *The policy-making process* (2nd ed.). Englewood Cliffs, NJ: Prentice Hall.

A lucrative loophole. (1992). *The Washington Post Weekly Edition, 9* (40), 13.

Mahaffey, M. (1982). Lobbying and social work. In Mahaffey, M., & Hanks, J.W., *Practical politics: Social work and political responsibility.* Silver Spring, MD: National Association of Social Workers.

McInnis-Dittrich, K. (1994). *Integrating social welfare policy and social work practice.* Pacific Grove, CA: Brooks/Cole.

Merida, K. (1996). Leading the poor to the polling booth. *The Washington Post National Weekly Edition, 13* (28), 12–13.

Michigan Program in Child Development and Social Policy. (1992). *Taking steps for children: A citizen's guide to child policy.* Ann Arbor, MI: Author.

Peck, S. (1991, March 2). Presentation on influencing legislators. Washington, DC: Children's Defense Fund.

Religious Action Center. (1989). *Register citizen opinion: A Congressional directory and action guide.* Washington, DC: Author.

Schmitt, E. (1996, November 7). Half the electorate, perhaps satisfied or bored, sat out voting. *The New York Times*, p. B6.

Simpson, G.R. (1994, May 2–8). Representative moneybags: Will the millionaires turn Congress into a plutocracy? *The Washington Post Weekly Edition, 11* (27), 25.

Stanley, H.W., & Niemi, R.G. (1994). *Vital statistics on American politics* (4th ed.). Washington, DC: CQ Press.

U.S. Bureau of the Census. (1991). *Voting and registration in the election of November 1990.* P20-453. Washington, DC: U.S. Government Printing Office.

U.S. Bureau of the Census. (1993). *Voting and registration in the election of November 1992.* P20-466. Washington, DC: U.S. Government Printing Office.

U.S. Bureau of the Census. (1996). *Statistical abstract of the United States, 1996* (116th ed.). Washington, DC: U.S. Government Printing Office.

U.S. General Accounting Office. (1990). *Voting: Some procedural changes and informational activities could increase turnout.* GAO/PEMD–91–1. Washington, DC: U.S. Government Printing Office.

© Joel Gordon

Chapter 14

The Role of Social Work

Social workers typically see themselves as providers of direct intervention or direct services to clients. The social welfare policy arena is perceived to be removed from the day-to-day work of human service providers. As has been shown throughout this book, however, this view is far from reality. The public policy decisions made at all levels of government, from local to the federal, have a direct impact on the daily responsibilities of social workers who struggle to help individuals deal with environmental challenges. The profession is based on a keen understanding of the individual's surroundings, and the political arena is part of that. There exists an "organic relationship between professional function and political responsibility" (Alexander, 1982, pp. 30–31).

Social issues drive the work of social workers. That is the reason we must be policy literate and prepared to practice in the social welfare policy environment. If we are not prepared to tackle public policy issues that affect our clients and ourselves, then we are forced to continue working within the existing social service programs. That is not to say that many of our current social welfare service programs and policies are not excellent or constructive social welfare efforts. Still, social welfare programs are created or evolve in response to identified social problems. Over time, social problems change and shift, and we need to assess whether our current efforts are adequate or whether we need to develop new ways to respond. The social welfare policy arena is often the best place to transform our responses to social problems. Social workers need to become social policy practitioners who can participate in the policy process. In this book, we have attempted to outline the processes and skills necessary to navigate the system and in turn influence the direction of social welfare policy: to engage in **policy practice**. This involvement is not new, although it has ebbed and flowed throughout the history of our profession. In this chapter, we trace the history of policy practice and social work, highlight the value of policy practice, and outline an agenda for future policy practitioners.

History of Social Work and Policy Practice

Examination of our nation's social history reflects swings between individual focus and social reform. Social work practice also reflects these historical shifts. In his history of social work practice, John H. Ehrenreich (1985) posits that there is an inherent tension in social work practice between individual work and social reform. He attributes this tension to the dilemma of whether to change people or to change social conditions. When individuals confront personal problems, they must deal with environmental realities, while when societies change, reform is shaped by many differing individual needs and characteristics. When trying to accomplish either of these goals—help the individual to change, or reform society—the other also comes into play. No matter how much a social worker chooses one form of intervention, there is always a pull from the other. Hence the reality that both forms of practice are ever-present.

The tension between individual work and social reform is underscored by periodic shifts in emphasis between private interest and public purpose, as identified by Schlesinger (1986) and described in chapter 3. These shifts in focus between the individual and social conditions have left social work practice with only periodic emphasis on policy practice. Although they are few, periods of strong public purpose in social work history have shaped the evolution of social welfare programs. Three key periods in our nation's history reflected a social work emphasis on policy practice: the Settlement Movement of the turn of the century, the New Deal of the 1930s, and the social reform efforts of the 1960s and 1970s. These three periods influenced the development and types of social change used by social workers.

Settlement Movement

The Settlement Movement is described in detail in chapter 2. The legacy of this movement in terms of policy practice is significant. The role of settlement organizers and residents in demanding social welfare policies that reflected social justice and protected those who were disadvantaged established a strong foundation for social work intervention on the policy-making levels. Child labor laws, protections for employees in the workplace (particularly women), public services such as waste removal, the establishment of public parks, and reforms in education were some of the public policies directly influenced by settlement workers (Davis, 1984). Settlement workers actively participated in the political process, and settlement houses often served as places for political organizing. The settlement workers were sometimes at odds with other social workers, particularly those who were committed to developing a profession and were focused on individual treatment.

The themes that characterized the settlements were participation and democracy (Garvin & Cox, 1995). Settlement workers encouraged the involvement of community residents in organizing services and advocating for social welfare policies. Working for changes in public laws was seen as a way to help communities. Thus, social reform was considered an integral part of the role of settlements and an effective way to improve the living conditions of those who resided in the communities.

The contributions of settlement workers to policy practice are exemplified in the work of Jane Addams. Although some may question whether Addams was identified as a social worker, she embodied the values of social work in advocating for social reform (Brieland, 1990). She was politically active on the local and national levels, influencing the development of public policies. She always maintained a close link with people through her residence at the Hull House settlement that she founded, and she used her first-hand knowledge of social conditions to inform her work (Stroup, 1986). These principles and actions still serve as a strong foundation for policy practice.

Although the impact of the settlements had waned by the time of World War I, the value of working to change social welfare policies and effect social reform had been proven. The settlement movement "demonstrated that private charity and philanthropy were not enough, that action by the government at all levels was necessary to combat the massive problems of urban, industrial America" (Davis, 1984, p. 245). The legacy of the settlement movement included and encouraged a place for social welfare policy practice and social reform in the social work profession.

New Deal

The Great Depression catapulted the federal government into the permanent role of provider of social welfare services. It also triggered events that led social workers to shift from a therapeutic focus in the 1920s to a broader interest in social welfare policies and social reform. The American belief in the power of individual achievement was seriously threatened by the advent of the Great Depression. People began to question the validity of individual responsibility in light of the massive economic downturn of the Depression. "Many came to regard government, rather than business, as the preferred means for developing a better society" (Garvin & Cox, 1995, p. 86). This shift in public sentiment was felt within social work practice. Social workers began to play a key role in the development of social welfare policies.

The two social workers most notable for influencing social welfare policies during the Great Depression were Frances Perkins and Harry Hopkins. They were instrumental in planning and implementing major parts of the New Deal programs. Both were trained in social work and had spent time as residents of settlement houses.

Frances Perkins, having studied at the School of Philanthropy in New York (the forerunner of the Columbia School of Social Work), spent years working in New York for labor reform and workers' rights. Her work led her to political involvement as the industrial commissioner of the State of New York appointed by Franklin D. Roosevelt. This made Perkins the first woman to serve on a governor's cabinet. When Roosevelt became president, he asked Perkins to follow him to the White House, where he made her secretary of labor. Again, Perkins established a political first, as she was the first woman to ever serve on the Cabinet of a president of the United States. Perkins used her political position to influence the course of social welfare policy and advocate for social reforms, particularly in relation to labor and workers' rights. She was involved in the establishment of the Federal Emergency Relief Administration, the Civilian Conservation Corps, and the Public Works Administration. The most notable policy achievement of Frances Perkins was her involvement in the development of the Social Security Act. Perkins chaired the Committee on Economic Security, which crafted the Social Security Act of 1935. She regarded the Act as a way to codify protection of workers from the uncertainties of the market (Berg, 1989; Martin, 1976). The Social Security Act as passed included protections from poverty resulting from unemployment, widowhood, and old age, and it set the stage for later changes that included economic protection for those who became physically unable to work. Perkins was instrumental in developing the policies of the Social Security programs and thus made a significant contribution to social welfare programs designed to protect people's well-being.

Harry Hopkins also served under President Franklin D. Roosevelt. A social worker by training, he became involved in politics in the State of New York while Roosevelt was governor. Having forged a strong personal and professional relationship, Hopkins had so much influence with Roosevelt that he was often referred to as the "assistant president" (McElvaine, 1993). Hopkins was a strong supporter of public relief and served as the first administrator of the Federal Emergency Relief Administration. Hopkins was instrumental in developing other major New Deal programs such as the Civilian Conservation Corps and the Works Progress Administration. As Roosevelt's presidency moved past the initial relief efforts, Hopkins became Secretary of Commerce in 1938. Unfortunately, one year later poor health prevented him from continuing in his official political roles during the rest of Roosevelt's time as president.

Since the time of Frances Perkins and Harry Hopkins, social workers have not enjoyed such a primary and key role in developing social welfare policies. Social work values of social reform and social responsibility were keenly reflected in the policies of the New Deal. It is likely that the influence of Perkins and Hopkins reflected the integration of their own social work values and experiences in the development of social welfare policies.

Community Organizing During the 1960s and 1970s

After the era of the New Deal, social reform efforts faded in importance for social work and the general society. World War II and its aftermath shifted public priorities. Concern again reflected focus on the individual and his or her own responsibility for social well-being. There were exceptions to this philosophy. The programs established under the Social Security Act were in place and began to grow, and public services were developed for returning veterans of World War II. Social reform did not surface to a measurable degree until the 1960s.

Perhaps in part as a reaction to the oppressive public policies of the 1950s and the growing acknowledgment of institutional racism and discrimination, the 1960s opened a new era in social reform. The Civil Rights movement and anti-war demonstrations highlighted a period of history when people organized and demanded democratic participation for all, regardless of personal attributes. Social work practice was greatly influenced by these events.

The 1960s and 1970s gave rise to community organization as a form of social welfare intervention. A blend of settlement work and labor organizing, **community organizing** grew out of grassroots movements. The evolution of community organization influenced social work practice and evolved into a practice method. As early as 1962, the Council on Social Work Education formally recognized community organization as a specialty within social work (Garvin & Cox, 1995).

Community organization can be viewed as an intervention method in which workers "seek to join with people who have endured exploitation and discrimination at the hands of certain social forces and social institutions" (Biklen, 1983, p. 85). Biklen also, however, differentiates community organizing from professional practice in that organizers do not give services or treatment and their targets for reform are not people but institutions.

As the federal government became more involved in responding to social problems during the 1960s, additional community programs were developed. The development of federally funded community action programs, community mental health centers, urban renewal programs, and employment training programs, to name but a few of these efforts, provided jobs for people trained as organizers (Garvin & Cox, 1995). The emphasis on community participation in key government-funded programs had the effect of raising the expectation for community members' participation in many other social welfare services.

For some theorists, community organizing in its strictest form cannot also be a social work mode of intervention because it does not support the current social welfare service structure. One way of trying to balance the different perspectives of community organizing and social work practice is to try to blend the two. This can be accomplished by defending existing social services, developing alternative services, and creating community-based systems that hold economic and political power (Reisch & Wenocur, 1986). These are some of the community organizing principles that social work practitioners and educators have integrated into the profession.

All schools of social work teach about communities, but the emphasis has shifted from organizing to intervention. Consequently, recent books on community work are less about organizing to change the social structure and more about professional practice. The shift from organizing to intervention demonstrates a change in ideology. Although the emphasis has changed, the need to understand how to practice on a macro level in communities is firmly entrenched in social work practice.

Shifting Emphasis of Social Work

In recent years, there has been mounting criticism that social work practice and professionals have lost their abilities or desires to integrate the two realms of individual focus and social change. Some argue that the reason social work has abandoned a commitment to both is to maintain a legitimate place in society as a viable profession. "The profession has moved away from its central core [commitment to both the person and the environment] and has instead opted to focus on therapeutic and supportive administrative skills" (Frumkin & O'Connor, 1985, p. 14).

More recently, other social work professionals have discussed their growing concern. "Social work has abandoned its mission to help the poor and oppressed and to build communality. Instead, many social workers are devoting their energies and talents to careers in psychotherapy" (Specht & Courtney, 1994, p. 4). The perception is that **professionalization**, the quest by social workers to gain recognition as legitimate professionals, has contributed to the "transformation of social work from a professional corps concerned with helping people deal with their social problems to a major platoon in the psychotherapeutic armies" (Specht & Courtney, 1994, p. 9).

The professionalization of social work has evolved out of a desire to establish the legitimacy and status of social work. The drive for professionalization has coincided, and in part been driven by, the pressures in today's society to emphasize personal responsibility and ignore social responsibility. The philosophical underpinning is that if the individual is responsible for his or her situation, including poverty or poor health, then the arena for change must be the individual person. Social work practice, critics argue, reflects this current societal view of individual responsibility. Such a view ignores one of the fundamental principles of social work: the importance of the environment in shaping people's social conditions.

Occupying a professional role that supports the current social welfare system rather than challenging it through social action can protect social workers from exclusion from the system. Social reformers are often viewed as outside "rabble rousers" and "troublemakers," whereas clinicians in established agencies are regarded as part of the system. One perspective posits that those with whom social workers interact are oppressed by the existing social and economic systems, and "social workers ought not to intervene in these systems, they ought to resist them" (Cloward & Piven, 1975, p. xv).

This is harsh criticism. It demands that social work professionals, and particularly those who train new social work professionals, examine the accuracy of these statements. Is there a necessary separation between those who practice individual work and those who advocate for social reform? Another point of view is that the division between individual focus and social reform, or micro and macro practice, is artificial:

> This division is an unnatural one. Effective direct services requires a strong knowledge of social welfare policies and programs. Developing effective social welfare policy requires a strong understanding of direct services. Professional social work practice means *integrating* social welfare policy and social work practice (McInnis-Dittrich, 1994, p. 3).

Individual social workers can begin to challenge these criticisms by adopting some of the activities outlined in chapter 13 and including them as part of their professional routine. Whether in clinical social work or community organizations, policy practice is critical. Every social work practitioner needs a working knowledge of how to influence the development of social welfare policy.

Benefits of Policy Practice

One of the premises of this book is the belief that policy practice is not only an integral part of social work practice and values, but also extremely valuable to social work and society. Policy practice can serve to enhance the relationship between workers and their clients and communities. Involvement in policy practice can aid social workers to better understand organizations and service delivery. It can also help to foster empowerment and influence the delivery of social welfare services in our country. While these values have been expressed throughout the book, it would be helpful to summarize them here as the reader completes his or her foundation in policy literacy.

Improved Client/Worker Relationships

The 1980s and 1990s have been periods of retrenchment, scapegoating, demands for greater accountability, and limited resources for social welfare services. The problems faced by agencies, workers, and clients when resources become scarce place stress upon the client/worker relationship. When workers cannot deliver what a client expects, strained relationships can develop between worker and client. Often this tension is the result of outside constraints. For example, changes in social welfare policy and federal legislation may result in funding cuts and redefined eligibility standards. Funding cuts may require agency reorganization, and consequently workers must take on additional responsibilities. Agency personnel changes and shortages may force workers to carry larger caseloads. Larger caseloads mean the worker has less time to interact with each client leaving clients feeling neglected, unimportant, and unworthy of services.

These constraints, which are the direct result of social welfare policy changes, place tremendous strain on the client/worker relationship. Understanding the impact of social welfare policy change can be beneficial in two ways: (1) when workers and clients are able to identify the source of stress, the helping relationship is preserved; and (2) an understanding of social welfare policy can provide a foundation for practitioner involvement in developing new approaches to resolving social problems.

Changes that occur on the macro level do not immediately touch the client/worker relationship. Therefore, workers rarely recognize the connection between what takes place in the macro policy arena and what happens between the worker and his or her client. Such a lack of recognition is to be expected. Workers are faced with meeting the needs of clients to the best of their abilities within the resources and boundaries of their agencies. Consequently, little time or energy is left to consider the effects macro policy may have upon them. Nevertheless, developing a more global perspective can give knowledge that can empower people to direct their energies toward what can be changed. This redirection can remove stress and lead to the development of innovative ways to resolve social problems.

For example, a social worker in a family service agency develops a counseling relationship with a single working mother of two school-aged children. Part of the woman's distress is related to worrying about the well-being of her children because while she is working there is no one to watch her children after school. A micro perspective would focus on her feelings: worry about the children's safety, guilt because she must leave them, anger at having to raise her children alone. Moving toward a macro perspective would mean the social worker would investigate community resources available to provide care for children after school. If these services are unavailable, the macro social reform perspective would require advocating for such services through local schools or local governments. This level of policy advocacy, which can be done by practitioners, grows out of the individual needs of clients.

Deeper Understanding of Organizations

The skills necessary for social welfare policy analysis and those techniques that foster social change can also be beneficial within organizations. The politics within organizations requires the "ability to assess the structure and operations of power in an organization and skill in coalition formation...other necessary skills include negotiation and bargaining, rhetoric and communication, cooperation, use of expertise and information, and structuring the presentation of data and policies" (Gummer & Edwards, 1985, p. 18). These skills are all directly or indirectly related to policy practice. Mastering these skills within organizations is important because organizations are political.

The benefits of becoming a savvy organizational member are numerous. Astute understanding of the workings of an organization can lead to better use of resources, sensitivity to clients' needs, protection from "burnout," and a clear sense of one's role within an organization. In addition, the larger environment in which social workers operate is political. To advocate and effectively provide services, practitioners must understand the larger context in which they and their organizations work. Policy practice methods provide a framework for understanding organizational politics.

Empowerment

The term **empowerment** refers to the "process of increasing personal, interpersonal, or political power so that individuals can take action to improve their life conditions" (Gutierrez, 1995, p. 205). Empowerment as a component of social work practice is rooted in community organizing. It stresses taking control and developing the power to effect social change. Empowerment includes collaboration, expansion of capacities and strengths, simultaneous attention to both the individual and the environment, active involvement of all, and emphasis on those population groups who have historically been excluded (Simon, 1994). These are also key principles of policy practice and social reform.

The tradition of empowerment in social work practice stems back to the work of settlement movements and is reflected today in the values of social work practice and education. According to the Council on Social Work Education Curriculum Policy Statement, schools of social work must teach students the skills necessary "to promote social change and to implement a wide range of interventions that further the achievement of individual and collective social and economic justice" (Council on Social Work Education, 1994, sections M6.7 & B6.5).

Empowerment leads to social and economic justice. When people, groups, and communities are able to take action to improve their well-being, then social justice prevails. Policy practice is a tool of empowerment. It can be used to foster collaboration, strengthen capacities and resources, and empower those who have historically been powerless and disenfranchised.

If providers and receivers of human services apply and analyze the substantive content of policies affecting them or those whom they represent, they are empowered. If practitioners and beneficiaries, professionals and recipients, workers and clients apply the skills to analyze the processes whereby policy comes into being, they are empowered. Empowerment is knowing that one is able to be a doer (Flynn, 1992, p. 1).

Empowerment focuses on strengths rather than weaknesses. Social work practice and social welfare policies are usually driven by social problems. This emphasis can focus significantly on what is negative and pathological. Policy practice benefits from emphasizing a different approach: the strengths perspective (Chapin, 1995). The goal of this approach is to create social welfare policies and programs that are based on clients' strengths. As did the settlement workers, New Dealers, and community organizers, we need to collaborate with client groups and develop social welfare policy proposals that emphasize empowerment and dignity.

Empowerment occurs in policy practice on two levels. First, policy practice can produce the outcome of changing social welfare policy and thereby sharing power and resources. Second, the process of advocating, organizing, and influencing policy-makers can also serve to empower those who are involved in it. Taking action and finding one's own voice can legitimize a person's feelings and experiences and be very empowering. It also emphasizes people's strengths rather than their weaknesses or limitations. The dual outcomes of policy change and personal growth make policy practice a valuable tool for empowerment in social work practice.

Changing the Course of Social Welfare Policy

The most obvious benefit of policy practice is worth repeating: the value of influencing the course of social welfare policy in America. While the other benefits are valuable components of policy practice, this is perhaps the key outcome. When all is said and done, improved client/worker relationships, keener understanding of social service organizations, and increased empowerment can be strengthened or weakened by public policies. Faulty social welfare policies put stress on those working in the field and on organizations trying to do more with less resources. Oppressive and punitive policies stifle empowerment and continue to disenfranchise people.

In the end, influencing the development and implementation of public policies is at the heart of social change and social reform. Developing skills in policy practice intervention can enable practitioners to participate in achieving the ultimate goal of influencing the course of social welfare policy.

Social work practitioners need to be their own judges of when to intervene on an individual level and when to advocate for social change. Through the course of one's work, however, both approaches must be applied. Most social work students graduate with an adequate level of comfort in the area of individual practice. Few graduates feel competent in the policy arena.

This needs to be changed if social work practitioners are going to fulfill their mission of promoting social and economic justice.

Techniques for Enhancing Policy Practice and Social Work

Chapter 13 outlines techniques for influencing policy in the political arena. While these activities should be incorporated into the practice of all social workers, there are other techniques that are particularly useful to direct service providers and social work educators. These activities include community-based research using the needs assessment approach and implementation of policy practice activities in the classroom (Brzuzy & Segal, 1996; Segal, 1989).

Needs Assessment

Conducting a **needs assessment** is usually thought of as a research technique, but needs assessment also can serve as a tool for organizing, policy analysis, and political analysis. The process of needs assessment can promote grassroots participation and empowerment. Needs assessment is "research aimed at documenting the needs of people living within a particular community or other geographical region or the needs of a particular subgroup within a region" (Schuerman, 1983, p. 86). The overall goal of needs assessment is to gather information through research techniques and community involvement as a means of identifying unmet needs.

Uncovering areas of unmet needs highlights what resources are and are not available. Such research identifies who is and who is not receiving resources. Thus, needs assessments are often conducted in a political context and bring to light questions about social welfare policy (Hobbs, 1987). Needs assessment research can thus be both a tool and an outcome of policy practice.

Three basic approaches are typically identified: (1) gathering statistical data to serve as quantifiable indicators of social need; (2) using the opinions of experts, usually referred to as key informants; and (3) going to those in the community who are directly affected by the possibility of unmet needs through community gatherings, surveys, or personal participation in community events (Cox, Erlich, Rothman, & Tropman, 1987; Monette, Sullivan, & DeJong, 1994; Witkin & Altschuld, 1995).

For policy practitioners, needs assessment serves as a way to influence policy-making. The act of gathering information has many benefits. First, the actual documentation of unmet social needs can provide evidence to support advocacy for a specific policy issue. For example, during the 1960s, community organizers invited politicians to witness first-hand the poverty they had "discovered" in their work in the rural South. There are famous photographs of Robert Kennedy, while serving as attorney general, visiting poor and malnourished families in rural Southern communities. Many believe his experiences prompted him to return to Washington and advocate for expansion of public assistance and anti-poverty programs.

The impact of documentation cannot be underestimated. Even when politicians choose to ignore the facts, advocates can use statistics and documentation as proof of policy-makers' insensitivity to the social needs of people. Identification of such insensitivity can also serve a political purpose. It can motivate people to organize and advocate for policy changes or new political representation. Documentation of need requires policy-makers to either address the proof or explain why they are choosing to ignore it. Such debate can be a powerful tool of political change.

Another value of needs assessment is that it is inexpensive and accessible to use. A general review of needs and community conditions can be conducted with a minimum of resources. Agency staff members or volunteers can meet with local officials to acquire data and background on community services and needs. Local residents can be invited to group gatherings and asked for their insights. The greatest expense in gathering such information is in people's time. This is one resource that policy practitioners can control and call upon when needed. Provided in Figures 14.1 and 14.2 are lists of guidelines to help structure a basic needs assessment.

Each policy practitioner must identify the relevant experts and community members to contact and also determine the best way to initiate that contact. One word of caution when conducting a needs assessment: it is important not to be swayed by your preconceived notions. What you may

Figure 14.1
Guidelines for Gathering Community Information

1. Define the problem: clarify issues and develop agreement on the problem.
2. Develop a population profile (age, race, sex).
3. Describe available services: extent, type.
   Quantify if possible:
   > Who needs services?
   > How many are served?
   > Who is not served?
   > Duration of service.
4. Determine geographic distribution of population and/or problem.
5. Identify networks.
6. Assess people's past perceptions and analyses of needs or problems.
7. Ask people's perceptions and analyses for the future.

Figure 14.2
Agency Interview Guidelines

1. Develop an agency profile:
   • Services offered;
   • Work force, training of personnel, extent of volunteers;
   • Agency resources;
   • Agency needs.
2. Determine extent of services: type and duration, number served.
3. Identify budgetary allotments.
4. Itemize cost of services provided.
5. Identify federal, state, and local support, resources, response.
6. Assess community response: extent of public awareness, local attitudes toward agency work.

think are the needs of people may not be those identified. Be open to all sources of information, and always ask participants to recommend other sources you might not know about. In this way, you can insure that your needs assessment research reflects the situation as it is experienced within the community.

The results of a needs assessment should promote policy practice. Armed with reliable information on communities, populations, and social needs, the policy practitioner can make a strong case for public policy changes. Having been directly involved in gathering information also makes you an expert who is available to advise and influence policy-makers. Linked with techniques such as lobbying, testifying, letter-writing, and other strategies outlined in chapter 13, needs assessment can be a powerful tool for policy practitioners.

Policy Simulations

Another excellent tool to assist social workers in becoming adept policy practitioners is to use role-plays and **policy simulations**. If you practice speaking about a policy issue and questioning policy-makers, you will be better prepared to do so when needed. Simulations can "bridge the gap between policy as theory and policy as practice" (Miller, 1987, p. 118).

There are a number of advantages to setting up mock policy debates or hearings within the classroom. Policy simulations can stress working together as a task group, force participants to feel what it is like to make difficult choices between options, help participants to examine individual and group values, prepare policy practitioners to articulate and defend policy positions, and help participants develop public speaking skills (Miller, 1987).

Before testifying or contacting an elected official, it is best to practice. Deliver your testimony to colleagues, fellow students, or any other group of people you trust. Ask them to be critical and prepared to analyze what you are presenting. Try to anticipate all the different positions you might encounter and prepare answers for them. If your research was thorough, you should already know the arguments against the policy position you are advocating.

After the simulation, ask all participants to help evaluate. What were the strengths? Weaknesses? What was most clear, and what was not? Discuss the delivery of the material. Might there be a more effective way to communicate your position? The simulation and post-simulation discussion should help to prepare policy practitioners to participate in the process. Elected officials use these techniques as part of their preparation for public debate and appearances, and policy practitioners would benefit from doing the same.

Final Thoughts on the Role of Social Work

Whatever the techniques used, social workers need to get involved in the social welfare policy process. This book should serve as a starting point. Use it as a reference and a guide. The key for the future of social work influence and social welfare policy in America is to participate. Begin by making sure you are registered to vote and cast your ballot at each election. Encourage your colleagues, clients, fellow students, and friends to also vote. Offer to discuss the issues and candidates with them so they can make educated decisions.

For the more adventurous among you, participate directly in the policy process through involvement in campaigns or actually running for political office. A number of guides exist to help you should you decide to pursue elective office (Mahaffey & Hanks, 1982; Haynes & Mickelson, 1991). Start at a manageable, local level and see what it is like to conduct a campaign. School boards and city councils can be very influential in deciding what social welfare policies should and should not be implemented locally. These are positions that are accessible to people interested in starting a political career.

Social workers have a strong history of involvement in policy-making, from Jane Addams and Frances Perkins to Senator Barbara Mikulski, who was elected to the United States Senate in 1986 and reelected in 1992. Many other social workers hold local and statewide offices or work as staff members and advisors to elected officials. The newly established Institute for the Advancement of Political Social Work Practice was developed to increase the number of social workers who are elected officials and to involve social workers in the political empowerment of clients. Policy practice actions may again be gaining strength within the social work profession. Whatever the role you choose—as a social worker committed to an individual focus, group work, community organizing, or administration—policy practice can and must be part of you repertoire of skills.

Key Concepts

policy practice	community organizing
professionalization	empowerment
needs assessment	policy simulations

Exercises

1. Check to see if there is a Community Action Program (CAP) agency or a settlement house in your community. If not, why not? If one exists call and ask if you can visit. What is the history of the agency? What services did it offer in its early years? What services are offered now? How have they changed, and how are they the same?

2. Ask for an organizational chart of the social service agency at your field placement or employment. What does it tell you about the organization? Does the chart accurately reflect what you have seen in the agency? Does the chart provide information helpful to understanding the flow of policies and rules within the agency?

3. Develop a plan for conducting a needs assessment in your community or any familiar geographic area. What steps would you take? Whom would you contact? What would be your goal?

4. As a class, choose a social welfare policy and plan a simulated debate. Choose pro and con speakers, and appoint people to act as elected officials. You may want to prepare policy briefs to help with the debate.

5. Contact the Institute for the Advancement of Political Social Work Practice [University of Connecticut, School of Social Work, 1789 Asylum Avenue, West Hartford, CT 06117, (860) 570-9166, Director: Dr. Nancy A. Humphreys]. Find out what services are offered, what activities are currently underway, and what resources are available.

References

Alexander, C. (1982). Professional social workers and political responsibility. In Mahaffey, M. & Hanks, J.W., (eds.), *Practical politics: Social work and political responsibility* (pp. 15–31). Silver Spring, MD: National Association of Social Workers.

Berg, G. (1989). Frances Perkins and the flowering of economic and social policies. *Monthly Labor Review, 112* (6), 28–32.

Biklen, D.P. (1983). *Community organizing theory and practice.* Englewood Cliffs, NJ: Prentice Hall.

Brieland, D. (1990). The Hull House tradition and the contemporary social worker: Was Jane Addams really a social worker? *Social Work*, 35 (2), 134–138.

Brzuzy, S., & Segal, E.A. (1996). Community-based research strategies for social work education. *Journal of Community Practice*, 3 (1), 59–69.

Chapin, R.K. (1995). Social policy development: The strengths perspective. *Social Work*, 40 (4), 506–514.

Cloward, R.A., & Piven, F.F. (1975). Notes toward a radical social work. In Bailey, R. & Brake, M. (eds.), *Radical social work*. New York: Pantheon Books.

Council on Social Work Education. (1994). *Curriculum Policy Statement*. Alexandria, VA: Author.

Cox, F.M., Erlich, J.L., Rothman, J., and Tropman, J.E. (1987). *Strategies of community organization* (3rd ed.) (pp. 327–337). Itasca, IL: F.E. Peacock.

Davis, A.F. (1984). *Spearheads for reform: The social settlements and the Progressive Movement*. New Brunswick, NJ: Rutgers University Press.

Ehrenreich, J.H. (1985). *The altruistic imagination: A history of social work and social policy in the United States*. Ithaca, NY: Cornell University Press.

Flynn, J. (1992). *Social agency policy* (2nd ed.). Chicago: Nelson-Hall.

Frumkin, M., & O'Connor, G. (1985, Winter). Where has the profession gone? Where is it going? Social work's search for identity. *Urban & Social Change Review*, pp. 13–18.

Garvin, C.D., & Cox, F.M. (1995). A history of community organizing since the Civil War with special reference to oppressed communities. In Rothman, J., Erlich, J.L., & Tropman, J.E., (eds.), *Strategies of community intervention*, (5th ed.) (pp. 64–99). Itasca, IL: F.E. Peacock.

Gummer, B., & Edwards, R.L. (1985). A social worker's guide to organizational politics. *Administration in Social Work*, 9 (1), 13–21.

Gutierrez, L.M. (1995). Working with women of color: An empowerment perspective. In Rothman, J., Erlich, J.L., & Tropman, J.E., (eds.), *Strategies of community intervention* (5th ed.) (pp. 204–212). Itasca, IL: F.E. Peacock.

Haynes, K.S., & Mickelson, J.S. (1991). *Affecting change: Social workers in the political arena* (2nd ed.). New York: Longman.

Hobbs, D. (1987). Strategy for needs assessments. In Johnson, D.E., Meiller, L.R., Miller, L.C., & Summers, G.F. (eds.), *Needs assessment: Theory and methods* (pp. 20–34). Ames, IA: Iowa State University Press.

Mahaffey, M., & Hanks, J.W. (1982). *Practical politics: Social work and political responsibility*. Silver Spring, MD: National Association of Social Workers.

Martin, G. (1976). *Madame secretary*. Boston: Houghton Mifflin.

McElvaine, R.S. (1993). *The Great Depression*. New York: Times Books.

McInnis-Dittrich, K. (1994). *Integrating social welfare policy and social work practice*. Pacific Grove, CA: Brooks/Cole.

Miller, P.A. (1987). Preparing leaders for influencing policy. *Journal of Teaching in Social Work*, 1 (2), 113–123.

Monette, D.R., Sullivan, T.J., & DeJong, C.R. (1994). *Applied social research: Tools for the human services* (2nd ed.). New York: Holt, Rinehart & Winston.

Reisch, M., & Wenocur, S. (1986). The future of community organization in social work: Social activism and the politics of profession building. *Social Service Review*, 60 (1), 70–93.

Schlesinger Jr., A.M. (1986). *The cycles of American history*. Boston: Houghton Mifflin.

Schuerman, J.R. (1983). *Research and evaluation in the human services*. New York: The Free Press.

Segal, E.A. (1989). Teaching community organization in the classroom. *Arete*, 14 (2), 42–47.

Simon, B.L. (1994). *The empowerment tradition in American social work: A history*. New York: Columbia University Press.

Specht, H., & Courtney, M. (1994). *How social work has abandoned its mission: Unfaithful angels*. New York: The Free Press.

Stroup, H. (1986). *Social welfare pioneers*. Chicago: Nelson-Hall.

Witkin, B.R., & Altschuld, R.W. (1995). *Planning and conducting needs assessments*. Thousand Oaks, CA: Sage Publications.

Index

Aaron, H. J., 118, 153
Abernathy, Ralph, 167
Abolitionists, 22
Abortion controversy, 53, 172–174
Abramovitz, M., 17, 35, 88, 100, 101
Absolute measure of poverty, 78
Acquired Immune Deficiency Syndrome
  (AIDS), 120. *See also* Human
  Immunodeficiency Virus (HIV)
  federal response to, 36
  incidence of, 120–121
  social welfare policy for dealing with,
    9–10, 121
Addams, Jane, 25, 26, 265, 276
Adoption Assistance and Child Welfare Act
  (1980), 134, 141
Adoption services, federal programs for,
  139–142
Affirmative action, 168–169
African-Americans
  impact of Progressive era on, 27
  impact of World War II on, 32–33
  post–Civil War treatment of, 22
  poverty of, 82, 85
  voting rights for, 164–166
Agency for International Development
  (AID), 225
Aging policy, 147–157
  in health care, 154–155
  history of, 148–149
  in intergenerational relations: conflict
    versus cooperation, 156–157
  and Older Americans Act (1965),
    155–156
  and social security, 150–154
Agriculture, U.S. Department of
  and administration of WIC program, 95
  economy food plan of, 80
AIDS. *See* Acquired Immune Deficiency
  Syndrome (AIDS); Human
  Immunodeficiency Virus (HIV)

Aid to Dependent Children (ADC)
  program, 31, 100, 133
Aid to Families with Dependent Children
  (AFDC), 90–91. *See also* Temporary
  Assistance for Needy Families
  (TANF)
  administrative flow for, 224
  caseload growth in, 35
  as child welfare program, 137–138
  cuts in, 36
  eligibility for, 135
  in federal budget, 219
  and Medicaid coverage, 113
  purpose of, 79
  shift to state control, 62, 102
  Unemployed Parent program in, 100
Aid to the Aged, 91
Aid to the Blind, 31
Aid to the Blind and Disabled, 91
Aldous, J., 193
Alexander, C., 263
Almanac of American Politics, 231, 236
Altschuld, R. W., 273
American Civil Liberties Union, 26
American Indian Movement (AIM), 179
American Indians
  civil rights for, 177–179
  post–Civil War treatment of, 22
  poverty of, 82, 85
American Medical Association (AMA), 108,
  109
American Public Welfare Association's
  Voluntary Cooperative Information
  System, 140
American Social Welfare Policy Response,
  15
Americans with Disabilities Act (1990)
  (ADA), 36, 174–175, 176
Analytical Perspective, 236
Anderson, O. W., 118
Anthony, Susan B., 166

SOCIAL WELFARE POLICY, PROGRAMS, AND PRACTICE
Edited by Janet Tilden
Photographs compiled by Cheryl Kucharzak
Production supervision by Kim Vander Steen
Designed by Jeanne Calabrese Design, Oak Park, Illinois
Composition by Point West, Inc., Carol Stream, Illinois
Paper, Finch Opaque
Printed and bound by Quebecor Printing, Kingsport, Tennessee